Thomas Wentworth Higginson

Young Folks' History of the United States

Thomas Wentworth Higginson

Young Folks' History of the United States

ISBN/EAN: 9783744786119

Printed in Europe, USA, Canada, Australia, Japan

Cover: Foto ©ninafisch / pixelio.de

More available books at **www.hansebooks.com**

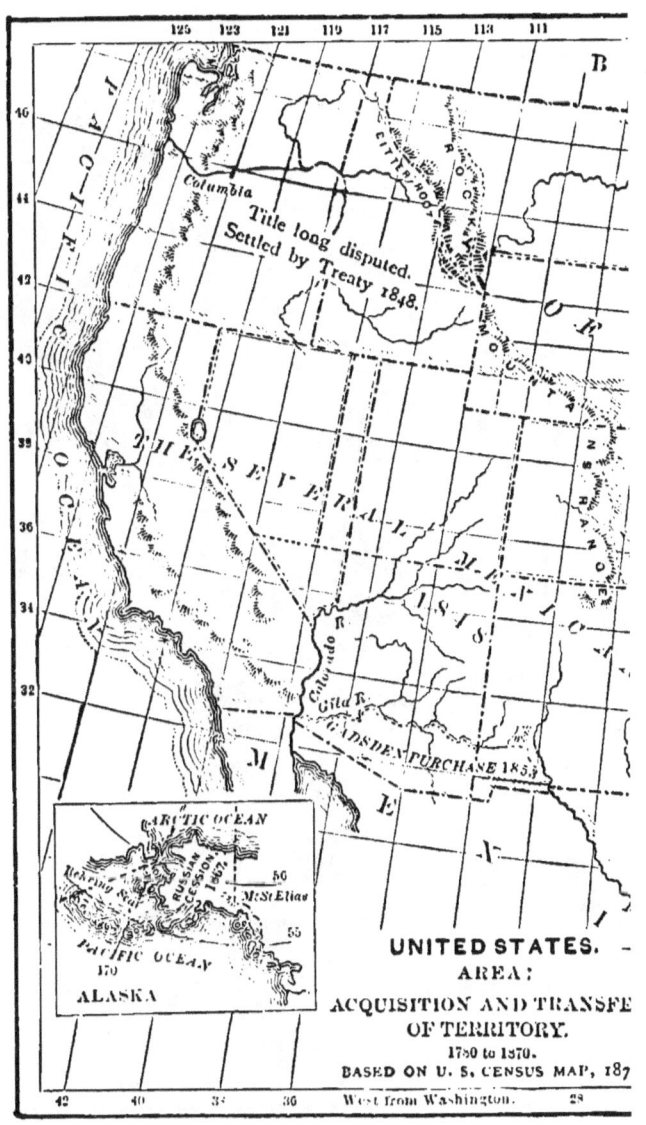

HISTORY OF THE UNITED STATES.

BY

THOMAS WENTWORTH HIGGINSON,

AUTHOR OF "ATLANTIC ESSAYS," "ARMY LIFE IN A BLACK REGIMENT,"
"MALBONE," ETC.

Illustrated.

BOSTON:
LEE AND SHEPARD, PUBLISHERS.
NEW YORK: CHARLES T. DILLINGHAM.
1887.

COPYRIGHT, 1875,
BY THOMAS WENTWORTH HIGGINSON.

COPYRIGHT, 1886,
BY THOMAS WENTWORTH HIGGINSON.

PRESS OF
S. J. PARKHILL & CO., 222 FRANKLIN ST.,
BOSTON, MASS.

PREFACE.

IT is the aim of this book to tell the story of the United States in a clear and simple manner, for young and old. In writing it, I have adopted two plain rules,— to omit all names and dates not really needful, and to make liberal use of the familiar traits and incidents of every day. If there is any merit in the design, it belongs largely to my honored friend, GEORGE B. EMERSON, Esq., of Boston, from whom the first suggestion of the work came, and by whose kind co-operation it has been carried through. I am indebted, also, to Rev. GEORGE E. ELLIS, D.D., to RICHARD FROTHINGHAM, Esq., and to FRANCIS PARKMAN, Esq., for valuable hints and criticisms; and to Rev. J. G. PALFREY, D.D., and the Maine Historical Society, for permission to use important maps, originally engraved for them.

It will be noticed that less space than usual is given, in these pages, to the events of war, and more to the affairs of peace. This course has been deliberately pursued. It is desirable, no doubt, that the reader should fully understand the way in which every important war began and ended, and that he should read enough of the details to know in what spirit it was carried on. Beyond this, the statistics of sieges and battles are of little value, and are apt to make us forget that the true glory of a nation lies, after all, in orderly progress. Times of peace, the proverb says, have few historians; but this may be more the fault of the historians than of the times.

T. W. H.

NEWPORT, R. I., Jan. 1., 1875.

TABLE OF CONTENTS.

CHAPTER	PAGE
I. The Earliest Inhabitants	1
II. The Mound-Builders	5
III. The American Indians	13
IV. The Coming of the Northmen	25
V. The Coming of Columbus	31
VI. The Successors of Columbus	40
VII. How America was explored and settled	46
VIII. The Massachusetts Colonies	55
IX. The other New England Colonies	65
X. Colonial Days in New England	74
XI. Old Dutch Times in New York and New Jersey	88
XII. The Friends in Pennsylvania and the Swedes in Delaware	101
XIII. The Old Dominion and Maryland	110
XIV. The Southern Colonies	124
XV. The Indian Wars	131
XVI. The French and Indian Wars	142
XVII. The Beginning of the Revolution	159
XVIII. Concord, Lexington, and Bunker Hill	178
XIX. Washington takes Command	188
XX. The Declaration of Independence	194
XXI. The Remainder of the War	202
XXII. After the War	214
XXIII. Washington and Adams	220
XXIV. Jefferson's Administration	235
XXV. Madison and Monroe, the War of 1812, and the Era of Good Feeling	248

TABLE OF CONTENTS.

CHAPTER	PAGE
XXVI. Adams and Jackson. — Internal Improvements. — Nullification and the Anti-slavery Movement	259
XXVII. Van Buren, Harrison, Tyler, and the Annexation of Texas	267
XXVIII. Polk and the Mexican War	273
XXIX. The Approach of the Civil War. — Taylor, Fillmore, and Pierce	280
XXX. The Opening of the Civil War. — Buchanan	286
XXXI. The Civil War. — Lincoln	293
XXXII. After the Civil War. — Grant	322
XXXIII. Hayes. — Garfield. — Arthur	330

APPENDIX.

I. Books of Consultation	343
II. List of Presidents and Vice-Presidents	349
III. List of States and Territories	350
IV. Area of the United States	351
V. Declaration of Independence	352
VI. Constitution of the United States	357

CHRONOLOGICAL TABLE 375

INDEX 387

YOUNG FOLKS' UNITED STATES.

CHAPTER I.

THE EARLIEST INHABITANTS.

WHO were the very first men and women that ever trod the soil of North America? Of what race were they, of what color, of what size? and how did they look? History cannot answer these questions. Science can only say, "Perhaps we shall find out; but we do not yet know." _{Important questions.}

We know already a good deal about the changes in form and appearance of the North American Continent itself. We know that a large part of it was at one time covered with a thick coating of ice, a sort of vast glacier which several times stretched itself farther southward, as the climate grew colder, and then shrank to smaller size again, as the climate, during unknown ages, grew milder. We know that the whole surface of the continent has risen or sunk, irregularly, at various times; so that the sea once covered much that is now dry land. We know that plants and animals of species now unknown have existed in many parts of the continent. The reindeer, which is now found only in the far _{Changes in the Continent.} _{Extinct animals.}

north, once roamed as far south as Kentucky. The monkey, which is now found in South America, was once an inhabitant of North America also. The rhinoceros is now found only in Asia and Africa; but several distinct species once existed in North America, one of these being as large as an elephant. There were, at least, five different species of camel, some of them reaching a very large size. Wild horses, or horse-like animals, of at least thirty different species, have at different times galloped or grazed in North America, though the first European explorers did not find a single species surviving. Some of these had three toes on each foot, some had four, instead of the solid hoofs of our present horses; and there were cloven-footed animals no larger than squirrels; while others, again, were as large as elephants. There were also gigantic animals of the sloth family, and, in short, a great variety of quadrupeds now unknown. No written history tells of them; we do not know whether human eyes ever saw most of them: but there are the bones in the soil; and new explorations, especially in Colorado, are constantly bringing more and more species to the light.

Extinct animals.

But most remarkable among all these fossil animals were two great quadrupeds akin to the elephant, and called the "mammoth" and the "mastodon." They once went trampling through the forests, tearing down the branches of trees for food; and they sometimes sank and died in the swamps, unable to move their huge weight out of the mire. They were ten or twelve feet high (taller than any living elephant); and their tusks have been found eleven feet long. We know their shape and size and appearance; and we know

Mammoth and mastodon.

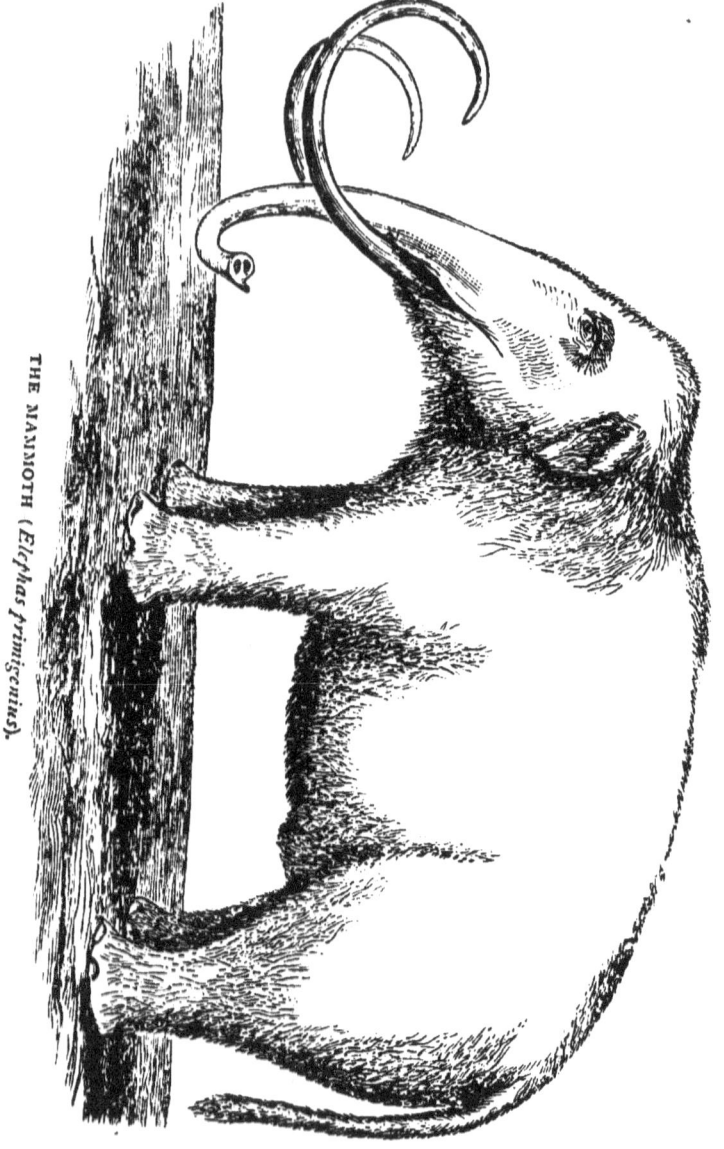

THE MAMMOTH (*Elephas primigenius*).

Man may have lived here with them.

that their race must have existed on the soil of North America for thousands of years. Whether men lived at the same time with them on the American Continent we do not know with certainty: yet there can be little doubt that it was so. In France there have been found rude drawings of the mammoth, made by men on ivory and slate, and mingled with remains of extinct animals in caves. In America no such positive proofs have been discovered; but human bones and flint implements have been found mingled with these animal remains. It is very possible that the mammoth and the mastodon were gradually destroyed by men. In Southern Africa all the men of a village go out to hunt an elephant; and, in spite of his great size, they kill him with bows and arrows. So it is possible that the flint implements found with the bones of these larger quadrupeds may be the very knives and arrow-heads that killed them; and perhaps this is all that ever will be known of the way in which that mighty race disappeared from the surface of the earth. But, at any rate, the mastodons and mammoths perished at last; and the men and women who had looked on them passed away likewise, leaving only obscure and scattered memorials of themselves.

CHAPTER II.

THE MOUND-BUILDERS.

AFTER the last mammoth was slain, it is possible that many centuries may have passed before the Mound-Builders came to occupy the soil where these animals had been. The Mound-Builders were a race of men who never saw the mammoth, we may be very sure ; or else they would have carved or painted its likeness, as they did those of the birds and beasts they knew. But, though they made pictures of these creatures, they unfortunately did not make equally distinct pictures of themselves ; so that we do not know what they looked like ; and, as they wrote no books, we do not know what language they spoke. All that we know of them is from the wonderful works of industry and skill that they left behind, and especially from certain great mounds of earth they built. It is from these great works that they derive their name.

Mound-Builders

THE SERPENT MOUND.

One of the most remarkable of these mounds is to

be seen in Adams County, Ohio. It represents an immense snake a thousand feet long, and five feet thick, lying along a bluff that rises above a stream. There you can trace all the curves and outlines of the snake, ending in a tail with a triple coil. In the open mouth, something in the shape of an egg seems to be held; and this egg-shaped mound is one hundred and sixty feet long. This shows on what a vast scale these earth-works are made. Sometimes they are shaped like animals, sometimes like men. In some places there are fortifications, often enclosing one or two acres of ground, and in some cases four hundred acres. Sometimes these earth-works have from fourteen to sixteen miles of embankment. In other places there are many small mounds arranged in a straight line, at distances nearly equal, and extending for many miles. These are supposed to have been used for sending signals from station to station across the country. Then, in other places, there are single mounds, sometimes sixty feet high, or even ninety, with steps cut in the earth upon one side, leading up to the top, which is flat, and sometimes includes from one to five acres of ground.

These mounds are scattered all down the valley of the Mississippi, and along many of its tributary streams. There are thousands of them, large or small, within the single State of Ohio. They are not made of earth alone, for some of them show brick-work and stone-work here and there, though earth is always the chief material. Some of them have chambers within, and the remains of wooden walls; and sometimes charred wood is found on top, as if fires had been kindled there. This

The Serpent mound.

Other mounds and their uses.

Where other mounds are.

fact is very important, as it helps us to understand the purpose of the higher mounds; for in Central America there are similar mounds, except that those have on their tops the remains of stone temples and palaces. So it is supposed that the higher mounds of the Mississippi Valley may have been built for purposes of worship; Mounds in Central America.

THE HOPETON WORKS, IN OHIO.

and that, although their summits are now bare, yet the charred wood may be the remains of sacrificial fires, or of wooden temples that were burned long ago.

It is certain that these Mound-Builders were in some ways well advanced in civilization. All their earth-works show more or less of engineering skill. They Engineering skill.

Shape of the mounds. vary greatly in shape: they show the square, the circle, the octagon, the ellipse; and sometimes all these figures are combined in one series of works. But the circle is always a true circle, and the square a true square; and, moreover, there are many squares that measure exactly one thousand and eighty feet on a side, and this shows that the Mound-Builders had some definite standard of measurement.

GRADED WAY IN OHIO.

Contents of mounds. There have been found in these mounds many tools and ornaments, made of copper, silver, and valuable stones. There are axes, chisels, knives, bracelets, and beads; there are pieces of thread and of cloth; and gracefully ornamented vases of pottery. The Mound-Builders knew how to model in clay a variety of objects, such as birds, quadrupeds, and human faces. They practised farming, though they had no domestic ani-

VASES FROM THE MOUNDS.

mals to help them. They had neither horses nor oxen nor carts; so that all the vast amount of earth required for these mounds must have been carried in baskets or skins; and this shows that their population must have been very numerous, or they never could have attempted so much. They mined for copper near Lake Superior, where their deserted mines may still be seen. In one of these mines there is a mass of copper weighing nearly six tons, partly raised from the bottom, and supported on wooden logs, now nearly decayed.

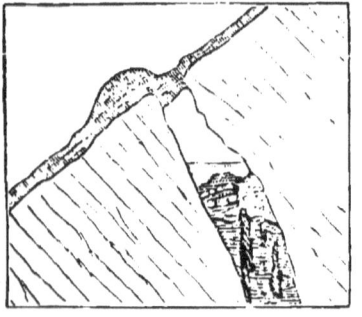

ANCIENT MINING SHAFT.

Population

Copper mining

It was evidently being removed to the top of the mine, nearly thirty feet above; and the stone and copper tools of the miners were found lying about, as if the men had just gone away.

Proofs of antiquity. Now, when did this ancient race of Mound-Builders live? There is not a line of their writing left, so far as is now known; nor is there any distinct tradition about them. But there is one sure proof that they lived very long ago. At the mouth of this very mine just described there are trees, nearly four hundred years old, growing on earth that was thrown out in digging the mine. Of course, the mine is older than the trees. On a mound at Marietta, O., there are trees eight hundred years old. The mounds must, of course, be as old as that, and nobody knows how much older. It is very probable that this mysterious race may have built these great works more than a thousand years ago.

Were they the ancestors of the present American Indians? It is very natural to ask whether the Mound-Builders were the ancestors of our present American Indians. It is not at all certain that they were, because the habits of the two races are quite different. Most Indian tribes now show nothing of the skill and industry required for these great works. The only native tribes that seem to have a civilization of their own are certain races, called Pueblo Indians (meaning village Indians), in New Mexico. These tribes live in vast stone buildings, holding, sometimes, as many as five thousand people. These buildings are usually placed on the summits of hills, and have walls so high as only to be reached by ladders. The Pueblo Indians dress neatly, live in families, practise various arts, and are utterly different from the roving tribes farther north.

Pueblo Indians.

But, after all, the style of building of even the Pueblo Indians is wholly unlike anything we know of the Mound-Builders; for the Mound-Builders do not seem to have erected stone buildings, nor do the Pueblo Indians build lofty mounds.

PUEBLO BUILDING, AS IT NOW APPEARS.

Perhaps the Mound-Builders will always remain a good deal of a mystery. They may have come from Asia, or have been the descendants of Asiatics accidentally cast on the American shore. Within the last hundred years no less than forty Japanese vessels have been driven across the Pacific Ocean by storms, and wrecked on the Pacific coast of North America; and this may have

Possible origin.

happened as easily a thousand years ago as a hundred. It is certain that some men among the Mound-Builders had reached the sea in their travels; for on some of their carved pipes there are representations of the seal and of the manati, or sea-cow, — animals which they

PUEBLO BUILDING, RESTORED.

could only have seen by travelling very far to the east or west, or else by descending the Mississippi River to its mouth. But we know neither whence they came nor whither they went. Very few human bones have been found among the mounds; and those found had almost crumbled into dust. We only know that the Mound-Builders came, and built wonderful works, and then made way for another race, of whose origin we know almost as little.

Our limited knowledge of them.

CHAPTER III.

THE AMERICAN INDIANS.

WHEN the first European explorers visited the Atlantic coast of North America, they found it occupied by roving tribes of men very unlike Europeans in aspect. They were of a copper-color, with high cheekbones, small black eyes, and straight black hair. They called themselves by various names in different parts of the country, such as Mohegans, Pequots, Massachusetts, Narragansetts, Hurons, and Wampanoags. But they almost all belonged to two great families, the Algonquins and the Iroquois; these last being commonly called the "Six Nations." The Europeans named them

Appearance.

Names of tribes.

INDIAN WIGWAMS.

all "Indians," because all the first explorers supposed that North America was only the eastern part of India.

Manner of living. These tribes of natives differed very much in some respects as to their mode of life. Some were warlike, others peaceful. Some lived only by hunting, others had fields of waving corn, and raised also beans, pumpkins, tobacco, American hemp, and sunflowers, — these *Dwellings.* last for the oil in the seeds. Some had only little tents of skin or bark, called "wigwams;" others built permanent villages, with streets, and rows of houses. These houses were sometimes thirty feet high, and two hundred and forty feet long, and contained as many as twenty families. They were built of bark, supported by wooden posts; they had a slit, about a foot wide, the whole length of the roof, to let the light in, and the smoke out. The fires were built on the ground, in a row, under the long opening.

Roving disposition. But, however carefully they may have built their houses, all these Indians were alike in being a roving race, living in the open air most of their time, and very unwilling to be long confined to one place. They were always moving about, changing their abode at different seasons of the year, or when they wished to pursue a different kind of game. One of their commonest reasons for removing was that they had burned the woods immediately around them. So when the first white settlers came, and the Indians were puzzled to know why these strangers arrived, some of them thought that it must be because they had burned up all the wood in the country from which they came, and that they visited the American continent merely to find fuel.

The Indians were not commonly equal to the Europeans in bodily strength; they were not so strong in *Comparison of Indians with Europeans.* the arms and hands, nor could they strike such heavy blows. But, on the other hand, their endurance was wonderful. They were very light of foot, so that their best runners could run seventy or eighty miles in a day; and they could bear the greatest torture without uttering a groan. In the woods they could hear sounds and observe signs which no white man could perceive; and they had the power of travelling for miles in a straight line through the thickest forest, being guided by the appearance of the moss and bark upon the trees.

When the colonists first arrived, they found the Indians dressed chiefly in the skins of animals, which they prepared by smoking them, instead of by tanning, as is now the practice. But they soon obtained blankets from the colonists, and decorated them with beads and shells and feathers. On great occasions, such as councils and war-dances, the chiefs wore a great quantity of these decorations, and also painted their faces with bright colors. The women, or "squaws" as they were called, had this same practice; and one old Puritan clergyman wrote with great indignation, "The squaws use the sinful art of painting their faces." The women were more plainly dressed than the men, and, like them, sometimes tattooed their bodies. But the women wore their hair long, while the men commonly shaved theirs off, except one lock, called the "scalp-lock," which *The scalp lock.* was left as a point of honor; so that, if one Indian killed another, he could cut off the scalp, lifting it by this lock. In summer they went about almost naked; and one of the first white settlers complained that it was hard fighting hand to hand with an Indian, becaues there was "nothing to hold on by but his hair," and not much of that.

Food. The food of the Indians was very simple; it consisted of what they obtained by hunting and fishing, with pounded corn, acorns, berries, and a few vegetables. They used tobacco, but had no intoxicating drinks till they got them from Europeans. They knew **Manufactures.** how to make rush mats and wooden mortars and earthen vessels. They made fish-hooks of bone, and nets out of the fibres of hemp. They made pipes of clay and stone, often curiously carved or moulded. They made stone axes and arrow-heads; and these are often found in the ground to this day, wherever there is the site of an Indian village. They made beads, called "wampum," out of shells. After the Europeans came, they supplied the Indians with their own beads, and with iron axes and arrow-heads, and, at last, with fire-arms.

But the most ingenious inventions of the Indians were the snow-shoe and the birch canoe. The snow-shoe was made of a maple-wood frame, three or four feet long, curved and tapering, and filled in with a net-work of deer's hide. This net-work was

Snow-shoes.

LEARNING TO USE SNOW-SHOES.

fastened to the foot by thongs, only a light elastic moccason being worn. Thus the foot was supported on the surface of the snow; and an Indian could travel forty miles a day upon snow-shoes, and could easily overtake the deer and moose, whose pointed hoofs cut through the crust. The peculiar pattern varied with almost every tribe, as did also the pattern of the birch canoe. This was made of the bark of the white birch, stretched over a very light frame of white cedar. The whole bark of a birch-tree was stripped *Birch canoe.*

BIRCH CANOE.

off and put round the frame, without being torn. The edges were sewed with thongs cut from the roots of the cedar, and were then covered with pitch made from the gum of trees. If torn, the canoe could be mended with pieces of bark, fastened in the same way. The largest of these canoes were thirty feet long, and would carry ten or twelve Indians: they were very light, and could be paddled with ease. They were often very gracefully shaped, and drew very little water. The birch canoe and the snow-shoe are still much in use, *How it was made.*

not only among Indians, but among white men, in the northern parts of the United States and in Canada.

Clans.

Many of the Indian tribes were divided into smaller classes, or clans, distinguished by a mark, or *totem*, tattooed on the breast; such as the wolf, deer, tortoise, beaver, bear, snipe, heron, hawk. Each class had one or more chiefs, or sachems, who represented it in the great councils.

Government.

The sachem was commonly a man, but sometimes a woman; and the first settlers in New England found a "great squaw sachem," who ruled over much country. These rulers did not govern by any written laws, but by fixed customs and tradition, which had great weight with the Indians; and the subjects carried their best fruit and game to the sachem.

The "totem."

Each class in a tribe was supposed to be particularly favored by the spirit of the animal represented in its *totem*. The Indians thought that all animals had protecting spirits; and they often addressed animals as if they were human. One of the early missionaries describes an Indian who shot at a large bear, and wounded him. The bear fell wounded, and lay whining and groaning. The Indian went up to him, and said, "Bear, you are a coward, and no warrior. You know that your tribe and mine are at war, and that yours began it. If you had wounded me, I would not have uttered a sound; and yet you sit here and cry, and disgrace your tribe."

Religion.

They believed that the winds and the stars had also spirits; and they had many wild legends about such things, some of which are preserved in Longfellow's "Hiawatha." They believed in a God, or sometimes in many gods; and they thought that they should live again after death. When any warrior died, they buried his weapons with his body, that he might use them again in the happy hunting-grounds of the blest in heaven. Their religious services were strange and noisy, with peculiar songs and dances; and they had "medicine-men," who were something between priests and physicians, and claimed to cure by magic spells, as well as by the simple remedies they knew. The Indians had no written language, but had ways of communicating to one another by signs on rocks and trees. They had no money, but used wampum-beads for coins; and these were so neatly made, and so convenient, that the first European settlers used them also, at the rate of four black beads, or eight white beads, for a penny. They had belts made with this wampum, which were used to record all important events in the history of the tribe; and treaties were thus kept in memory for years. *Language.* *Their money.*

Schoolcraft gives a copy of a drawing made by two Indian guides on a piece of birch bark. It was placed upon an upright pole, for the purpose of informing their comrades that a party of fourteen white men and two Indians had encamped at that place. *Their method of writing.*

The eight figures in the upper row, with hats on, and with muskets beside them, represent as many white soldiers. In the second row, No. 1 represents the officer in command, with a sword; No. 2, with a book, the secretary; No. 3, with a hammer, the geologist; 4, 5, 6, attendants, one of these being the interpreter. Nos. 7 and 8 represent the two guides, who are distinguished as Indians by being without hats. Figure 11 represents a prairie-hen, and 12 a tortoise, which had been eaten by the party. Figures 13, 14, 15, mean that there *Explanation of picture on next page.*

were three separate fires. The slant of the pole showed the direction of the proposed march, and three notches in the wood showed that it was to be a three-days' expedition.

The character of the Indians.

The Indians had great courage, self-control, and patience. They were grave and dignified in their manners, on important occasions: in their councils they were courteous to one another, and discussed all important

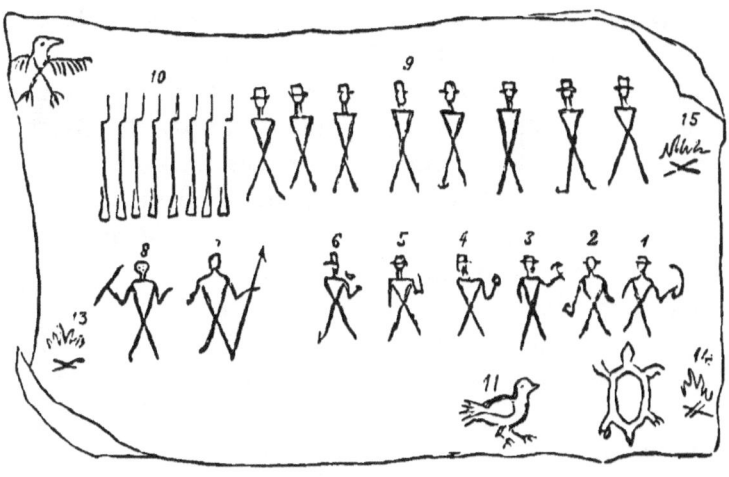

questions at great length. They were often kind and generous, and sometimes even forgiving; but they generally thought that sternness was a virtue, and forgiveness a weakness. They were especially cruel to captives, putting them to death with all manner of tortures, in which women took an active part. It was the custom among them for women to do most of the hard work, in order that the bodies of the men might be kept supple and active for the pursuits of the chase and war.

Treatment of their captives and women.

When employed on these pursuits, the Indian men seemed incapable of fatigue; but in the camp, or in travelling, the women carried the burdens, and, when a hunter had carried a slain deer on his shoulders for a long distance, he would throw it down within sight of the village, that his squaw might go and bring it in.

Most of the Indian tribes lived in a state of constant warfare with one another. When there was a quarrel between tribes, and war seemed ready to break out, strange ceremonies were used. Some leading chief would paint his body black from head to foot, and would hide himself in the woods or in a cavern. There he would fast and pray, and call upon the Great Spirit; and would observe his dreams, to see if they promised good or evil. If he dreamed of a great war-eagle hovering before him, it was a sign of triumph. After a time he would come forth from the woods and return among his people. Then he would address them, summon them to war, and tell them that the Great Spirit was on their side. Then he would bid the warriors to a feast at his wigwam. There they would find him no longer painted in black, but in bright and gaudy colors, called "war-paint." The guests would be also dressed in paint and feathers, and would seat themselves in a circle. Then wooden trenchers containing the flesh of dogs would be placed before them; while the chief would sit smoking his pipe, and would not eat anything.

Preparations for war.

After the feast, the war-dance would follow, perhaps at night, amid the blaze of fires and lighted pine-knots. A painted post would be driven into the ground, and the crowd would form a wide circle round it. The

War-dance

war-chief would leap into the open space, brandishing his hatchet, and would chant his own deeds and those of his fathers, acting out all that he described, and striking at the post as if it were an enemy. Warrior after warrior would follow, till at last the whole band

INDIAN WAR DANCE.

would be dancing, shouting, and brandishing their weapons, striking and stabbing at the air, and filling the forest with their yells.

Departure from camp. Much of the night would pass in this way. In the morning the warriors would leave the camp in single file, still decorated with paint and feathers and ornaments; and, as they entered the woods, the chief would fire his gun, and each in turn would do the same.

Then they would halt near the village, would take off their ornaments and their finery, and would give all these things to the women, who had followed them for this purpose. Then the warriors would go silently and stealthily through the forest to the appointed place of attack. Much of their skill consisted in these silent approaches, and in surprises and stratagems, and long and patient watchings. They attached no shame to killing an unarmed enemy, or to private deceit and treachery, though to their public treaties they were always faithful. They were desperately brave, and yet they saw no disgrace in running away when there was no chance of success. Their weapons were, at first, the bow and arrow, and a sort of hatchet called a "tomahawk;" and they had shields of bison-hide, and sometimes breastplates of twigs interwoven with cord. Afterwards they learned the use of fire-arms from the whites, and became skilful with these weapons, losing much of their skill with the bow and arrow. Some tribes built strong forts, with timber walls, palisades, banks, and ditches. In these forts they had magazines of stones to hurl down upon those who attacked them; and there were gutters by which to pour down streams of water, should the fort be set on fire.

Mode of warfare.

Weapons.

Defensive works.

When first visited by Europeans, the Indians along the coast were already diminishing in number, through war and pestilence; and they have diminished ever since, in the older parts of the country, till many tribes have wholly disappeared. At first they were disposed to be friendly with the white men; but quarrels soon arose, each side being partly to blame. The savages often burned villages, carried away captives, and laid

Their numbers growing less.

The Indians driven westward.

whole regions waste. In return, their villages and forts were destroyed, and their tribes were driven westward, or reduced to a mere handful. Some of these wars will be described farther on in this history; and to this day some of the western settlements of the United States live in constant fear of attack from Indians. But the wilder tribes are passing away; and in another century there will hardly be a roving Indian within the limits of the United States. Only those tribes will survive which have adopted, in part, the habits of civilization.

Civilized Indians of the present day.

Of the Indians now within the limits of the United States, more than 150,000 are wholly or partly civilized. About half of these live on what are called "reservations," in the Indian Territory; while the rest are scattered through various Territories and States. Many of those in the Indian Territory, especially the Cherokees, Choctaws, and Creeks, are quite prosperous, having good farms, herds of cattle, and graded schools. Many boys and girls from the wilder tribes are being educated in schools at Hampton, Va., and Carlisle, Pa.

CHAPTER IV.

THE COMING OF THE NORTHMEN.

THERE is in the city of Newport, R.I., a pictu- *Old Stone* resque old building, the precise history of which *Mill.* is not known. It is commonly called the "Round Tower," or the "Old Stone Mill." It is built of stone, and consists of a low, circular tower, supported on eight arches. Within the memory of living men, there still remained a floor above these arches, making a second story to the building. There are two windows and a fireplace, but nothing to show for what use the building was originally employed. Yet it is not exactly a ruin, since the cement in which the stones are embedded is as strong as ever, and the whole structure seems complete, except that it is roofless. The first mention of this building is by Gov. Benedict Arnold in his will, dated 1677; and he calls it "my stone-built windmill." But it is so unlike any other windmill in America, that it was for a long time doubted whether it could have been built for that purpose.

Some thirty-five years ago, Professor Rafn, of the *Book about* Royal Society of Northern Antiquaries at Copenhagen, *the North-* published a book showing that the Northmen, or Scandinavians, undoubtedly visited the shores of North America about A. D. 1000, and that they probably entered Narragansett Bay. It then occurred to some American antiquarians that this old building at Newport might have been erected by those early voyagers. Examination was also made at about the same time of an inscription on a rock near Dighton, Mass., called the "Dighton Rock;" and it was thought that some words of this were in the Norse language. Then it was remembered that a skeleton in a brass breastplate had been dug up at Fall River, Mass., a town lying between Dighton and Newport; and it was thought that this might be the remains of a Norse viking, or rover. The poet Longfellow has written a ballad about this "Skeleton in Armor." The skeleton was unfortunately destroyed not long after; so that we do not know much about it; but it is now known that the Norsemen did not use brass armor, while the American Indians sometimes used for breastplates pieces of brass kettles, which they got from the English colonists. The inscription at Dighton Rock is now supposed to have been made by the Indians, as it resembles many sculptured rocks in the interior of the continent; and the skeleton may have been that of an Indian warrior. And as for the "Old Stone Mill," it is found to be very much like some still standing in that very county in England from which Governor Arnold came. So it is not at all likely that any of these memorials could date back as far as the time of the Northmen; and yet it is altogether probable that the Northmen visited America at a very early time.

Dighton Rock.

Skeleton in armor.

Conclusions concerning these antiquities.

We must remember that the Northmen were great sailors, like their descendants, the Danes, Norwegians, and Swedes. It is rare to find a large crew of sailors without a man in it who belongs to one of these nations; and their ancestors had the same love of the sea. Now, when we look on the map, we see that it does not look very far from Norway to Iceland, nor from Greenland to Labrador. When once arrived at Labrador, any bold sailor would be tempted to follow down the coast of North America. But the Northmen

THE "OLD STONE MILL."

certainly settled Iceland a thousand years ago: and it is known from the annals of Iceland that a colony was sent thence to Greenland, and there remained for a long time; and some of these emigrants may easily have sailed on to Labrador; or some vessel bound for Greenland may have been driven too far west, and so reached the mainland without intending it. At any

Settlements of the Northmen.

rate, it is recorded in the Norse traditions that the Northmen, in sailing west, actually arrived, about A. D. 1000, at some country beyond Greenland.

Story of Leif the Lucky.

This is the way the story is told in the Norse books. A prince, named Leif the Lucky, son of Erik the Red, sailed west from Greenland with thirty-five men, one of whom was a German. After they had landed on a strange land, this German, named Tyrker, strayed off one day and was thought to be lost. When he came back, he talked German and rolled his eyes around and seemed out of his senses. But at last he said in the Norse language, "I have not been far; but I have found something to tell of: I have found vines and grapes."

"But is it true, my foster-brother?" asked Leif.

"Surely it is," he answered; "for I came from the land of grapes and vines."

"Then they slept for the night," the Norse narrative says; "but in the morning Lief said to his sailors, 'Now we shall have two jobs. Each day we will either gather grapes, or hew grape-vines, or fell trees, so there will be a cargo for my ship;' and that was the counsel taken. It is said that their long-boat was filled with grapes. Now was hewn a cargo for the ship, and when spring came they got ready and sailed off; and Lief gave a name to the land, after its sort, and called it 'Vinland.' They sailed then afterwards into the sea, and had a fair wind until they saw Greenland."

Story of Thorwald.

A year or two afterwards Leif's brother, Thorwald, wished to visit Vinland; for he thought that the land had been too little examined. They came to the place where Leif had built huts. There they spent the winter, and in the spring went exploring along the shore "to the westward." At last they saw three boats made of skin, with three men in each. These the Northmen attacked, and killed all but one. They were apparently Indians, called in the Norse legends "Skraelings." Then came from within the firth innumerable skin-boats, and made toward them. Thorwald said then, "We will set up our battle-shields, and guard ourselves the best we can, but fight little against them." So they did; and the Skraelings shot at them for a while, but then fled as fast as they could. But they had wounded Thorwald by an arrow, so that he died; and this party of Norsemen also became discouraged and went back to Greenland the next spring.

But Vinland was now well known; and still larger parties of Northmen came afterwards. They sent home very enthusiastic accounts of their new dwelling-place; praising the grapes and the salmon and the soil, and saying that the day and night were more nearly equal than in Greenland or Iceland. The Indians, or Skraelings, soon came in skin-boats to trade with them. In one case the Skraelings were all busy selling furs for red cloth, when a bull that belonged to the strangers came bellowing out of the wood; and the Skraelings jumped into their canoe and rowed away. The next time the Skraelings came it was as warriors; and they attacked the Northmen with their arrows and could not be easily beaten off. So the strangers did not have an easy time. But they stayed there several winters; and a woman named Gudrid had a son named Snorri, who was perhaps the first white child born on this continent.

Visits of other Northmen

There is much more of this same sort in the traditions of the Northmen; but there is nothing to yield us any more definite knowledge. There is little doubt of their having reached the North American coast; but whether Vinland was Rhode Island, or Nova Scotia, or some other place, we perhaps shall never know. For a time it was thought that it must be Rhode Island. The Norse narratives describe a mild climate, with wild grapes; and it was thought that this must refer to Newport, R.I., where there are plenty of these grapes on the islands in the harbor. But wild grapes grow in Nova Scotia also; and the climate there might seem mild to those who had come from Iceland. This is all we know about the matter. Perhaps there may yet be found along the coast of New England some real memorial of the Northmen; and in the mean time, if it were not for their own legends, it would be hard to believe that they ever came.

Localities probably visited by the Northmen.

CHAPTER V.

THE COMING OF COLUMBUS.

WHATEVER may have been the truth about the visit of the Northmen to America, it is certain, that, if they came, they sailed away again, never to return. Even their colony in Greenland was at last abandoned; and the memory of Vinland almost disappeared. For nearly five centuries, so far as we know, not a European vessel crossed the Atlantic. Some of the older people in Iceland may have remembered that their grandparents had told them of a country far to the west, where vines grew; and perhaps they used to tell these legends, in the long, dark evenings, to the Spanish and English sailors who went on trading voyages to Iceland. There came a time of great commercial activity among the nations of Southern Europe; and voyages began to be

TOMB OF COLUMBUS.

America still unknown to Europeans.

attempted in all directions. And one voyage was at last undertaken that was destined to make the New World known to the Old World.

Christopher Columbus.
There was born at Genoa, in Italy, about 1435, a boy named "Cristoforo Colombo," or, in English, "Christopher Columbus." His father was a weaver of cloth, but his ancestors had been sailors; and the little Columbus was sent to school at ten years old to learn navigation. At fourteen he went to sea; and from that time, so long as he lived, he was either making voyages or else drawing charts. He lived in Portugal, then in Spain, these being the great seafaring nations at that day; and he sailed to almost all the ports then known. Most of his voyages, however, were in the Mediterranean Sea. In these there was almost as much fighting as sailing; for that sea was full of pirates. On one occasion his ship was burnt, and he swam six miles to shore with the aid of a spar. And throughout all these adventures he was gradually forming the plan of sailing farther west upon the Atlantic than anyone had yet dared to sail.

Common belief about the shape of the earth.
But it must be remembered that the people of Europe, in those days, did not know the real shape of the earth, as it is now known. Most persons did not suppose it to be a sphere. They thought it was a flat surface, with the ocean, like a great river, lying round about its edges. What was on the other side of this river, they hardly dared to guess. Yet some scientific men had got beyond this ignorant view; and they supposed the earth to be a sphere, but thought it much smaller than it really was. They did not dream that there could be room on it for two wide oceans and for two great bodies of land. They thought that there was

What learned men thought.

MAP I.
ABORIGINAL AMERICA.

but one continent on the globe, and one great ocean, and that, by sailing across the Atlantic, you would come, after a time, to India and Tartary and Cathay (as they called China) and Cipango (as they called Japan). Many beautiful things were brought from those countries overland, — gold and pearls and beautiful silks; and so the kings of Europe would have been very glad to find a short way thither. This map shows clearly how the wisest men thought it might be done. The drawing was made by a friend of Columbus, in the very year when he made the first western voyage across the Atlantic. It shows the names of all the places just mentioned; and it shows, moreover, how near at hand they were supposed to be, when the navigators of those days were making the maps.

Columbus studied such maps, or helped to draw them, and grew more and more convinced, that, if he could only cross the unknown ocean, he would find India on the other side. Things often happened to confirm him in this opinion. Sailors from the Canary Islands told him of seeing land far in the west. His brother-in-law had seen a piece of curiously-carved wood, that had been washed on shore in Portugal, after a westerly gale. An old pilot had picked up a carved paddle at sea, a thousand miles west of the European coast. At Madeira, Columbus heard of pine trees that had been washed up; and at the Azores they had found tropical cane-stalks on the beach; and once the bodies of two men, of foreign dress and aspect, had been cast on shore. Then it is supposed that Columbus went to Iceland; and there he may have heard legends of the early expeditions to Vinland.

Conclusion reached by Columbus.

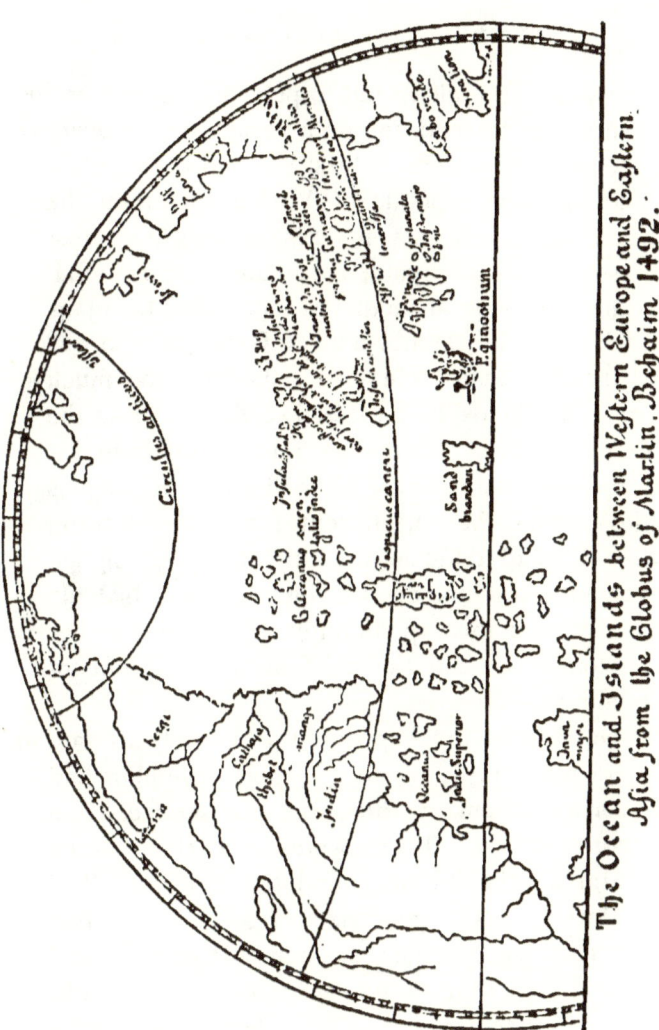

The Ocean and Islands between Western Europe and Eastern Asia from the Globus of Martin Behaim 1492.

THE COMING OF COLUMBUS.

For ten years he endeavored to persuade some Euro- *Efforts of Columbus to obtain aid.* pean government to send him on a voyage of discovery across the Atlantic Ocean. First he tried the republic of Genoa, then the republic of Venice, and then the court of Portugal. For seven years he tried to interest the two sovereigns of Spain, Ferdinand and Isabella. At last they gave him an audience, and liked his plans very much; but the Archbishop of Granada, who was present, thought that Columbus asked for too much power over the lands he expected to discover: so the archbishop objected. Columbus refused to lower his claims, and left the court. He had gone two leagues (six miles), when the queen sent for him to return; and, when he had done so, the king and queen signed an agreement with him on his own terms. Isabella decided to fit out the expedition at the expense of her own kingdom of Castile, the chief of the kingdoms of which Spain was composed.

In three months the expedition was ready to sail. *His outfit.* But sailors were unwilling to go; and Columbus had to drive some of them by force into the service, as he had authority to do. There were three ships, — the "Santa Maria," the "Pinta," and the "Nina." The "Santa Maria" was a good-sized vessel, ninety feet long, and carrying sixty-six seamen. It was decked all over, and had four masts, — two with square sails, and two with lateen-sails. The other vessels were smaller, and without decks: and they were all provisioned for a year. There were, in all, one hundred and twenty persons on this bold expedition.

They sailed from Palos Aug. 3, 1492. It took *His first voyage.* them a month to reach the Canary Islands; but after they had passed those, and found themselves on the lonely ocean at night, many of the sailors wept, and declared they never should return. Columbus quieted them, and they sailed on, day by day; sometimes hopeful, and sometimes mutinous. Once the sailors plotted

FLEET OF COLUMBUS SAILING FROM PALOS.

Signs that land was near at hand.

to throw Columbus overboard. Often they thought they saw signs of land: once they were sure of it, and it proved only a cloud. At last land-birds were seen, and floating twigs with red berries, and a piece of wood rudely carved, and drifting seaweed, to which live crabs were clinging. Finally, one evening at ten o'clock, Columbus saw a light glimmering across the water;

and the next morning a gun was fired from one of the smaller vessels, as the signal agreed upon for "making land." It was a very welcome sound; for they had been seventy-one days in crossing the ocean, which is now crossed by steamers in less than nine. The vessels "lay to" that night; and the next morning the crew saw a wooded island six miles away, and crowds of natives running along the beach.

We may imagine how Columbus felt, when, at daybreak, he was rowed to the shore, with waving banners, and to the sound of music, and when he stepped upon the beach where no European had ever before landed! He bore the great flag of Spain, gorgeous with red and gold; and his other captains bore each a green flag, inscribed with a cross. All knelt, and kissed the ground; then Columbus, rising, and drawing his sword, took possession of the island in the name of Spain, and called it "San Salvador." *Landing of Columbus.*

He soon sailed farther on, visiting Cuba, Hayti, and other West India islands; but he did not reach the mainland during this voyage. Returning to Spain, he was received with great honor: and a second expedition was fitted out under him, consisting of seventeen vessels and fifteen hundred men. With these he discovered the Windward Islands, — Jamaica and Porto Rico, — and founded a colony in Hayti; the island being then called "Hispaniola," or "Little Spain." *His other discoveries.*

On his third voyage, in 1498, he had six ships, and reached the mainland of South America, though not till it had been visited by another navigator, Amerigo Vespucci, or Americus Vespucius. The voyage of Americus Vespucius was made in the winter of 1497–98. He *Voyage of Vespucius.*

was long supposed to have deceived the world in giving this date to his discovery; but it is now pretty well established that he spoke the truth. Ten years after, a European geographer gave the continent the name of "Americi Terra," or the land discovered by Americus; and thus it has borne his name ever since. It would have seemed more just that it should have borne the name of Columbus; and Americus Vespucius, who was his friend, had probably no intention of taking this honor from him; but this was the way it happened. Meanwhile Sebastian Cabot had reached the North American Continent before Columbus; so that the great navigator was not the first to set foot on the mainland, North or South.

Naming the Continent.

On this third voyage of Columbus, he touched at his colony of Hispaniola, where he found them all quarrelling; and he was presently arrested by a Spanish commissioner, Bobadilla, who had been sent out by the enemies of Columbus. He was carried on board ship in chains; and when the officers of the ship wished to take them off, he refused, saying, "I will wear them as a memento of the gratitude of princes." Reaching Spain, he was released, but could get no redress from the king. The truth was, that King Ferdinand was quite dissatisfied with the new countries, because they did not yield wealth enough. However, Columbus fitted out one more expedition, with four ships, and went on a final voyage, reaching the coast of North America at last, although he thought all his life that it was Asia he had visited. This last voyage was a sad one for him, as his own colony at Hispaniola refused to let him land; and he was now old and weary, and as poor as ever. His one firm

Injustice to Columbus.

His last voyage.

friend, Queen Isabella, had died; and he died himself *Death of Columbus.* in 1506, aged about seventy years. Some years after, King Ferdinand ordered a marble tomb to be placed upon his grave, with the inscription, "To Castile and Leon, Columbus gave a New World." But, more than two centuries after that, the remains of the great voyager were transferred to the great cathedral at Havana, that they might rest in the soil of that New World which he had discovered.

CHAPTER VI.

THE SUCCESSORS OF COLUMBUS.

John Cabot's patent.

THE next important voyage to America was planned by John Cabot, a merchant born at Venice, but living in Bristol, England. There had long been some commerce between Bristol and Iceland; and it is very likely that John Cabot, like Columbus, had heard from Icelanders the tradition of the old Norse voyages. After a time he got from King Henry VII. of England a "patent," or permission, allowing himself and his three sons to cruise about the world, at their own expense, with five ships; and to take possession, in the name of England, of countries hitherto unknown to Europeans. It was agreed that, whenever he had done so, nobody but the family of Cabot was to be allowed to trade with any such countries unless the Cabots gave permission. They were allowed to sail in any direction, — east, west, or north; but what they really desired was to get to India by a northwest passage. At any rate, wherever they might go, one-fifth of the profits of their trade must be given to the King of England.

First Voyage.

So John Cabot and his sons set sail in 1497. Sebastian is the best known of these sons, and became more famous than even his father. We do not know exactly

THE SUCCESSORS OF COLUMBUS. 41

what their ships were; but they probably looked like this picture, which is taken from a map made by Sebastian Cabot. We do not know much of their voyage; only that they reached Labrador, and found it, as we may well suppose, cold and dismal. They said, when they got home, that the country was very barren, and that they had seen a great many white bears. They *He reaches Labrador.*

had not much more to say; for they had not remained long, having reached home again in three months. Their maps and journals are all lost; but we know that they were the first Europeans, after the Northmen, to visit the mainland of North America.

A letter from a Venetian merchant, who was then in London, says that great honors were paid to John Cabot on his return to England. He was called "The Great Admiral," went about richly dressed in silk, and *John Cabot's return.*

was followed by crowds of admirers. The merchant's letter adds, "These Englishmen run about after him like mad people; so that he can enlist as many of them as he pleases, and a number of our own rogues besides."

Sebastian Cabot.

A year after, in 1498, Sebastian Cabot sailed again with two ships and three hundred men; some of these being Italian "rogues," very likely. Such expeditions were very popular among reckless and daring men in those days. The explorers again went to Labrador, and then sailed three thousand miles along the coast, as far as Maryland. They were gone six months, and then had to go back for provisions. This second voyage convinced Sebastian Cabot that the land they had discovered was not Asia, after all, but a new continent. He made still another voyage after this, and explored Hudson's Bay. Sebastian Cabot lived to be a very old man, and had a pension from the king, and the title "The Great Seaman." He loved the sea so much, that, even while he was dying, his wandering thoughts were upon the ocean. It was said of him, "He gave England a continent — and no one knows his burial-place."

SEBASTIAN CABOT.

Ponce de Leon.

The next expedition of which I have to tell is that of Ponce de Leon to the coast of Florida. There was a story told in Spain, and believed by many people, that there was somewhere in the regions discovered by

Columbus a wonderful fountain, whose waters would restore youth to any one who should bathe in them. Ponce de Leon was a Spaniard and a brave soldier; he had sailed with Columbus on his second voyage, and was finally made governor of the Island of Porto Rico. But he had heard of the fountain of youth, and resolved to discover it; and so sailed westward from Porto Rico in March, 1512, on that errand. At last, on Easter Sunday,—a day which Spaniards call Pascua Florida, or Flowery Easter,—land was seen. It was the peninsula of Florida, then thought to be an island; and its blossoming forests seemed to him so beautiful, that he gave it this name. *The wonderful fountain.*

Ponce de Leon landed near what is now St. Augustine. He explored the coasts and islands for many weeks, and then returned home. He visited the flowery land again, five years after, meaning to establish a colony, but was driven away by the Indians, was wounded with an arrow, and went back to Spain to die, without ever finding the fountain of youth.

It would be interesting to tell of other voyages that took place in those years, when the New World seemed to Europeans so very new. It is exciting to hear how Balboa, crossing the Isthmus of Darien in 1513, came for the first time in sight of an unknown sea,—the vast Pacific Ocean; how he knelt on the mountain-top from which he saw it, and thanked God for this great discovery; and how, descending to the shore, he waded in, waist deep, and, waving his sword, took possession of the ocean for the king of Spain, and pledged himself to defend it for his sovereign. It is interesting to read the adventures of Cortez, who conquered Mexico, *Other discoverers.*

and of Pizarro, who overcame Peru. But, as these things do not strictly belong to the history of the United States, this is not the place to describe them; and I shall only speak of one more of the early voyages, that of Verrazzano, or Verrazzani, an Italian in French employ.

Voyage of Verrazzano. This voyage is important, because Verrazzano has left us the earliest full description of the North American coast. He sailed from France, by way of Madeira, in 1524, leaving that island with a single vessel, and spending fifty days before seeing land. At last he reached the shore of North Carolina, and followed it southward for a time; then sailed northward, carefully examining the coast. He put into what is now the harbor of New York, and afterwards into what is now the harbor of Newport, R. I. There he stayed a fortnight, trading with the Indians, and he mentions that he found vines and grapes there, just as the Northmen described them in Vinland, long before. Then he sailed along the New-England coast to Nova Scotia, still trading with the Indians on the way. His narrative, as translated in an old collection of voyages, describes the savages as " coming to the seashore upon certain craggy rocks; and we standing in our boats, they let down with a rope what it pleased them to give us, crying continually that we should not approache to the land, demanding immediately the exchange, taking nothing but knives, fish-hookes, and tooles to cut withal; neither did they make any account of our courtesie."

Appearance of the coast Think how strange it would be, if we were to sail along the Atlantic coast, and not meet so much as a fishing-vessel! It would be strange never to see a lighthouse, a buoy, or a wharf; and to enter New York harbor, and see only a few wooded hills and uninhabited islands, but no sign of human life, except, perhaps, a half-naked Indian standing on the shore. Yet this is what Verrazzano did. He carried home full accounts of what he saw. He thought that the savages were "like the people in the uttermost parts of China," and that "these new countries were not altogether destitute of the drugs and spicery, pearls and gold," for which everybody was so eager. King Francis I. was quite delighted. He said that he "did not think God had created those new countries for the Castilians alone:" but it is not certain whether he sent out a second expedition; or whether Verrazzano made any more voyages, or what became of him.

In those early days.

Verrazzano's report.

CHAPTER VII.

HOW AMERICA WAS EXPLORED AND SETTLED.

THESE were some of the first voyages to America, made by Columbus, the Cabots, Ponce de Leon, and Verrazzano. But after the continent was fairly discovered, the next question was, Who should explore it, and claim it, and settle it?

First explorers compared to a family of boys. It has always seemed to me that the first explorers of North America were very much like a family of boys who have discovered a large pond in the woods, somewhere within reach of their dwelling-house. The boys wish to be always on the water, and are constantly exploring. They have different objects: some go merely for the fun of it; others to catch fish; others, to look for blackbirds' nests among the reeds; others, to find a shorter route to the village or to the schoolhouse. What wonderful stories they tell their little sisters about the things they have seen by the side of the lake! By degrees they know the whole shore very well, and can find their way anywhere. Yet if they were to sit down at night to draw the outline of that shore from memory, — with all the ins and outs, all the bays and the islands, — no two would draw it alike; and the different maps would look very strangely side by side.

Now, this is precisely the way it was with those who

HOW AMERICA WAS EXPLORED AND SETTLED. 47

first came to the shores of the North-American Continent. Everybody wished to see the new country. Everybody who came saw something wonderful; and each described even more wonders than he had seen. The returning sailors told of giants and Amazons, of countries where the sands sparkled with gems, and

Eagerness to visit the New World.

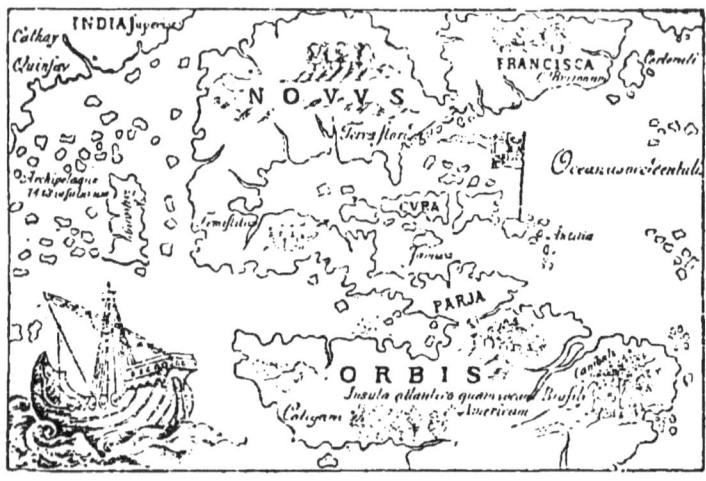

FROM MAP OF 1540.

of rivers in which were found golden pebbles as large as hens' eggs. So there was immediately the greatest eagerness to undertake voyages to these new lands. Some large towns in Spain lost half their inhabitants, so many people went on these expeditions. The Spaniards generally went for gold; the Portuguese, for slaves; and the French and English, for the sake of fishing. Many people still believed that this new country was India, of which they had known something before. But the more learned people — the geographers,

Different ideas at this time.

and those who made the maps — now thought that these new lands were not a part of India, but were a series of islands, called "Cuba," "Florida," "America," and so on; and they expected to find among these islands a passage that would lead to China and Japan. It may be seen by this map, made in 1532, thirty-eight years after the first voyage of Columbus, just how these wise men supposed these islands to lie; and it will be seen that India and China (Cathay) and Japan (Cipango) are placed just behind them, as if easily to be reached.

Maps of the coast.

When there was so much curiosity about exploring the New World, we should suppose that they would have soon learned its outline thoroughly. But they were just like the boys by the lake. There was not a harbor along the Atlantic shore, from Labrador to Terra del Fuego, that had not been entered before this map was made. But no one captain had visited all the harbors. Nobody knew about the interior of the country, or its general form; and so no two explorers agreed about the actual shape of the coast. When they came to draw its outline, we can see what work they made, if we look at this series of sketches, taken from old maps made between 1534 and 1560. The River St. Lawrence seemed to puzzle them particularly: sometimes they made it run south, and sometimes east; and, as for Cape Cod, it appears in all manner of shapes.

But even after Europeans had begun to understand how large the new region was, and after they had improved in map-drawing, there came the still more puzzling question, To whom was it all to belong?

Here, again, these great nations were very much like

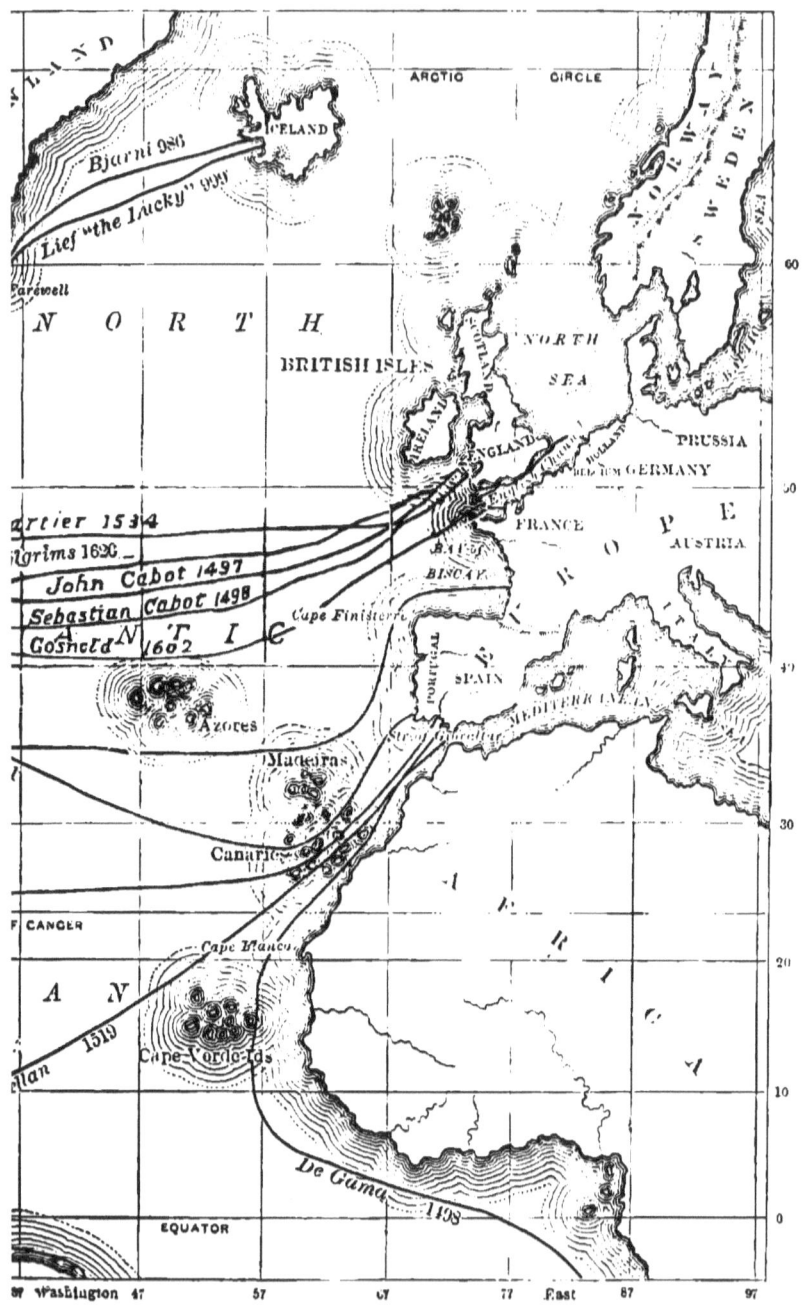

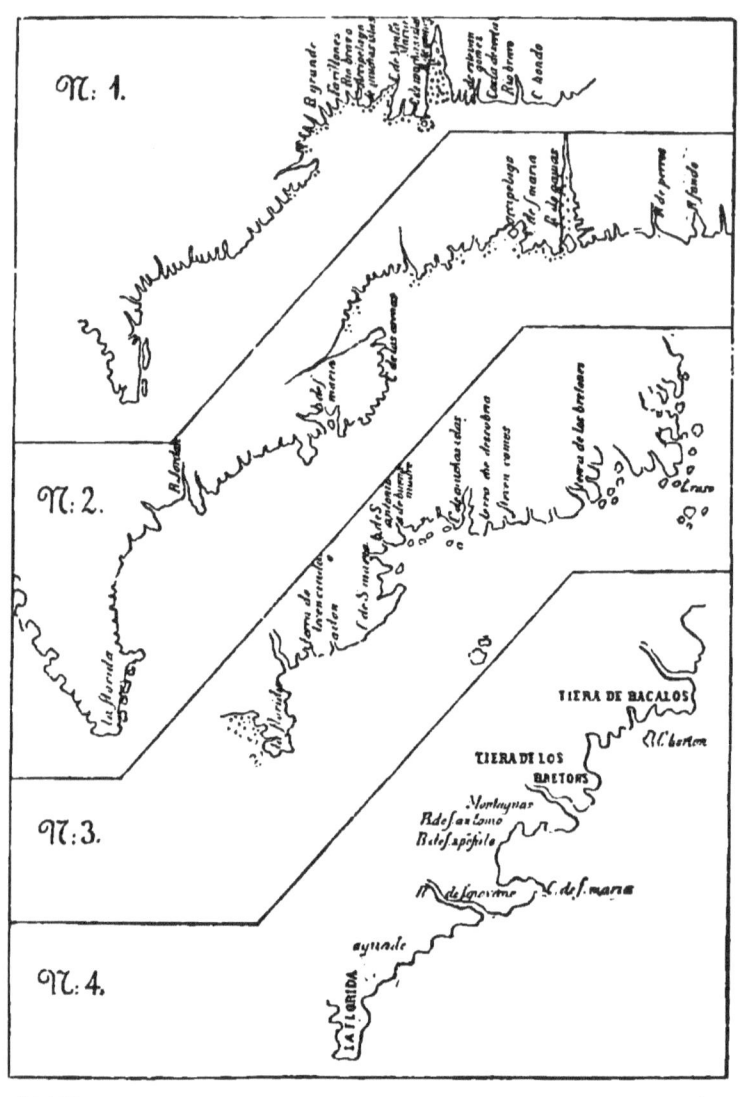

COAST OF NORTH AMERICA, FROM MAPS MADE BETWEEN 1534 AND 1560.

YOUNG FOLKS' UNITED STATES.

Claims of the different Nations.

boys who have explored the shores of a lake, and who play at taking possession of its different islands and capes. Perhaps a boy has claimed a part of the shore for his own, and has given his name to it; perhaps he has cut his name on a tree as a sign of ownership: but, as soon as he is gone, another boy may come and seize it, and give it another name. There is no way to keep it, except to stay and guard it; and this is what few will take the trouble to do. Just so it was with these nations. The Spaniards wished to own all they had explored; so did the French; so did the English: but nobody liked very well to stay there and keep possession. Each claimed a certain portion by right of discovery: the trouble was to occupy what they claimed.

First permanent settlement.

But at last the Spaniards made some permanent settlements in Mexico, and one at St. Augustine, Fla. There is the quaint old town to this very day, with some of the fortifications they built. It was founded in 1565, and is the oldest town in the United States. Then the French settled Nova Scotia (in 1605); but it looked very much as if there would never be any English settlements in North America.

Different names of the Continent.

We must remember that in those days the name "North America" had been scarcely heard. As you will see on the map of the new discoveries, the name of "America" was given first to South America, which Americus Vespucius had visited and described, and which was supposed to be an island. But North America was usually called "Florida" by the Spaniards; while the French called it "Francesca," or "Canada," or "New France." After a while, it came to be generally understood between these two nations that, somehow or other, they owned it all between them. In the National Library at Paris I saw an old French globe, made about three hundred years ago, and one of the largest globes ever made. On this globe the northern part of the Atlantic shore is called, in great capital letters, "Canada, or New France" ("La Nouvelle France"); and all the southern part is called "Florida." The name "North America" does not appear at all. The New York Historical Society owns a smaller globe, with much the same divisions: this was made in Spain, in 1542. That was the view the French and Spaniards took of the subject in those days. They did not dream that the time was coming when neither France nor Spain would own a foot of land in North America.

But the English had never forgotten, all this time, that John and Sebastian Cabot, with English ships, had first reached the mainland of North America. So Sir Walter Raleigh and other gallant men made several unsuccessful attempts to found colonies. They were determined to take possession of that great region between Canada and Florida; and they named it "Virginia," after their queen, Elizabeth, who liked to be called "the Virgin Queen." But it was very hard to make the colonists stay there in the wild forests and among the Indians; and so colony after colony failed. One is said to have been attempted, for instance, on an island now called "Cuttyhunk," in Buzzard's Bay, Mass. The leader was Bartholomew Gosnold; but he only stayed a few months, and it is doubtful if he ever meant to stay longer. Another famous colony was very unfortunate,—that on Roanoke Island in Virginia (now North Carolina). The first child of English parents on Amer- *English efforts to found colonies.*

Bartholomew Gosnold.

ican soil was born there, and was named "Virginia Dare." She was grandchild of the governor of the settlement. He went to England without his family, and was gone several years; and, when he came back, the whole colony had disappeared; and no one has ever discovered what became of little Virginia and her companions.

Potatoes and tobacco. Thus colony after colony proved unsuccessful; and for a long time the most important results of the new discoveries, so far as England was concerned, appeared to be the introduction of potatoes and tobacco. They are both said to have been made known through Sir Walter Raleigh; and it is said that when, after one of his voyages, he sat smoking in his room in England, some one threw a pail of water over him, supposing him to be on fire.

Charter granted by James I. Finally, in April, 1606, King James I. granted a charter to two companies formed in England. This charter gave them the whole continent of North America, from the thirty-fourth to the forty-fifth parallel of latitude. That left the French undisturbed at the north, and the Spaniards at the south; and yet it included all the present States along the Atlantic, north of South Carolina, except a part of Maine. As was said before, all this territory was called "Virginia" by the English. The books of that day said, "Virginia is that country of the earth which the ancients called Morosa, between Florida and New France."

Division of the territory. Moreover, the king decided that this territory should be further divided into two parts. The London Company must take the southern half, and the Plymouth Company the northern half; and their nearest settlements must be a hundred miles apart, so that there should be no quarrelling.

Then the two companies sent out their colonies about the same time. The southern colony reached Jamestown, Va., in April, 1607; and the northern colony arrived at the mouth of the Kennebec River in August of the same year. The southern colonists remained, and founded what is now the State of Virginia; but *The two colonies.*

ENGLISH SHIP OF THE SIXTEENTH CENTURY.

the Maine colonists gave up their enterprise very soon. Most of them went back to England in the autumn; but a portion stayed till spring, building a storehouse, with a fort, which was called "Fort St. George." But they suffered great hardships; and in the spring their leader, George Popham, died, and all the survivors returned home. If they had remained, Maine would have been permanently settled almost as early as Virginia. The colonists under Popham did some good by *Maine colonists return to England.*

helping to establish the English title to the country; but they did harm by telling everybody, after their return, that New England was too cold to be inhabited, This so discouraged the people who had thought of emigrating, that it was more than twelve years before another colony came to New England. Thus Virginia was the oldest of the English colonies; but I shall tell their story in geographical order, beginning with the New-England States, because this arrangement will be easier to remember, and less confusing, than to regard only the order of time.

<small>Virginia the oldest of the English colonies.</small>

CHAPTER VIII.

THE MASSACHUSETTS COLONIES.

THE PLYMOUTH COLONY.

MORE than two centuries and a half ago, there *Religious* was a time of great religious persecution in *intolerance in England.* England. People had not then learned to leave each other free to worship, or to abstain from worship, in their own way. If a man did not attend the services of the Established Church of England, he was liable to be severely punished; and, if he attended any other religious service, it might lead to exile or death. So *The Pil-* a great many of the persecuted people went to live *grims in Holland.* in Holland, where there was more religious freedom. There they dwelt in peace, and won the respect of all. The Dutch magistrates said, "These English have lived among us now these twelve years, and yet we never had any suit or accusation against any of them."

But when children began to grow up around them, *Their rea-* these exiles thought that they would rather teach their *sons for leaving* boys and girls the English language and give them an *Holland.* English education. Besides, war between the Dutch and Spaniards was just beginning again, after ten years of peace; and this caused the English emigrants much anxiety. They had to work very hard, too, and began to wish that they could be laboring to found a settlement of their own, where they could feel at home. Above all, they wished to do something, as they said, "for the propagating and advancing the gospel of the kingdom of Christ in the remote parts of the world." So they decided to leave Holland for the unexplored continent of America, where there was as yet no English settlement but in Virginia. Even before they had resolved on this, they had been called familiarly by the name of "Pilgrims;" because they were wandering from place to place on the way "to heaven, their dearest country," as they said.

Preparations for leaving.
So, out of several hundred English Pilgrims in Holland, about a hundred were selected to go to America, — "such of the youngest and strongest as freely offered themselves." They procured two small vessels, the "Speedwell," of sixty tons, and the "Mayflower," of one hundred and eighty tons; this last being intended to sail from Southampton, England. In July, 1620, the "Speedwell" sailed from Delft-Haven. The Pilgrims had religious services before sailing; and their old minister, John Robinson, said in his address to them, "I charge you, before God and his blessed angels, that you follow me no further than you have seen me follow the Lord Jesus Christ. The Lord has more truth yet to break out of his holy word." Then they were feasted at the pastor's house; and one of them wrote, "We refreshed ourselves, after tears, with singing of psalms, making joyful melody in our hearts, as well as with the voice; there being many of the congregation very expert in music: and indeed it was the sweetest melody that mine ears ever heard."

"After this," he adds, "they accompanied us to Delft- *The Pilgrims leave England.*
Haven, to the ship, but were not able to speak, one to
another, for the abundance of sorrow to part. But we
only, going aboard, gave them a volley of small-shot,
and three pieces of ordnance; and so, lifting up our
hands to each other, and our hearts for each other and
the Lord our God, we departed."

THE "MAYFLOWER."

Thus the Pilgrims set sail without aid from govern- *The voyage to America.*
ment, and without any royal charter, for the New
World. After touching at three English ports, they still
had a long passage of sixty-three days. The "Speedwell" proved unseaworthy, and put back; while the
"Mayflower" went on alone. Instead of reaching the
Hudson River, where they had meant to go, they were
driven by storms to the Massachusetts shore. For a

58   YOUNG FOLKS' UNITED STATES.

<small>The search for a good harbor.</small> month they sailed up and down, looking for a favorable harbor along the coast. It was a barren region; but it seemed pleasant to them after the sea. They saw pines, junipers, sassafras, "and other sweet woods," growing on the shore. They found, their narrative says, "the greatest store of fowl that ever we saw." They saw whales; and, when they fired at one, the gun exploded, when "the whale gave a snuff, and away." When they first went ashore, sixteen men landed, "with every man his musket, sword, and corselet," headed by Capt. Miles Standish. They saw "five or six people, with a dogge, who were savages." These all ran away, and "whistled the dogge after them." At last, in a valley, the Pilgrims saw a deer, and found springs of fresh water; "of which we were heartily glad," the narrative says, "and set us downe, and drunke our first New England water with as much delight as ever we drunke drink in all our lives." Then they found a grave, with mats and bowls, and the skeleton of a man and that of a little child buried together. Perhaps it was pleasant to them to see that parents and children loved each other, even among wild Indians. Then they found a great basket of Indian corn, buried in the ground. This they took, and afterwards, finding the owners, paid for it. They killed three fat geese and six ducks, which they ate "with soldier stomachs," their story says.

<small>The landing at Plymouth.</small> At last they came into a harbor to which an earlier explorer, Capt. John Smith, had given the name of "Plymouth." They fixed on this as a good place for their settlement; and on the 21st of December, 1620, they landed. A young girl named Mary Chilton is said

THE PLYMOUTH COLONY.

to have been the very first to step on Plymouth Rock. But, before landing, they had held a meeting in the cabin of the "Mayflower," and agreed that every man in the colony should have an equal share in the government. They chose John Carver for their first governor; and they also formed a military company, with Capt. Miles Standish to command it. The soldiers had each a coat of mail, and a sword, and a match-lock musket; and we shall see hereafter how well they defended the colony.

Plymouth Rock.

Then they brought on shore all their possessions, such as we may see at this day preserved as relics in Pilgrim Hall, at Plymouth, — arm-chairs and spinning-wheels, and Miles Standish's great iron dinner-kettle, and little Lora Standish's sampler, and the cradle of Peregrine White, the baby who was born on board the "Mayflower," and who was named "Peregrine" from the peregrinations of the Pilgrims.

PEREGRINE WHITE'S CRADLE.

Landing in early winter on that cold, bleak shore, they began at once to build houses. There were one hundred and two persons to be provided with shelter. First they built a common house as a temporary abode for all; then they divided themselves into nineteen families; and by degrees a house was built for each. These houses were of logs and mortar, with thatched roofs, and with windows of oiled paper. The rooms were so crowded that they were "as full of beds as they could lie, one by another." Then they built a

Hardships of the first winter.

great shed for the public goods, and a small hospital for the sick, and a church, which had four cannon planted on the top for defence. Here they could have their religious services in safety, with good Elder Brewster for their minister. As for food, they lived by hunting and fishing till they could raise corn. Sometimes they killed deer and wild turkeys. They caught shad and cod; took lobsters and shell-fish. The Indians taught them to shoot fish with arrows, and to tread eels out of the mud with their feet. Once they tried to eat an eagle, and thought it tasted "very much like a sheep." For several years they had no cattle, and could scarcely have kept any, because of the lions, as they called the wolves, which came close to the town. Often they suffered for want of food; often "they knew not at night where to have a bit in the morning." "I have seen men," says one of their number, "stagger by reason of faintness for want of food." What with hardship and exposure, just one-half of their number died during the first winter, including their first governor; and they planted corn-fields to conceal the graves, so that the Indians might not know how weak they were growing. Yet in the spring, when the "Mayflower" returned to England, not one of these brave colonists went back. Women with sick children preferred to stay in this comfortless country rather than live in comfort at home.

How they lived.

THE MASSACHUSETTS COLONY.

The voyage to Salem.

While the Pilgrims were thus establishing themselves at Plymouth, there were some temporary English settle-

THE MASSACHUSETTS COLONY.

ments made at other places along the coast. But the principal colony was yet to be founded. On the 29th of June, 1629, there came sailing into what is now Salem harbor five vessels, one of these being the self-same "Mayflower" that had first brought the Pilgrims. They had been six weeks and three days at sea; and the passengers called the voyage "short and speedy." It had been a prosperous voyage; and the only person who described it says, "Our passage was both pleasurable and profitable; for we received instruction and delight in beholding the wonders of the Lord in the deep waters, and sometimes seeing the sea round us appearing with a terrible countenance, and, as it were, full of high hills and deep valleys; and sometimes it appeared as a most plain and even meadow." Then, when they came along the coast, the same writer says, "By noon we were within three leagues of Cape Ann; and, as we sailed along the coast, we saw every hill and dale, and every island, full of gay woods and high trees. The nearer we came to the shore, the more flowers in abundance; sometimes scattered abroad, sometimes joined in sheets nine or ten yards long, which we supposed to be brought from the low meadows by the tide. Now, what with pine-woods and green trees by land, and these yellow flowers painting the sea, made us all desirous to see our new paradise of New England, whence we saw such forerunning signals of fertility afar off." How unlike the first approach of the Pilgrims to Cape Cod in the frosty autumn weather!

Arrival at Salem.

This new colony was called the Massachusetts Bay Colony. John Endicott had preceded it, with a few men, the year before, and had been appointed governor

The leading men.

of the colony. He left no account of his voyage. Those who came in the five ships whose arrival I have just described were Rev. Francis Higginson and two hundred more. They came in 1629. Then, the next year, Gov. John Winthrop came with eight hundred. The Massachusetts Bay Colony was large, strong, and rich, compared with that at Plymouth. It included many highly-educated men and some rich men. They had powerful friends in England; and they had a charter from the king, securing to them the right to govern themselves, so long as they did nothing contrary to the laws of England. They founded the town of Salem, which they called by that name, because in Hebrew it signified "Peace." Afterwards they settled Boston, —

Comparison of the two colonies.

TRIMOUNTAIN.

at first called Trimountain, from its three hills, — and also Roxbury, Dorchester, Charlestown, Watertown, and other places.

Difference between Pilgrims and Puritans.

These colonists were not "Pilgrims" from Holland, or "Separatists," as the Plymouth colonists were sometimes called; but they were "Puritans," or religious reformers, who came from England, hoping to find more freedom for themselves in America. They had been persecuted for their opinions at home, though not so severely as the Pilgrims; and the Puritans at first

THE MASSACHUSETTS COLONY. 63

thought that the Pilgrims did not feel kindly enough toward the mother-country. It is reported that Francis Higginson said, as his ship sailed away from the English shores, "We will not say, as the Separatists were wont to say at their leaving of England, 'Farewell, Babylon! Farewell, Rome!' But we will say, 'Farewell, dear England! Farewell, the Church of God in England, and all the Christian friends there!'" However, when they got to America, there was not much difference between the Pilgrims at Plymouth and the Puritans at Salem. At least, both colonies soon grew quite independent of the ways and authority of the Church of England."

But, for all their larger numbers and greater wealth, the Massachusetts colonists suffered almost as much hardship as the Plymouth settlers had undergone. They had, to be sure, from the beginning, horses and cattle and tools. But one of the early colonists wrote, "Bread was so very scarce, that sometimes I thought the very crumbs of my father's table would be sweet unto me. And, when I could have meal and water and salt boiled together, it was so good, who could wish better? . . . The Indians did sometimes bring corn, and truck with us for clothing and knives; and once I had a peck of corn, or thereabouts, for a little puppy-dog. Frost-fish, mussels, and clams were a relief unto many." Another writer describes how the women in the seaside settlements used to go down to the beach every day, at low tide, and dig for shell-fish. "It would have been a strange thing," says another, "to see a piece of roast beef or mutton or veal." One day, just as Governor Winthrop was giving away the last handful of meal he

The scarcity of food.

possessed to a poor man, they saw a ship from England, with provisions, just entering the harbor.

Contentment in the midst of hardships.

A good many died of hardship and fatigue during the first year or two; but, after that, they grew quite healthy. They found the climate bracing; and one said, that "a sup of New England's air was better than a whole draught of Old England's ale." Even in their worst times, very few went back to England; and, notwithstanding their poverty, there was not an instance of theft among them for four years. Governor Winthrop wrote to his wife, "We here enjoy God and Jesus Christ; and is not that enough? I thank God I like so well to be here as [that] I do not repent my coming. I would not have altered my course, though I had foreseen all these afflictions. I had never more content of mind."

Union of the two colonies.

These two colonies, Plymouth and Massachusetts Bay, were for many years independent of one another; but the Plymouth Colony, though the older of the two, grew far more slowly than the other, and was at last united with it in 1692, under the name of Massachusetts; the name being taken from one of the tribes of Indians inhabiting the soil. The meaning of the word is said to be "Blue Hills."

CHAPTER IX.

THE OTHER NEW ENGLAND COLONIES.

THE two colonies afterwards united under the name of Massachusetts have been described before the other New England colonies. This is because Massachusetts, being first settled, was in a manner the parent of these later colonies. Let us take up the rest in the ordinary geographical order.

Maine was not for many years considered as a separate colony; and yet it was one of the first parts of the country to be visited and explored by Europeans. It was visited by the navigator Gosnold in 1602; and an English colony tried to establish itself there in 1607, as has already been told; and a French colony came soon after. But the English settlers went home; and the Frenchmen were driven away by the Virginia settlers, who did not wish to have them so near, and sent an expedition against them. Capt. John Smith explored the coast of Maine, and wrote a description of it; and an Englishman, Sir Ferdinando Gorges, had a patent from the king, Charles I., for a part of it; and it was named Maine by him, probably in honor of Queen Henrietta Maria, who is said to have owned a French province of that name; though this is doubtful. Then the Massachusetts Colony claimed the whole; and so

Early history of Maine.

Capt. Smith's explorations.

there was a good deal of confusion about the ownership of that region. But Maine was, after all, reckoned a part of Massachusetts during almost all the colonial period, and for many years after.

Origin and slow growth of settlements.

The first settlements grew gradually out of fishing-stations; and it is hard to say when the earliest permanent town settlements were founded; before 1630, at any rate. People sought Maine for hunting and fishing, rather than for farming: so the villages grew slowly, and they suffered greatly in the Indian wars. The laws were milder in that part of New England than in Massachusetts and Connecticut. There was much religious freedom, and no persecution for opinion's sake; so that persecuted people often took refuge in Maine. But, on the other hand, the nearness to Canada was a disadvantage; because the French and Indians were for many years the great source of terror to the English colonists. So these settlements had much to keep them back; and Maine was not counted as a separate colony among those that finally combined to form the United States.

Early history of New Hampshire.

New Hampshire was also visited very early, in 1603, by an explorer named Martin Pring; and Portsmouth and Dover were settled in 1623. Portsmouth was first called Strawberry Bank. The settlements made there were chiefly for fishing; and it is said that when a travelling preacher went among the people, ten years later, and told them that they must be religious, for that was their main end in coming thither, they replied, " Sir, you are mistaken. You think you are speaking to the people of Massachusetts Bay. Our

THE OTHER NEW ENGLAND COLONIES. 67

main end was to catch fish." The colony grew very slowly; and, thirty years after the settlement of Portsmouth that town contained only fifty or sixty families. New Hampshire was several times connected with Massachusetts in government, and at one time with New York; but, after 1741, it was a separate province, under a royal governor, who lived in much style and elegance at Portsmouth. There are still to be seen in that part of the State the fine dwellings of colonial days. {The government.}

Gov. Benning Wentworth of New Hampshire claimed that the lands of that colony extended through what is now Vermont; and as his Excellency asserted the right to give away townships west of the Connecticut River, and to reserve for himself five hundred acres in every township, it is plain that it was a profitable thing to be a colonial governor in New Hampshire. Then the more northern townships were gradually filled up by immigrants from Scotland and Ireland; and, by the time of the American Revolution, New Hampshire was a strong and independent colony. It took its name from the English county of Hampshire, whence some of the early settlers came. {New Hampshire grants.}

Vermont was first explored in 1609, by Champlain, a French officer, after whom Lake Champlain was named. It had, however, no European settlers for more than a century after that; and, down to the time of the American Revolution, it was not recognized as a separate colony, but was known as the "New Hampshire Grants," on account of the townships that Governor Wentworth had granted. But the governor of New {Vermont}

York also claimed to control these same "grants;" and Ethan Allen and the other "Green Mountain Boys," as they were called, refused to submit to New York, and wished to be independent of the other colonies. It was, however, long before they succeeded in this; and the history of their efforts must therefore be postponed for a good many pages. The name "Vermont" means simply "Green Mountain."

<small>Settlement of Rhode Island.</small> Rhode Island was founded quite differently from any of the other New England settlements; for it was established mainly by those who had fled from religious persecution in another colony. The founders of Massachusetts came to America to secure freedom for the exercise of their own religious opinions; but they did this because they thought those opinions were right, not because they believed in the general principle of toleration. The idea of liberty in matters of religion was not very common in those days; and the very men who were most conscientious in maintaining their own views of things were often the most zealous in putting down all those who differed from them. <small>Roger Williams.</small> But one young minister came out to America who believed in religious freedom, not only for his own opinions, but for those of all others. His name was Roger Williams. He said that the magistrates of a country should behave like the captain of a ship, who lets his passengers have any kind of religious meeting they please on board, so long as they keep the peace, and do not quarrel. He thought that the law ought to be used to keep people from crime, but that it had nothing to do with their religious belief. He did not approve

THE OTHER NEW ENGLAND COLONIES.

of obliging people to attend church, unless they wished to do it. He did not think it right to choose the magistrates from the church-members only, or to make people pay to support the church, unless they wished. He was not always moderate or judicious in his way of expressing these opinions: but most people would now admit that his views on toleration were right and wise. He, however, held also some peculiar opinions as to the authority of civil magistrates in any case; and those views gave to the Puritans some just ground of complaint.

At last he talked so boldly against the established laws that the Massachusetts magistrates decided to send him back to England. He heard of this intention, and fled, in mid-winter, from his home in Salem, and wandered in the wilderness for fourteen weeks, "sorely tost in a bitter season, not knowing what bread or bed did mean." This was in January, 1636. First he settled at Seekonk, within the Plymouth Colony; but, being advised by Governor Winthrop to "steer his course" to the Narragansett Bay, he crossed, with five companions, in an Indian canoe. The first place where he landed he called "Providence;" thus acknowledging his gratitude to God. There were then no white settlers in that region; and Canonicus, chief of the Narragansetts, gave Roger Williams a large tract of country. But he kept nothing for himself: "he gave away his lands and other estate to them that he thought most in want, until he gave away all." "I desired it might be a shelter for persons distressed for conscience," he said. Many such persons came to him, and settled in different parts of the colony he founded. Among these

Flight of Williams.

Providence

Noted persons who joined him. were Anne Hutchinson, a famous woman-preacher of those days, whom the Massachusetts magistrates had exiled; and Samuel Gorton, another independent religious teacher. Another was William Coddington, who bought the island of Rhode Island, then called Aquidneck, from the Indians. Indeed, so many people of various opinions went there, that it used to be said that any man who had lost his religion would be sure to find it again at some village in Rhode Island.

The charter and laws. The new colony finally obtained a charter under the name of "Rhode Island and Providence Plantations;" the first part of the name being given from a supposed resemblance of that island to the Island of Rhodes. **Unequalled civil and religious liberty.** The laws of the colony were based on the plan of perfect religious toleration. Roger Williams maintained that "a permission of the most Paganish, Jewish, Turkish, or anti-Christian consciences," should be granted "to all men of all nations and countries," and that "Papists, Protestants, Jews, or Turks" should be protected in their worship; and the General Assembly in 1647 passed a law to the same purpose. That was an amount of liberty not then equalled under any Christian government, not even in the Maryland colony, which was the most liberal in America. And, in general, the inhabitants of Rhode Island were so fearful of establishing any tyranny, that, when Roger Williams had refused the office of governor, the colony **Rhode Island and the rest of New England.** went on without one for forty years. After a time the character and habits of the people became more like those of the other New England colonies; but the others always felt some jealousy of Rhode Island, and it was not admitted into the alliances made by the rest. Yet Rhode Island took an active part in the wars of the colonies against the French, and was ready to join with the others in raising troops when the time of the American Revolution came.

The coast of Connecticut was first explored by one of the early Dutch navigators, Adrian Block, who was the first European to sail through Hurlgate. This was in 1614; and the island called Block Island still bears the name of the bold sailor. Other Dutch navigators afterwards went up the Connecticut River, and claimed its banks, and the whole shore of Long Island Sound, as far as Cape Cod. But the river was also claimed by an English company; and an exploring party from Plymouth chose a site for a trading-house on the bank, in answer to an invitation from an Indian chief named Seguin. Then the Dutch bought of another chief, Sassacus, the land where Hartford now stands, and built there a trading-house and fort, called the "House of Good Hope." They forbade any English from ascending the river, and threatened to fire on the party from Plymouth when they came in sight; but the Plymouth men sailed on up the stream, and built their trading-house at Windsor. This was in 1633; and for many years after there was a rivalry between the Dutch and the English in settling the Connecticut valley. The Dutch of New Amsterdam were nearer to the spot; but the English were more numerous and more enterprising; and they soon began to come by land as well as by water. Some whole churches formed colonies, and came through the unbroken forest to Hartford and Windsor and Wethersfield. It was an untried way for white men; but the

Adrian Block.

Origin of the Dutch and English claims to Connecticut.

Arrival of English settlers.

YOUNG FOLKS' UNITED STATES.

Indians had told them of the beautiful river, and had said that its banks were more fertile than the rugged soil of the Massachusetts shore. The first party of settlers, in 1635, suffered greatly in their first winter; and some of them waded back through the snows before spring. But in the spring a much larger party went westward, under guidance of a celebrated minister, Thomas Hooker. They drove their cattle before them; they had no guide but their compass; they hardly travelled ten miles a day through the forests; and Mrs. Hooker, who was an invalid, was borne on a litter: but they, too, reached the river at last. In 1639 the first constitution for the Connecticut Colony was made, permitting all men to vote who had taken the oath of allegiance to the commonwealth. The name of the colony was taken from that of the river; and it is said to mean "Long River." While this colony was being established, another large party came from England, in 1638, and founded a second settlement farther south, at what they called New Haven. This colony had for a long time no laws but the Bible, and allowed none but church-members to vote. In this respect it was like the Massachusetts Colony in early times; but religious controversies were milder in the Connecticut settlements, and there was very little persecution for opinion's sake.

Constitution and name.

The New Haven Colony.

End of the troubles with the Dutch.

The troubles with the Dutch of New Netherlands continued until 1664, when the whole province of New Netherlands itself passed into the hands of the English, and its name was changed to New York. After that time, there was no more trouble from Dutch neighbors. The New Haven Colony was, during the next year, united with the Connecticut Colony; and they went on prospering, being only visited by such troubles as attacked all the New England colonies together. These troubles must be told in a separate chapter. We shall there see how the people of New England lived, down to the time of the American Revolution, which combined all the scattered colonies into one nation.

Union of the two colonies.

CHAPTER X.

COLONIAL DAYS IN NEW ENGLAND.

Similarity of New England colonies.

WE must remember that although the New England colonies had jealousies and differences, yet they were in many respects alike. They were composed almost wholly of Englishmen and Protestants; and most of their pioneers had come from motives of conscience, as well as for their worldly advantage. Their leaders were men of strict morality, and they aimed to have no others among them. In the very first year of the Massachusetts Bay Colony, Governor Endicott broke up a settlement at "Merry Mount," composed of people who led gayer and idler lives than he approved; and this same John Endicott cut the red cross out of the English flag, because he thought it meant superstition. The other New England colonies were not so stern in their discipline as was Massachusetts; but the habits of that age would seem to us very peculiar, and they had their influence even in the more liberal colonies, such as Rhode Island.

New England village on Sunday morning.

If we could carry ourselves back to those days, and were to approach a New England village about nine o'clock on Sunday morning, we should hear some one beating a drum, or sounding a horn, or blowing a conch-shell, or possibly ringing a bell, to call people to worship. As we came nearer still, we should see a flag waving from a little log-built church, or "meeting-house." Entering the village, we should observe a strong fence of stakes around this meeting-house, and a sentinel in armor standing near it; and we should see some of the men, as they went in, leaving their muskets under his care. We should, perhaps, find a cannon or two planted near the meeting-house; and we should also notice some strange wooden frames not far off, these being the stocks and the pillory, put there to punish offenders. Looking at this church itself, we should see that it had very few glass windows, and that these had very small and thick panes, diamond-shaped, and set in leaden frames. We should observe that the other windows had oiled paper instead of glass; and we should see between the windows the heads of wolves that had been killed and displayed there during the past year.

EARLY NEW ENGLAND CHURCH.

If we were to look inside the little church, we should *Church services* not find families sitting together, as now; but they would be distributed according to age, or sex, or rank. In those days the old men sat together in one place in church, the young men in another, the young women in another. The boys all sat on the pulpit-stairs and gallery-stairs, guarded by constables. Each of these constables had a wand, with a hare's foot on one end, and a hare's tail on the other. These were to keep people awake. If any woman went to sleep, the constable touched her on the forehead with the hare's tail; but, if a small boy nodded, he was rapped with the other end, not quite so gently. No doubt the wand was often used; for the services were sometimes three or four hours long, the sexton turning the hour-glass before the minister at the end of every hour. The only music consisted of singing by the congregation, from a metrical version of the Psalms, called "The Bay Psalm Book." The whole number of tunes known to the people did not exceed ten; and few congregations could go beyond five. This was the Puritan form of religious service. And people were not allowed to stay at home from it; for men called tithing-men were sent about the town to look for those who were absent. Men were fined for every unnecessary absence; and, if they stayed away a month together, they might be put in the stocks, or into a wooden cage.

Puritan dwellings. Looking round at the houses of the Puritan village, we should see that the older ones were made of earth or logs, one story high, with very steep roofs, covered with thatch. Entering any of these, we should find the fireplaces made of rough stones, and the chimneys either of boards, or of short sticks crossing each other, and smeared with clay. Here and there we should see newer and better houses, made of wood and brick, two stories high in front, and one story behind; or houses of stone, like this of which a picture is given, and which represents the house of Rev. Mr. Whitfield at

Guilford, Conn., built in 1639, and still standing, probably the oldest house in the United States north of Florida. We should observe that the windows were very small, and opened on hinges; and we should find the fireplaces of these houses large enough for burning logs four feet long, and for the children to sit in the corners to look up at the sky. We should find the houses facing exactly south, so that the sun at noon might "shine square" into them, and the family might know when to have dinner.

MR. WHITFIELD'S HOUSE.

If we could see the people occupying these houses, we should find the men wearing jerkins, small-clothes, ruffs around their necks, and, when in the open air, short cloaks and steeple-crowned hats, under which the elders wore velvet caps. We should find the young men, on public occasions, wearing showy belts, gold and silver buttons, and great boots rolled over at the top. We should find the young women wearing plain and homespun

Puritan dress.

A PURITAN.

clothing when about their work, but appearing on Sundays in silk hoods, lace neckerchiefs, slashed sleeves and embroidered caps. But the law required that they should dress according to their means; and, if they wore such things, they must prove that they were rich enough to afford it. This was the practice in England in those days, and the Puritans brought such laws with them. Thus it appears in the records, that one Alice Flynt was accused of wearing a silk hood; but when she proved before court that she was worth two hundred pounds in money the complaint was dropped. Jonas Fairbanks, about the same time, was prosecuted for wearing "great boots;" but the evidence was not sufficient to convict him, and he was happily acquitted.

The muster. If we were to remain in this Puritan village during the week, we might see, perhaps, a monthly muster of the soldiers; that is, of all men over the age of sixteen. We should perhaps see the officers with swords like that sword of Capt. Miles Standish, which is still preserved, bearing an unknown Oriental inscription, in the Antiquarian Hall at Plymouth. We should see some of the soldiers armed with pikes ten feet long, and others carrying muskets called "matchlocks," from being fired by a slow-match instead of a percussion-cap, as now. We should observe that each soldier had also a "rest," or iron fork, to be stuck in the ground for the support of his heavy weapon; and we should notice that he had girt round him a belt, or "bandolier," holding a sword and a dozen tin cartridge-boxes. He would probably wear, also, a steel helmet and an iron breastplate; so that he would need to be a strong man to make a long march thus laden. Or perhaps he would wear merely a coat thickly quilted with cotton-wool, which would turn the Indian arrows, and would be much lighter in weight. Such would be the soldiers. Or, if a town-meeting were being held, we should find those same men, dressed in civil costume, gravely and patiently discussing the affairs of the town, or the interests of the church; most of the voters everywhere being church-members also. Or, if a vote were to be taken, we should see them doing it by putting in corn or beans; each kernel of corn counting in the affirmative, and every bean in the negative. *The town meeting.*

The laws of the Puritans were, in many ways, more severe than was wise, as we should now think. Those who had done wrong were often publicly whipped, or placed in stocks or the pillory; these being wooden frames that held people by the feet or neck, so that they could not get away. Or sometimes an offender had to stand on a stool in the church, during public worship, bearing the name of his crime embroidered on his clothes, or written on a paper pinned to his breast. A woman who scolded her family might be silenced by a cleft stick applied to her tongue, or by being ducked in running water. Such punishments are not now applied in civilized communities; but we must remember that they were common in that age, and that the aim of such laws was to produce a sober and virtuous people, fearing, above all things, to do wrong. *The laws.*

"Let it never be forgotten," said one of the early Puritan preachers, "that our New England was originally a plantation of religion, and not a plantation of trade. And if there be a man among you who counts religion as *twelve*, and the world as *thirteen*, let such a *The remark of a Puritan preacher.*

one remember that he hath neither the spirit of a true New England man, nor yet of a sincere Christian."

Their desire to control the religious opinions of others. Unhappily, the people honestly believed at that time that it was their duty to control the religious opinions of those about them, as well as their moral conduct; and those who differed from the majority in their opinions often suffered very much. One reason was, that the English Government always complained that the Puritans were a fanatical and unreasonable kind of people, and so the Puritans naturally did not wish to be confounded with anybody still more fanatical, or to account for any strange actions but their own. Unfortunately, the way they took to remedy the evil was much worse than the evil itself.

Persecutions of the Quakers. Now the Quakers, or Society of Friends, in those days, though they were in some respects wiser and better than those who persecuted them, were yet in some ways quite troublesome. The Quakers were honestly opposed to many things that the Puritans thought necessary to good government. They would not pay taxes, or acknowledge the government, or fight in war: therefore the Puritans wished them to go away, and to found a settlement for themselves in the wilderness, leaving the Puritan settlements in peace. But this the Quakers did not choose to do. They thought they had as much right in New England as anybody else; and they, moreover, had among them some foolish persons, who did very mistaken things, not at all approved by the main body of the Society of Friends. Some of these excited people would run naked through the streets, meaning this as a protest against the vanities of dress; sometimes they would come into the

Sunday meetings, dressed in sackcloth, and with ashes on their heads. But besides these half-crazy persons, the Puritans persecuted even the good and sober among the Quakers. These poor people were sometimes branded with hot irons (H. for "heretic," and R. for "rogue"): they were whipped publicly through the streets, and four of them were hanged on Boston Common. All this was very wrong and cruel; but we must remember that such severity was the practice of those days in most countries; and that men had not then learned to tolerate freedom of opinion in one another. Indeed, they have not entirely learned it even now.

Then another great source of anxiety among the Puritans was what was called the witchcraft excitement. All over Europe, two centuries ago, it was firmly believed that certain persons were witches, and had power to bewitch and injure other people by magic arts. Perhaps some old woman, living by herself, would be accused of exerting this magic power on men or animals, and of causing disease or death. Then the poor woman would be accused before a magistrate, and would be examined, and perhaps tortured to make her confess; then she would become so frightened, or excited, as to say that she was really a witch, and perhaps accuse others: and so the delusion spread from one to another. In Scotland, about that time, four thousand persons suffered death on charge of witchcraft in ten years' time, and it is not strange that twenty were executed in America. Sometimes the very persons who were accused would do and say such strange things, that it was hard to know what

Witchcraft

Witchcraft in Scotland.

course to take with them. A young girl, for instance, would jump up in church, and shout out, "Parson, your text is too long!" or, "There's a great yellow bird sitting on the parson's hat in the pulpit;" and, when people did such strange things, the magistrates themselves became excited. But, the more severely such persons were treated, the more their number increased; so that the persecution of witches made more witchcraft; and some of the Puritans were afterwards very much ashamed of what they had done. One brave old judge, Samuel Sewall, confessed in his later years that he had done wrong in yielding to the public excitement about witches; and he used to keep a solemn day of fasting and prayer, every year, to atone for the sin he had committed.

The charters. Then the Puritan colonies had a great deal of trouble about their charters. The charters were the parchments given by the British Government, securing to the colonists the right to make their own laws, and to appoint their own magistrates. The colonists knew that without these charters they would be liable to a great deal of injustice, and that governors and magistrates might at any time be sent out from England to govern them without their consent. These magistrates might deprive them of their religious freedom and destroy their whole prosperity. Besides, it was a time of civil war in England, between Charles I. and the parliament; and the colonists did not wish to have anything to do with the contest. If they sided with either party, the other party would be very likely to oppress them whenever it came into power: so they tried to keep out of that war altogether and to hold to their charters. Several times the English Government attempted to take away the charters; and at last, in 1686, Sir Edmund Andros was sent out for this very purpose, and was authorized to act as royal governor for all New England. He came with great show and display, glittering in scarlet and lace; and Massachusetts and Rhode Island submitted to his authority. Connecticut appeared to do the same; but a brave man, William Wadsworth, took the charter and hid it in a hollow tree. Sir Edmund Andros was very angry, and took the book of records of the Connecticut Colony, and wrote under it "Finis," which means "the end." But in 1688 there was a revolution in England; and the people of New England soon rebelled against the new governor. The men of Boston put Sir Edmund Andros in prison; the charter of Connecticut was brought out from its hiding-place; and the word "Finis" disappeared from the colonial records. *Arrival of Andros.*

There had been, ever since 1643, a league of part of the New England Colonies to aid each other against the Indians, and for other purposes. It included the two Massachusetts Colonies and the two Connecticut Colonies; but they would not admit Rhode Island. Maine and New Hampshire were not yet independent colonies; and Vermont was not settled at all. This league lasted more than forty years, though its importance was much diminished during the latter part of that time. But when Sir Edmund Andros came to Boston as royal governor, the league was dissolved; and even after the people had rebelled, and had banished him, three years later, it was not restored. Massachusetts and New Hampshire were separated into distinct colonies, and *Union of 1643.* *End of the league.*

had royal governors from England, very much against their will; while Connecticut had kept its charter through all changes, thanks to William Wadsworth and the oak-tree; and Rhode Island began again to govern itself under its old charter, and was not molested. But all these contests about charters left a very sore feeling behind, and helped to prepare the way for that separation from the mother-country which was destined to take place.

Employments. But, while this great event was drawing near, the people of the New England Colonies all thought themselves true and loyal Englishmen; and they grew in numbers and in strength. At first they were all farmers or hunters or fishermen; but by degrees they introduced cotton and woollen manufactures, made glass and gunpowder, got lumber and tar from the woods, and exported fish cured with salt of their own making. The first vessel they built was called "The Blessing of the Bay;" and after a while there were many such blessings.

Money. There was very little coin among them to use for business purposes, because they had often to send it to England for buying supplies, and it did not return. So they had to trade by barter; afterwards they used wampum for money, and beaver-skins and Indian corn and bullets; and finally, in 1652, the Massachusetts legislature set up a mint, and coined twelvepenny, sixpenny, and threepenny pieces of silver. These bore on one side the inscription, "Massachusetts," always spelled "Masathusets," with a tree in the centre, and "N. E.," or "New England," with the date, on the other. These are commonly known as "pine-tree" shillings, sixpences, and threepences.

While the colonists were poor, there was necessarily much simplicity of living among them. People of all stations made their morning and evening meal of boiled corn-meal and milk, or of pork and beans, or pork and peas. Tea and coffee were not yet introduced; but home-made beer and cider were largely employed. Bread was commonly made of "rye and

Food.

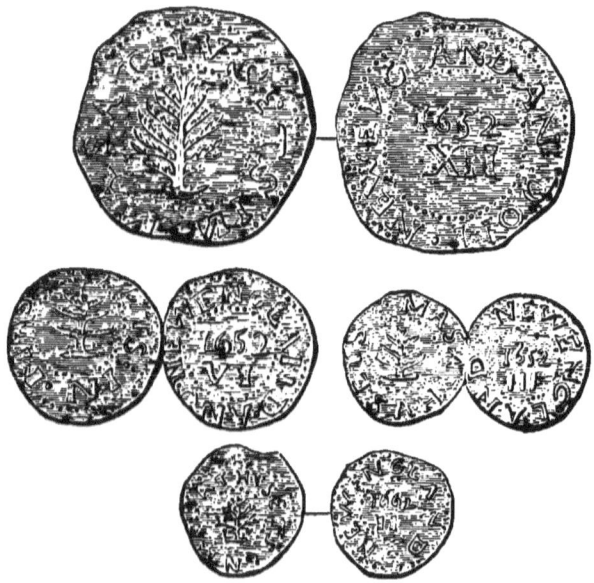

EARLY NEW ENGLAND COINS.

Indian," and seldom of flour. There were few amusements; dancing and the theatre were prohibited; musical instruments were rare; and no one was allowed even to own a pack of cards or a pair of dice. In their desire to promote virtue, the Puritans, no doubt, were too austere in their way of living; yet the standard of morality among them was certainly very high.

Amusements.

Social life and education. With this simplicity of living there was a great deal of equality in the early days. Only a few people of the highest social position, such as the clergy and the magistrates, were called by the titles of *Mr.* and *Mrs.*; the common designation being *Goodman* and *Goodwife*. Yet there was much deference paid to people of higher education or authority, especially to the clergy. The standard of education was high in the early colonies; many of the very first emigrants being men educated at the English universities. They introduced schools without delay, and then colleges. Harvard College

HARVARD COLLEGE IN 1720.

is almost as old as the colonies themselves, having been founded in 1636; and Yale College followed it in 1700. The first printing-press in the New England colonies was established at Cambridge in 1639; and the **The first newspaper.** first newspaper in any of the colonies appeared in 1704, and was called "The Boston Newsletter." Booksellers prospered very early in Boston; and many books were printed there, most of these being sermons or theological pamphlets.

As wealth increased in New England, social distinctions became greater; and the royal governors, especially, brought with them much show and display. In

Boston and Cambridge, in Portsmouth, N. H., and in some parts of Rhode Island, there grew up much elegance of living and magnificent hospitality; and there still remain in these places old houses which show the splendor that prevailed in colonial days. Slavery existed in all the early colonies, but in a very mild form; slave-labor being rarely employed in the fields, but mainly in private houses. At its first introduction it had been earnestly opposed; and when, in 1646, a cargo of Africans came from the Guinea coast to Boston, the legislature ordered them to be sent back to their native country, with a letter of indignation; and they were so scrupulous as to send and bring back one who had been already taken to Maine. In the Connecticut Colony, in 1650, and in New Haven soon after, man-stealing was made a capital offence. In Rhode Island, also, the first act of the General Assembly in regard to slavery, in 1652, ordered that no "blacke mankind or white" should be held in slavery for more than ten years, or after the age of twenty-four. But these scruples were gradually disregarded, and slavery was established. Many influential men still protested against it, especially Chief Justice Samuel Sewall, who published, in 1700, a tract on the subject, called "The Selling of Joseph." An answer to this tract was soon published; and Judge Sewall says in his letters that he met with "frowns and hard words" for it, but that he was sustained by the influence of some of the leading clergymen, such as Rev. John Higginson of Salem. It was not till after the Revolution, however, that slavery disappeared from the New England Colonies.

<small>Slavery.</small>

<small>Protests against slavery.</small>

CHAPTER XI.

OLD DUTCH TIMES IN NEW YORK AND NEW JERSEY.

Henry Hudson.

THERE was once an English sailor, named Henry Hudson, who made some very daring voyages. The European nations were trying hard to discover a shorter passage to India, either by sailing to the north of Europe, or by finding some opening through the new continent of America. Henry Hudson had made two voyages for this purpose, in the employ of English companies. Twice he had sailed among the icebergs, and through the terrible cold, as far as Spitzbergen; and twice he had turned back, because he could get no farther. But he was still as resolute and adventurous as ever, always ready for something new, — ready to brave the arctic cold or the tropic heat, if he could only find that passage to India which so many had sought in vain. At last, on the 4th of April, 1609, the Dutch East India Company sent him out once more to make discoveries. The Dutch at that time were the great commercial nation of the world; and Amsterdam was the centre of the commerce of Europe. There was not a forest of ship-timber in Holland; but it owned more ships than all Europe beside.

Enterprise of the Dutch people.

Discovery of the Hudson River.

Henry Hudson's vessel was named the "Half-Moon." He had a crew of twenty Englishmen and

Dutchmen; and his own son was among them. First he sailed north, as he had done before, trying to reach Spitzbergen and Nova Zembla; but he found icebergs everywhere, and his men almost mutinied because of the cold. Then he resolved to sail farther westward. He passed near Greenland, then southward to Newfoundland, then to Cape Cod, then as far south as Virginia; then he turned northward again, observing the shore more closely, and found himself at the mouth of what seemed to him a broad strait or river. On the 3d of September, 1609, he anchored near what is now Sandy Hook. There the Indians came out to trade with him; and after a few days he set sail again, following the stream farther and farther, thinking that he had found the passage to India at last.

It must have been an exciting thing to sail with Henry Hudson up that noble river, where no white man had ever sailed before. He said in his narrative that the lands on both sides were "pleasant with grass and flowers and goodly trees." "It is as beautiful a land as one can tread upon," he declared, "and abounds in all kinds of excellent ship-timber." The Indians came out to meet him in canoes "made of single hollowed trees;" but he would not let them come on board at first, because one of them had killed one of his sailors with an arrow. After a while the Dutchmen put more confidence in the Indians, and let them bring grapes and pumpkins and furs to the vessel. These were paid for with beads, knives, and hatchets. At last the Indians invited the brave sea-captain to visit them on shore, and made him very welcome; and one of their chiefs "made an oration, and showed him all

Sailing up the river.

Trading with the Indians.

the country round about." Henry Hudson sailed up as far as where the town of Hudson now stands; and there, finding it too shallow for his vessel, sent a boat farther still, — as far as what is now Albany. Then he turned back, disappointed, and sailed out of the "great river," or "Groot Rivier" as he called it, and went back to Holland.

Discovery of Hudson's Bay. He never saw that beautiful river again. The Dutch East India Company did not care to explore it, since it did not lead to India; and Hudson, on his next voyage, went to the northern seas, hoping to find the passage to India that way. He entered the bay that now bears his name; and there his men mutinied, tied him hand and foot, put him on board a boat, with his son and a few companions, among the floating ice, and set him adrift. Nothing more was ever heard of him.

Dutch legends. But to this day some of the descendants of old Dutch families on the Hudson River tell legends of the daring navigator who first explored it, and call him by the Dutch form of his name; and, when the thunder rolls away over the Highlands, they say, "There are Hendrick Hudson and his crew playing ninepins among the hills."

New Netherlands. In a few years trading-posts began to be established on the Hudson River. King James I. of England had lately chartered two companies (as has already been told) for the purpose of colonizing North America. One was to take the northern part of the Atlantic coast, and the other the southern half; but he required that their nearest settlements should be a hundred miles apart, so that there should be no quarrelling between them. It did not occur to him, that, if he left this wide space open, some other nation might slip in between, and found colonies; so that there might be quarrelling after all. Yet this was just what happened. After Henry Hudson's discoveries, Holland laid claim to all the land along the "great river," and called the whole territory "New Netherlands." Then, the next year, there came a bold sailor, named Adrian Block, the first European who ever sailed through Hurlgate, as has been already described in a previous chapter. He loaded his ship, the "Tiger," with bear-skins at the mouth of the Hudson, and was just ready to sail when the ship caught fire, and he had to land on Manhattan Island, where New York City now stands. There his men spent the winter of 1614. They put up some log-huts, and a fort of logs; and before spring they built a new vessel of sixteen tons, called the "Onrust," or "Unrest," a very good name for the restless navigators of those days. This was the second vessel built on this continent by Europeans. This settlement, which was called "New Amsterdam," was the foundation of what is now the great city of New York; and, ten years after that, the whole of Manhattan Island was bought from the Indians for twenty-four pounds sterling. Staten Island received its name from Henry Hudson, in honor of the Dutch government, "Staaten" being Dutch for "states."

New Amsterdam.

Staten Island.

Settlers at first came slowly to New Amsterdam; but the Dutch established several trading-posts, at different points, where they might buy the skins of beavers, bears, and otters, which the Indians had trapped or shot. At first only poor immigrants came; but, after a while, certain richer and more influential men were

Patroons.

sent out, with special privileges, from the Dutch West India Company. Each of these had authority to found a colony of fifty persons, and to own a tract of land sixteen miles in length, bordering on any stream whose shores were not yet occupied, and running back as far as he pleased into the interior. He was required to pay the Indians for their land, and to establish his colony within four years. He could exercise authority on his own "manor," as it was called, without regard to the colonial government; but he could not engage in the woollen or cotton manufacture, because that was a monopoly of the Dutch West India Company. And this company also agreed to supply the manors with negro slaves, whom they imported from Guinea. These great proprietors were called "Patroons."

Troubles of the Dutch with their neighbors. This was a very different system from the simple way in which New England had been colonized, where all men were equal before the law, and each man had a voice in the government. The Dutch and English settlers did not agree very well, especially when both nations had begun to explore the Connecticut valley, and both wished to secure possession of it. The Englishmen thought that the Dutchmen had no business on the continent at all, and that they certainly had no claim to the Connecticut valley. On the other hand, the Dutchmen said that they had ascended the Connecticut River first, and that their eastern boundary was the cape now called Cape Cod. Then the Englishmen charged the Dutchmen with exciting the Indians against them; and, on the other hand, the Dutchmen said that the English settlers were apt to get the better of them in making bargains. So the colony of New

Netherlands got into more and more trouble with these active and sharp-witted neighbors; and, besides that, the Indians were very troublesome; and there was also a standing quarrel with the Swedish settlers in Delaware; so that, on the whole, the Dutchmen had not so peaceful a time as they might have desired.

If we could have visited a Puritan village in Massachusetts during those early days, and then could have sailed in a trading-vessel to New Amsterdam, we should have found ourselves in quite a different community from that we had left behind. The very look of the houses and streets would have seemed strange. To be sure, the very first settlers in both colonies had to build their cabins somewhat alike, — with walls of earth or logs, and thatched roofs, and chimneys made of small sticks of wood set crosswise, and smeared with clay. But, when they began to build more permanent houses, the difference was very plain. The houses in New Amsterdam were of wood, with gable-ends built of small black and yellow bricks, brought over from Holland. Each house had many doors and windows; and the date when it was built was often marked in iron letters on the front. The roof usually bore a weathercock, and sometimes many. The houses were kept very clean inside and out, — as clean as they still are in Holland, where you may see the neat housekeepers scrubbing their doorsteps, even when the rain is pouring down upon their heads. The furniture in these houses was plain and solid, — heavy claw-footed chairs, polished mahogany tables, and cupboards full of old silver and china. Clocks and watches were rare; and the time was told by hour-glasses and sun-dials. The floors were

New Amsterdam unlike a New England village.

Dutch dwellings.

Their furniture.

covered with white sand, on which many neat figures were traced with a broom. There were great open fireplaces, set round with figured tiles of different colors and patterns, commonly representing scriptural subjects, — the ark, the prodigal son, and the children of Israel passing the Red Sea. In the evening they burned pine-knots for light, or home-made tallow-candles. Every house had two or more spinning-wheels; and a huge oaken chest held the household linen, all

DUTCH HOUSE.

of which had been spun upon these wheels by the women of the family.

Habits of the Dutch. Many of the citizens had also country-houses, called "boweries," with porches, or "stoeps," on which the men could sit and smoke their pipes; for the Dutch colonists did not work so hard as those in New England: they moved about more slowly, and took more leisure, and amused themselves more, in a quiet way. They were not gay and light-hearted, and fond of dancing, like the French settlers in Canada; but they liked plenty of good eating and drinking, and telling stories, and hearty laughter, and playing at "bowls" on smooth grass-plots. It was the Dutch who introduced various festivals that have been preserved ever since in America; such as "Santa Claus," or "St. Nicholas," at Christmas-time, colored eggs at Easter, and the practice of New-Year's visiting. They kept very early hours, dining at eleven or twelve, and often going to bed at sunset. Yet an early Swedish traveller describes them as sitting on the "stoeps" before their houses, on moonlight evenings, and greeting the passers-by, who, in return, were "obliged to greet anybody," he says, "unless they would shock the general politeness of the town." He also says that the Dutch people in Albany used to breakfast on tea, without milk, sweetened by holding a lump of sugar in the mouth; and that they dined on buttermilk and bread, "and, if to that they added a piece of sugar, it was called delicious." But the Dutch housekeepers of New Amsterdam had a great reputation for cookery, and especially for a great variety of nice cakes; such as doughnuts, olykoeks, and crullers. _{Santa Claus.}

The people of New Netherlands were not quite so fond of church-going as those who had settled Plymouth and Salem; but they were steady in the support of public worship, and had a great respect for their ministers, whom they called "dominies." Sometimes the dominies had to receive their salaries in beaver-skins, or wampum, when money was scarce. The dominie of Albany had one hundred and fifty beaver-skins a year. As for the dress of these early colonists, the _{Dominies.} _{Dress.}

women used to wear close white muslin caps, beneath which their hair was put back with pomatum; and they wore a great many short and gayly-colored petticoats, with blue, red, or green stockings of their own knitting, and high-heeled shoes. The men had broad-skirted coats of linsey-woolsey, with large buttons of brass or silver: they wore several pairs of knee-breeches, one over another, with long stockings, and with great buckles at the knees and on the shoes; and their hair was worn long, and put up in an eelskin cue. As to their employments, the people of New Amsterdam used to trade with the West Indies and with Europe, exporting timber and staves, tar, tobacco, and furs. They used to build their own ships for this commerce, giving them high-sounding names; such as "Queen Esther," "King Solomon," and "The Angel Gabriel."

Employments.

One of the Dutch governors, named William Kieft, used to be called "William the Testy," from his hot temper; and he kept the colony in a great deal of trouble, especially through his cruelty to the Indians, who injured the settlers very much in return. Gov. Kieft was very much displeased at the colonies sent from Massachusetts into Connecticut; for he wished to see that region settled from New Amsterdam only. So he issued a proclamation against the New England men. But they, instead of paying the least attention to it, attacked the Dutch fort at Hartford, and drove the garrison away. They also took possession of the eastern part of Long Island; threw down the coat-of-arms of Holland, which had been set up there; and put a figure of a "fool's head" in its place. This failure, and the severity of Kieft's government, made him very

William the Testy.

unpopular; and the people were very glad, when, in 1647, Gov. Peter Stuyvesant was appointed in his stead. *Peter Stuyvesant.*

Gov. Stuyvesant was a brave and honest man, but was so obstinate, that he was often called "Hardkoppig Piet," or "Headstrong Peter." Sometimes he was called "Old Silverleg," because he had lost a leg in war, and used to stump about on a wooden leg ornamented with strips of silver. Under his government the colony was well defended, for a time, against Indians, Swedes, and Englishmen. The trouble was, that he was quite despotic, and was disposed to let the people have as little as possible to do with the government. They did not feel that they had as much freedom as those who lived in the other colonies; and they were not so ready to fight for their patroons and for the East India Company, as were the English colonists for their own homesteads. Then the English settlers increased very fast in wealth and numbers; and the Dutchmen rather envied them, even while quarrelling with them. At last, in 1664, an English fleet, with many recruits from New England on board, appeared before New Amsterdam; and very soon the town was surrendered to the English by the general wish of the inhabitants, though quite against the will of "Headstrong Peter." He tore in pieces the letter from the English commodore requiring the surrender of the town; but the people made him put it together again, and accept the terms offered. From that time forth, except for one short interval of time, the English held possession of New Netherlands. *Surrender of Dutch possessions to the English.*

The name of the colony was then changed to New

York, in honor of the king's brother, the Duke of York, to whom King Charles II. gave the province. That part of New Netherlands south of the Hudson was, however, made into a separate province, under the name of New Jersey. The Duke of York allowed his own province to hold an assembly, that the people might make their own laws; and in 1683 they obtained a charter for themselves, much like those of the colonies farther east. When the duke became king, under the name of James II., he tried to take away this charter, but never succeeded. New York remained an English province, and lost some of its Dutch peculiarities: but some of these traits lingered for a good many years; and Dutch was long the prevailing language. There were still Dutch schools, where English was taught only as an accomplishment; but there was no college till King's College (now Columbia) was founded, in 1754. After the English had taken possession, a great many immigrants came to New York, though not so many as to Philadelphia; and these new-comers represented many different nations. Indeed, Holland itself had long been the abode of men from a great many nations, both because of its commercial prosperity, and from its offering an asylum to those persecuted for their religion. So there was an unusual variety of people in New Amsterdam from the first; and it is said that eighteen languages were already spoken there when it was transferred to the English. Thus New York seemed marked out, from the very beginning, for a cosmopolitan city, — for the home of people from all parts of the globe.

The Colony under the Duke of York.

New Jersey made a separate province.

Many people come to New York.

NEW JERSEY.

When the first Dutch settlers built their fort on Manhattan Island, in 1614, they also built a redoubt on what is now the New Jersey shore, opposite; and they afterwards claimed the whole region as a part of New Netherlands. Danish settlers also came very early, and settlers came from the English and Swedish colonies; but this the Dutch did not approve: so they first used the help of the Swedes in driving out the English, and then drove out the Swedes themselves, sending most of them back to Europe. When the English got possession of New Netherlands, in 1664, and the king gave it to his brother, the Duke of York, he in turn sold the southern part of it to two English noblemen, Lord Berkeley and Sir George Carteret. The latter had been governor of the Island of Jersey in the British Channel; and so he chose that name for the colony. His wife was named Elizabeth; and he named a village Elizabethtown, after her. His part was called East New Jersey, and Lord Berkeley's was West New Jersey; and the colony was commonly called "The Jerseys," for many years. The whole region was gradually purchased by the Society of Friends, or Quakers, and was chiefly settled by them. Other persecuted people came there also, especially Presbyterians from Scotland. They had perfect liberty of conscience; and their charter said, "No person shall at any time, in any way, or on any pretence, be called in question, or in the least punished and hurt, for opinion in religion." At last, in 1702, the colony was given up by the proprietors to Queen Anne, that a royal governor might be appointed.

First settlers of New Jersey.

The name.

Subsequent history to the time of the revolution.

The two provinces were then made into one, though they had separate legislatures for a long time. Free schools were introduced; and the College of New Jersey, now Princeton College, was founded in 1746. The colony remained quiet and at peace, down to the time of the American Revolution. "In all its borders," said a traveller, "there is not a poor body, nor one that wants."

Princeton College.

CHAPTER XII.

THE FRIENDS IN PENNSYLVANIA, AND THE SWEDES IN DELAWARE.

PENNSYLVANIA.

William Penn.

STATUE OF PENN IN PHILADELPHIA.

PENNSYLVANIA was founded in a different way from any of the other colonies, for it was entirely planned by one great and good man, who was the proprietor of the soil where the colony was established. His name was William Penn. He was a young Englishman, highly educated, and rich. He had studied at Oxford University, and at a college in France; but he was expelled from Oxford for taking part in Quaker meetings and in some trouble that grew out of them;

and he was afterwards imprisoned several times for the same offence. He became a very thoughtful and conscientious man. It was said as a joke, among his former fashionable friends, that "William Penn was a Quaker, or some very melancholy thing." He spent his money freely in aiding those who were punished for conscience' sake; and finally he resolved to found a colony in America, where such persecuted people could take refuge.

His grant of land. It happened that his father, who was a famous admiral in the English navy, had left, at his death, a claim for a large sum of money which he had lent to Charles II. before he came to the throne; and William Penn proposed to the king to give him a province in America instead of that money. This the king was very glad to do; for he had plenty of American lands, and very little of English gold and silver. So William Penn became the sole proprietor of a great tract of country, on condition of paying two beaver-skins annually to the king. *The name.* Penn wished to have this territory named Sylvania, because it was covered with forests (*sylva* being Latin for "a forest"); but his name was added to the word, against his wish, by the king; and the whole region was called Pennsylvania. *Previous history.* It had been visited by the Swedes and Finns in 1627, and had afterwards submitted to the Dutch of New Netherlands, and had passed, with all the Dutch possessions, into English hands. *Arrival of Penn.* William Penn sent out some emigrants in 1681, and came in person the year after. He was received with great enthusiasm. It seemed very appropriate that he should come in the ship "Welcome." It was right that he should be welcomed; for he had permitted every poor emigrant to settle on this land which the king had given to Penn himself, and he had promised to secure freedom of thought and speech to all. He called it a "free colony for all mankind," and wrote to the people, "You shall be governed by laws of your own making. I shall not usurp the right of any or oppress his person." So when the Quaker King, as he was sometimes called, had landed, the English, Dutch, and Swedish settlers came together; the deeds given William Penn by the king were publicly read; and he addressed the people, who heard him with delight. The next year he bought the ground for his chief city from some Swedes, who had bought it from the Indians; and he laid out the city, and gave it the name "Philadelphia," which means "brotherly love." He built it on the plan of the ancient city of Babylon; and he wished to have it "a faire and greene country towne." At first it consisted of three or four little cottages; and some of the people lived in hollow trees; but in three years it gained more than New York gained in fifty, though New York has since outstripped it, being far better situated for commerce. *Philadelphia.*

William Penn remained only two years in his colony, and then went back to England, where he stayed a long time. During almost all this time, the people governed themselves, choosing their own officers and making their own laws. There was no tax to support the poor, because none was needed. Every man who paid a tax for other purposes had a right to vote, without regard to religious belief or to nationality. No oath was required of witnesses in court. Theatrical exhibitions were forbidden; and some other laws were *The colony during Penn's absence in Europe.*

made that resembled those of the Puritans; but there was no religious persecution, and there was but one trial for witchcraft, and then the prisoner was convicted only of being "suspected of being a witch." Nevertheless, some of the cruel punishments that were usual in that age came gradually into use in Pennsylvania; and the whipping-post, the pillory, and the stocks were set up in the market-place. Slavery also existed in Pennsylvania; and, if a slave killed his master, it was the law that he should be burned, though there is no record that this ever happened there.

Penn's return.

After fifteen years of absence, William Penn returned to his colony, and stayed two years, finding it very much changed since he left it. He was personally very popular; and every one knew how generously he had thrown open to all settlers the estates that had been given him by the king. He himself felt that he had made great sacrifices. "O Pennsylvania," he once wrote, "what hast thou not cost me! Above thirty thousand pounds more than I ever got for it, two hazardous and most fatiguing voyages, and my son's soul almost." This referred to a son of his, who had behaved very badly during the father's absence The people of the colony knew what he had done for them, and were grateful; and yet, after all, they were not so well contented as in those colonies where every man owned his own clearing. And, after William Penn had died, the settlers did not pay so much respect to the rights of his successors as they had paid to his rights; and there was a good deal of discord in the colony.

Employments.

The early inhabitants of Pennsylvania were a very steady and industrious race. They lived by farming, commerce, and ship-building; constructing many vessels for sale, as well as for their own use. The great coal-mines of the State were not then discovered; but some iron furnaces were quite early established. Most of the English settlers preserved the simplicity of Quaker ways; but they led very comfortable and even luxurious lives. They did not establish schools and colleges *Schools.* quite so early as the eastern colonies; yet the first girls' school in America is said to have been established at Lewistown, at a time when Delaware was a part of Pennsylvania. The University of Pennsylvania was founded in 1749.

Philadelphia remained, almost down to the Revolution, "a faire greene country towne," such as William Penn had desired. The houses were generally of brick or stone, surrounded by gardens and orchards. *Interesting facts concerning Philadelphia and its citizens.* A German traveller said, in 1748, that peaches were so abundant around the town, that the very pigs were fed on them; and that the country-people in Europe guarded even their turnips more carefully than people in Pennsylvania guarded the most delicious fruits. Any one who chose could get over any wall, and help himself. Every Philadelphian, he said, had so much liberty and abundance, that he could live in his own house like a king. Yet in those days a Philadelphia shop was only a common dwelling-house with goods in the lower rooms, and with something hung over the door to show what was sold within, — perhaps a basket, a book, a wooden beehive, or a model of an anchor or a ship. In the street before the shop there was no pavement, only a narrow flagging in the middle of the sidewalk. There were weekly market-days, which *Philadelphia stores* were a kind of holiday; and there was a public fair twice a year. At first the people were of a sober kind, and had few amusements; but later there was a dancing-school, and then a public ball-room, and a race-ground, and a pack of hounds. As for travelling about, there was not very much of that to be done. Not only were there no railroads, but the common roads were bad, and the conveyances slow. In 1772 a stage, called "The Flying Machine," was advertised to go through from Philadelphia to New York in "the remarkably short time of two days."

Great prosperity of this colony. The Pennsylvania Colony was for many years more prosperous and comfortable than any other. Most of the foreign immigration came to the port of Philadelphia; and sometimes twelve thousand Germans arrived in a single year. About a third of the population were Quakers; and these were a thrifty and orderly people. At the time of the American Revolution, Pennsylvania ranked third among the colonies in population and power; being only surpassed by Virginia and Massachusetts.

DELAWARE.

Facts in the early history of Delaware. It happened once that an Englishman, Lord de la Ware, who was then governor of Virginia, made an exploring expedition up the coast, and entered a beautiful river, which was afterwards called the Delaware, from his name. This was in 1610. Twenty years after, the Dutch tried to found a colony there; but the colonists were all killed by the Indians. Some years after that, it was permanently settled by Sweden. It was the only colony that Sweden ever founded.

It happened in this way. Gustavus Adolphus, the most famous king of Sweden, — so famous that he was called "The Lion of the North," — had heard about America, and resolved to plant a colony there. So a company was formed, which invited colonists, from every part of Europe, to go out under the control of the Swedish Government. The company resolved, in particular, to allow no slaves among them. "Slaves," they said, "cost a great deal, labor with reluctance, and soon perish from hard usage. The Swedish nation is laborious and intelligent; and surely we shall gain more by a free people with wives and children." Gustavus Adolphus called the proposed American colony "the jewel of his kingdom," and thought that it would be a benefit to "all oppressed Christendom." *Plan of the Swedish colony.*

Unfortunately the great Gustavus was killed in battle in 1632; and his daughter Christina, a little girl only six years old, became queen in his place. But the Swedish prime-minister, Oxenstiern, was one of the wisest statesmen in Europe; and he was resolved to carry out the plan of the American colony: so he sent out, in 1638, a large number of Swedes and Finlanders, who built a fort, and called it Christiana after their little queen. The colony itself they called New Sweden. Many more colonists followed, and their settlements extended into what is now Pennsylvania; so that the governor's house was at one time only a few miles from what is now Philadelphia. But this did not please the Dutch settlers in New Netherlands; for they considered that they had taken possession of the region first, and that the Swedes were intruders. The Swedes were *New Sweden.* *Troubles between the Dutch and Swedes.*

very enterprising, and rivalled the Dutch in buying tobacco from Virginia traders, and in selling beaver-skins and other furs. Still the Dutch did not attack them, because the Swedish Government was powerful in Europe, and would be sure to sustain its colonies. However, the Dutch built a fort of their own, near Christiana; but the Swedes captured it. Then the Dutch company would bear it no longer; and they ordered their governor, Peter Stuyvesant "to revenge their wrongs, to drive the Swedes from the river, or to compel their submission." So, in 1655, the Dutch governor sailed up the Delaware River, took back his own fort, and then took the Swedish forts. The Swedish Government had, by that time, grown much weaker in Europe, and did nothing to defend its only colony; and, after seventeen years of separate existence, New Sweden was merged in New Netherlands.

Subsequent history. Then came the English, in 1664, and drove out the Dutch from the whole of New Netherlands; so that Delaware belonged, in turn, to three different nations. After this it was at one time a part of Pennsylvania, and then at last (1703) a separate colony; but it was always a small and peaceful community, being sheltered from the Indian attacks by the other colonies around it.

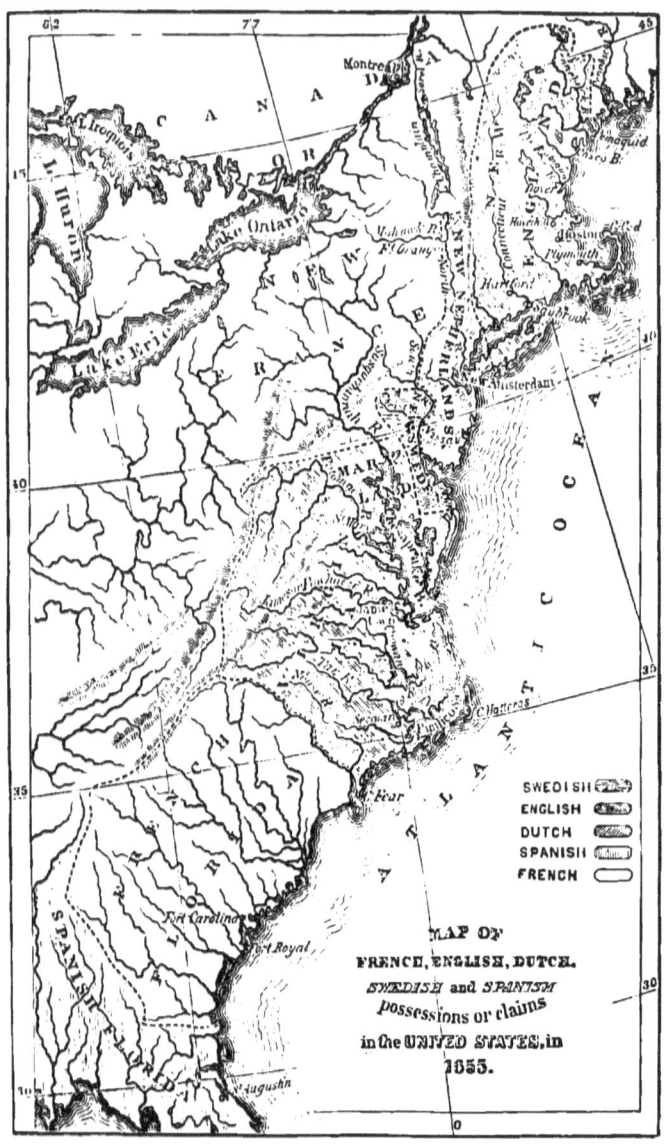

CHAPTER XIII.

THE OLD DOMINION AND MARYLAND.

VIRGINIA.

The "Old Dominion."

I HAVE described the early colonies in geographical order, beginning with New England, because this order is so much easier to remember than any other. But no colony can claim to date back so far as Virginia, "The Old Dominion" as it is sometimes called. Nothing but a ruined church, at a place called Jamestown, now marks the spot where the first Virginia settlement was made, in the year 1607, thirteen years before the landing of the Pilgrims at Plymouth. When King James I. gave a charter to two companies, one of which was to settle south of a certain region, and the other north of it, leaving a vacant space between them, it was the southern or Virginia company that settled Virginia.

John Smith.

The commander of the vessels that brought out the first Virginia colony was Capt. Newport; but the leading person among those on board was Capt. John Smith, a man who had led a very strange life. He was born in Lincolnshire, England, in 1579. When he was a boy of thirteen, he sold his school-books and satchel, meaning to run away to sea. Then his father died sud-

denly; and he decided that he ought to stay at home.
But he was willing to stay only two years; after which

RUINS OF JAMESTOWN.

he left England, went to France and Holland, and fought in various armies for several years. He had all sorts of wild adventures in these wars. Once, when sailing from Marseilles to Italy, he was accused by some superstitious fellow-passengers of being the cause of a storm that

Smith's travels and adventures

had arisen: so they threw him overboard. He swam to an island, and was presently taken off by a French ship. This ship engaged in a sea-fight while he was on board; and he so distinguished himself, that a part of the plunder of the hostile ship was given to him. Afterwards he went to fight against the Turks; and, during a long siege, a certain Turkish officer requested that some Christian officer would meet him in single combat "to amuse the ladies."

CAPT. JOHN SMITH.

Smith accepted the challenge, and killed not only this officer, but two others in succession. After a time he was taken prisoner, was sold as a slave, and was pitied and aided by his mistress, whose name was Tragabizanda. Then, making his escape, he reached Russia, went thence to Austria, Spain, and Morocco, and came back to Europe at last all ready for fresh adventures.

He soon heard of Captain Newport's expedition to Virginia, and eagerly joined it.

The first permanent English colony in America. They sailed Dec. 19, 1606, with three vessels; the party consisting of a hundred and five men in all, without women or children. When they at last entered Chesapeake Bay, the explorers were delighted with all they saw; and Captain Smith wrote that "heaven and earth never agreed better to frame a place for man's habitation." They called the capes between which they entered the bay, "Cape Henry" and "Cape Charles," after their young princes. They named "Old Point Comfort" for the good anchorage which they found there after a severe storm; and they called James River "the King's River," and their first settlement "James City" (now Jamestown) in honor of their king. They landed at this place May 13, 1607, and founded the first permanent English colony in North America.

It had been intended that Smith should be one of the directors of the colony; but the others were all jealous of him, and so prevented him from taking that position. But they could not prevent him from being the ablest man among them; and so they often had to turn to him, and finally made him their president. The truth was, that the colonists were a troublesome class to deal with. Many of them were not at all industrious or energetic. There were very few mechanics or farmers among them, though these are the men most needed in a new settlement. Many of them were "useless gentlemen;" and some were pardoned criminals. Some of them expected to reach the Pacific Ocean soon after landing, and were discouraged because they did not. Others went looking everywhere for gold, and loaded one of their ships with earth, mistaking it for precious ore. Smith wrote once to the company in England who had fitted out the colony: "When you send again, I entreat you rather send thirty carpenters, husbandmen, gardeners, fishermen, blacksmiths, and diggers-up of the roots, well provided, rather than a thousand of such as we have." Then

Smith's management of them.

they were reckless and wasteful, and built, says an old traveller, "a church that cost fifty pounds, and a tavern that cost five hundred." So Capt. John Smith had a good deal to do in keeping them to their duty, teaching them to cut down trees, and to build houses, drilling them as soldiers, and exploring the country to procure food for them. His punishment for idleness was starvation; and, in order to cure profane swearing, he had a daily account kept of every man's oaths; and at night, in penalty for each oath, he poured a can of cold water down the offender's sleeve. He himself worked harder than anybody; so that the others were put to shame by his example. And after a while, when the wives and children of these men came out to them, and they began to have comfortable homes, they did a great deal better; and Captain Smith wrote home that they had become "accomplished wood-cutters." Yet still one of their governors said that what the colony most needed was "a few honest laborers, burdened with children."

The discomforts of the colony.

Captain Smith wrote some vivid accounts of the early discomforts of the colony. He says, "When I first went to Virginia, I well remember, we did hang an awning (which is an old sail) to three or four trees, to shadow us from the sun : our walls were rails of wood; our seats unhewed trees, till we cut planks; our pulpit a bar of wood nailed to two neighboring trees. In foul weather we shifted into an old rotten tent, for we had few better; and this came by way of adventure for new. This was our church, till we built a homely thing like a barn set upon crotchets, covered with rafts, sedge, and earth, as were also the walls. The best of our houses were of the like curiosity, but, for the most part, far worse workmanship, that could neither well defend wind nor rain." . . . "Notwithstanding," he afterwards says, "out of the relics of our mercies, time and experience had brought that country to a great happiness, had they not so much doted on their tobacco, on whose firmest foundation there is small stability." It seems from this that Captain Smith foresaw what really happened, and feared that the cultivation of tobacco would exhaust the soil of Virginia, and would be in other respects injurious.

Captain Smith, at different times, made expeditions along the coast as far as Maine. He visited the Isles of Shoals in New Hampshire, which were formerly called "Smith's Isles," and on which a monument is now erected to his memory. It was he who first gave the name of "New England" to that part of the country; and the names of "Plymouth" and "Cape Ann" and "Charles River" appear first on a map made by him. He also made expeditions into the interior of the country. On one of these he was made prisoner by the Indians; and his few companions were killed. He, however, amused his captors by showing them his compass, and by explaining to them the movements of the earth and sun; so that they spared him. Then he puzzled them very much by writing a letter to be sent to his friends; for the Indians could not well understand how a message could be put on a piece of paper. Then he was condemned to death by Powhatan, an Indian chief; but the chief's daughter Pocahontas, a girl twelve years old, threw herself between the prisoner and the uplifted tomahawk, and Captain Smith was spared. This story

Expeditions along the coast.

Capture of Smith by the Indians

Pocahontas.

has been doubted in later times and may not be true, but it is certain that there was such a person as Pocahontas, and that, when she grew to be a woman, she became a Christian, was married to an Englishman named Rolfe, and went with him to England, where, as an English writer of that day says, "She did not onely accustom herself to civilite, but carried herself as the daughter of a king."

SMITH SHOWING COMPASS TO THE INDIANS.

The "Starving Time." She died soon after. Capt. John Smith also went to England in 1609, to be cured of a severe wound; and he never returned to the colony. After his departure, things grew worse and worse among the emigrants; and in six months they left Jamestown in despair, meaning to return to England forever. When Captain Smith had left them, there had been five hundred of them; but now there were only sixty. "None dropped a tear," they wrote; "for none had enjoyed one day of happiness." But, as they went down the James River, they met the long-boat of a vessel; and it proved to belong to an English ship which had brought them out a supply of provisions and a new governor, Lord De la Ware, or Delaware. Then they returned, and went on living in Jamestown; but that period of suffering was always remembered as "the starving time."

The settlers in Virginia did not generally live in villages, like those of the more northern colonies. The soil of Virginia was so productive, and the cultivation of tobacco so profitable, that the men paid little attention to commerce or the fisheries; and they were not, like the eastern colonists, obliged to live near one another for protection against the Indians. So no large towns or villages were established; but they cultivated separate plantations, and it became the practice to send out "apprenticed servants" from England, who were sold for a certain number of years to the planters. These servants were men who had committed crimes, or rebelled against the government, and who were sent to America in order that they might be of some use. After a time, in the year 1619, a Dutch man-of-war brought a cargo of twenty negroes from Africa; and the planters eagerly bought them, thus laying the foundation for the institution of slavery, which prevailed through the Southern States until within a very few years. The slaves became the field-laborers on the plantations, and were also the mechanics: all articles of luxury being brought from England, and being paid for, like all else, with tobacco. Taxes

The Virginia plantations.

Introduction of slavery.

Tobacco.

were payable in tobacco; and so were the salaries of the clergy, and all private debts. In the early days of the colony, ninety respectable young women were sent out by the company from England; and whoever took one of them for a wife must pay a hundred pounds of tobacco. Fines were paid in the same commodity. If a woman was convicted of slander, her husband had to pay five hundred pounds of tobacco. Legacies were left by will, in the form of so much tobacco. A good deal of comfort was enjoyed in Virginia at that period; and there was a good deal of rough and generous hospitality and a manly out-of-door life; but there was very

Education. little education. A Virginia governor, writing in 1671, said, "I thank God there are no free schools, nor printing; and I hope we shall not have them these hundred years." Another governor gave orders "to allow no person to use a printing-press on any occasion whatever;" and still another taxed schoolmasters at twenty shillings a head. Yet William and Mary College, in Virginia, is, next to Harvard, the oldest college in America, having been founded in 1692. It had twenty thousand acres of land from the English king and queen, for whom it was named; and duties were levied for its support.

The laws. At first the Virginia settlers had no power given them to make laws for themselves; and everything was done by a council appointed by the king. Many of the early laws were very severe, especially about religious matters. In 1610 it was the law, that, if any man absented himself from church for a single Sunday, he must lose his provision and allowance for a week; and, if he repeated the offence, he must lose his allowance

VIRGINIA.

and be whipped; and, if he offended a third time, he must suffer death. At a later time it was decreed, that, for the first absence from church, he must be tied neck and heels that night, and be a slave to the colony for the next week; for the second offence, he must be a slave a month: and, for the third offence, a year and a day. There were severe laws against swearing and scolding; and a woman who was an habitual scold might be ordered to be ducked three times in running water. In Virginia men and women might be punished by being publicly whipped; or by being placed in the stocks; or by standing in church, during the service, with white sheets over them, and white wands in their hands; or by standing at the church-door with the names of their crimes pinned upon their breasts. There were also laws against the entrance of Quakers and Roman Catholics into the colony; and they were severely punished if they came. All these things were the practice of that period; and very few communities were free from them. *Laws against swearing.*

The influence of the clergy was not so great in Virginia as in the New England Colonies; and the character of the early clergymen was not so high. Many instances are recorded of drunken and disorderly ministers of the Church of England, who came to the Virginia Colony, and set a very bad example in the way of drunkenness, gambling, and other vices. Society in Virginia was free, hospitable, and not very severe as to morality. Many of the colonial gentlemen lived on large plantations, owned many thousand acres of land, held many slaves, and kept open house. There was a good deal of show and ceremony on public occasions. *Character of the clergy.* *Style of living.*

One of the early governors, whenever he attended church, did so with a formality thus described by his secretary: "Every Sunday, when the lord-governor and captain-general goeth to church, he is accompanied by all the counsellors, captains, other officers, and all the gentlemen, with a guard of Halbardiers in his lordship's livery (fair red cloakes), to the number of fifty, on each side, and behind him. His lordship hath his seat in the Quoir, in a great velvet chair, with a cloth, with a velvet cushion spread before him, on which he kneeleth; and on each side sit the council, captains, and officers, each in their place; and, when he returneth home again, he is waited on to his house in the same manner."

House of Burgesses. After a time the people of Virginia secured the right to govern themselves They had a legislature of their own choosing, called "the House of Burgesses," whose laws only needed the approval of the company in England; and a written constitution was obtained at last.

Effects of slavery. The existence of slavery among them caused much ignorance and idleness, as the wisest Virginians admitted; but there grew up an aristocratic class, among whom there were many men of high character and energy. There still remain in Virginia the ruins of many old churches, and of stately houses built of imported brick, and having carved mahogany stairways, the memorials **Virginia at the time of the Revolution.** of a proud and wealthy colony. At the time of the American Revolution, Virginia was the leader among the colonies: it was the first to propose separation from the mother-country, and furnished many of the ablest men, both in congress and in camp.

MARYLAND.

The first settlement in what is now Maryland was made by a party from Virginia, headed by Capt. William Clayborne, who had a permit from the king of England to make discoveries, and to engage in the fur trade. He settled on Kent Island, in Chesapeake Bay, in 1631. But that region had been explored, just before, by an Englishman, George Calvert, Lord Baltimore; and he had persuaded King Charles I. to give him a charter for a colony there. Lord Baltimore died before the charter was signed; but his son Cecil, the second Lord Baltimore, took his place. In this charter, the new province was named "Terra Mariæ," or "Mary's land," in honor of Queen Henrietta Maria, wife of the reigning king. Lord Baltimore sent out an expedition under his brother, Leonard Calvert. There were some two hundred colonists; and they sailed in two vessels, the "Ark" and the "Dove." They landed in March, 1634; and their first settlement was called "St. Mary's," in honor of their queen. They often called themselves "the pilgrims of St. Mary's."

Maryland was the only early colony which the king expressly agreed to let entirely alone. Lord Baltimore was to govern it without help or hindrance from England. The king even promised not to tax the colony, on condition that it should send him two Indian arrows every year in token of subjection, and should pay him one-fifth of any gold or silver that might be found within its borders. The charter provided that the settlers should have a certain share in making the laws; but, in fact, the laws were chiefly made by Lord

The first settlements in Maryland

The government of the colony

Baltimore, or by the governors whom he appointed. This the people did not like very well; although Lord Baltimore was a good and enlightened man, and was particularly wise in regard to religious toleration. He was a Roman Catholic, and so were many of the first colonists; but, from the very foundation of the settlement, it was understood that all Christian denominations were to be on an equality in Maryland. In 1649 the Assembly passed an act providing that "no person professing to believe in Jesus Christ" should "be molested in their religion, or in the free exercise thereof, or be compelled to the belief or practice of any other religion, against their consent." This did not, like the Rhode Island law, afford toleration to Jews, and all others who were not Christians; but hardly any other government in that age was so liberal as Maryland in this respect. The Quakers were sometimes punished for refusing to do military duty, but never for preaching their religious doctrines. The colony was sometimes called "the land of the sanctuary."

Religious toleration.

Many Puritans, driven from Virginia by persecution, took refuge in Maryland, and, after a time, made a good deal of trouble, because they and their leader, Clayborne, could not get along harmoniously with the Roman Catholics. The Puritans were at last strong enough to pass an act declaring that the Roman Catholics were not entitled to protection in the colony which they had founded. Then the king settled the matter by establishing the Church of England in Maryland, in 1691; and, some twenty years after, he gave the colony into the hands of one of Lord Baltimore's descendants,

Religious troubles.

who had become a Protestant. Apart from this trouble about religion, Maryland was prosperous, and was much like Virginia in the occupations and habits of the people. It was a slaveholding community: there were few large towns; and the people generally lived on plantations and raised tobacco. Like the Virginians, they paid their bills with this plant, and their State House cost forty thousand dollars' worth of tobacco. The Indians molested them but little; and, even in the French and Indian wars, it was only the far western settlements in Maryland that were disturbed. There was, to be sure, a good deal of trouble between Maryland and Pennsylvania about their boundary line; but that was settled at last by appointing two surveyors, Mason and Dixon, to determine it; and the line they drew in 1750 has always been called "Mason and Dixon's line." For many years this line was of special importance, because it divided the slaveholding States of the Union from the free States.

Prosperity of the colony.

Mason and Dixon's line.

CHAPTER XIV.

THE SOUTHERN COLONIES.

NORTH AND SOUTH CAROLINA.

The first colony in Carolina.

THE name of Carolina was first given to the region that now bears it, by a little colony of French Protestants, under Jean Ribault, who arrived as early as 1562, fleeing from persecution at home. They landed at Port Royal; built there a fort of concrete, a part of the walls of which may still be seen; and raised a stone monument engraved with the lilies which were the symbol of France. They named the new country Carolina, after Charles (or Carolus) IX., then king of France. But the colony failed, like almost every one planted on the American continent during that century. The surviving Frenchmen all went back to France; and the attempt was abandoned. It was almost a hundred years before settlements began to be made from Virginia, from the New England Colonies, and from Barbadoes. Then, after a while, a great plan was formed in England for colonizing Carolina. North and South Carolina may be described at first as if they were one; for they were not separated till long after.

Carolina granted to eight men.

In the year 1663 King Charles II. of England granted the whole region called Carolina to eight proprietors, most of whom were noblemen at his court. They were men of wealth and influence; and they resolved to have a much more aristocratic form of government than any yet existing in America. At the request of the king, the plan for this was drawn up by a philosopher named John Locke. It was skilfully arranged in order to keep all the power in the hands of a very few persons. There was to be a regular order of nobility, as in European countries. These nobles were to be called earls and barons; and the lands were all to belong to them, while the condition of the common people was to be little better than that of slaves. But it turned out that the men who planned all this knew very little about colonies, and about the strong desire the people would show for self-government. King Charles and John Locke thought that the way to have the colony prosper was to give the mass of the people hardly any power; but it had been found in all the other colonies that the way to secure prosperity was to let the settlers own their lands, and govern themselves as far as possible. So it turned out, at last, that the proprietors and earls and barons, who claimed to own Carolina, stayed at home; and the plan of government from which so much was expected hardly went into operation at all. *Locke's plan of government.*

Meanwhile settlers came from all directions into Carolina. There were English, Irish, Scotch, Dutch, and French. These last were Huguenots, or Protestants, fleeing from persecution, like those other Frenchmen who had given Carolina its name and set up the lilies of France there a hundred years before. These Huguenots had quitted France forever, and *Growth and prosperity of the colony* sought religious freedom under the English flag. Personal freedom was not valued so highly in the colony; and negro slaves were introduced from Barbadoes in 1665. Except in this respect the colony prospered for a long time. The rice plant is said to have been accidentally obtained out of the cargo of a vessel from Madagascar, that put into the port of Charleston, and it was soon very extensively cultivated; but it was long before cotton was introduced, though it has since become the chief product of the southern part of Carolina. It soon became the habit of the people of that southern region to live on large isolated plantations, as in Virginia; while in the northern part of Carolina the settlers lived yet farther from one another, in the woods, where there were no roads; and they could travel only by paths "blazed" through the woods by notches made here and there upon the trees. There they supported themselves by cutting timber, making tar and turpentine, hunting the bear, and trapping the beaver; all this being done with the aid of slaves, whom they had brought with them from Virginia. So the northern and southern parts of Carolina came to have different habits and interests, even before they were separated into two distinct colonies.

At one time, when Spain and England were at war, the province of Carolina was drawn into hostilities with the Spanish settlements in Florida. The colonists sent an armed expedition against St. Augustine; and, in return, the Spaniards excited the Indians against the colonists. Both portions of Carolina had much trouble from these Indians, especially from the tribe of Tuscaroras, who were at last conquered, and had to emigrate to New York, where they joined the Five Nations, in 1722. During the French and Indian wars, the French attacked Carolina from Havana; and the colonists were much harmed by these various enemies. They were also very much dissatisfied with the government of the English proprietors of the soil; and at last they rebelled, imprisoned the secretary of the province, and banished the governor. Finally they petitioned the king of England to buy out the proprietors, and make two royal provinces of the whole. This was done in 1729, after which North and South Carolina were permanently separated. Each province had a royal governor, with an assembly chosen by the people. As time went on, these royal governors became almost as unpopular as those whom the proprietors had before appointed. So the desire for self-government grew stronger and stronger among the people, down to the time of the American Revolution. *The division.*

GEORGIA.

The colony of Georgia was founded by a very remarkable man, Gen. James Oglethorpe. He became an officer in the British army when very young, and was a great favorite with every one, on account of his courage, fine manners, and good looks. After a time he volunteered for duty in the army of Prince Eugene of Savoy, who was then fighting against the Turks. After distinguishing himself at the siege of Belgrade, Oglethorpe returned to England, and became a member of parliament. While in that position he was particularly interested in the condition of the poor *James Oglethorpe* debtors in England, who were then cruelly treated. This led him to plan a colony, to be established in America, whither all who were poor and unfortunate might come, and all who were persecuted for their religion. So he applied to King George II. for lands to be thus used; and the king gave him a large tract between Carolina and Florida. It was quite large enough indeed; for it was supposed to reach to the Pacific Ocean. But, as it had been claimed by both the English and Spanish, there was some doubt about the title to it; and this doubt led to much trouble afterwards. However, Oglethorpe fitted out a colony to his new possessions, in 1733, and went himself as their governor. The colony was named Georgia, after the king. The land was given to Oglethorpe and his associates "in trust for the poor;" and the seal of the colony represented a family of silkworms with a Latin motto, meaning, "Not for themselves, but for others."

Settlement of Georgia.

When Oglethorpe first arrived in the wilderness, he pitched his tent under four large pine-trees, where now Savannah stands. This tent was for a year his only abode. He had a royal title to the land; but he took care to pay the Indians of that region for it, and they were always friendly to him. Some of the chiefs presented to him a buffalo-skin, with the head and feathers of an eagle painted on the inner side. They said, "The feathers of the eagle are soft, signifying love; the skin is warm, and is the emblem of protection: therefore love and protect our little families." Oglethorpe always acted on this request; and he was not only a friend to the Indians, but also to the negroes; and, though slavery existed in the neighboring

Wise measures of Oglethorpe.

colony of South Carolina, he would not have it introduced into Georgia. He said that if slaves were to be introduced into Georgia he could "have no further concern with the colony." He also forbade the importation of rum; and it was not allowed until after his departure.

Many of the settlers in Georgia were Moravians, a persecuted sect of Christians from Austria. Some celebrated English preachers came out to visit these people, — John and Charles Wesley, the founders of the great Methodist denomination; and George Whitefield, who founded an "Orphan House" at Savannah, and supported it with sums of money gained by his preaching. But Whitefield was not so consistent as Oglethorpe in one respect; for Whitefield was in favor of slavery, and it was by his influence that it was introduced into Georgia at last, after Oglethorpe's departure. The Wesleys, on the other hand, called slavery "the sum of all villanies." The Wesleys and Whitefield.

After a time, when there was war between Spain and England, Georgia, like Carolina, was led into hostilities with the Spanish colony of Florida. Oglethorpe was made commander of the whole colonial force of a thousand white men and some Indians, and made an attack on St. Augustine in 1740. This failed; and he afterwards had to defend his own colony against an attack of the Spaniards. They came with three thousand men, and landed on St. Simon's Island, where they were at last utterly defeated. Soon after this, Oglethorpe left the colony for England. The other trustees, who had been appointed by the king, were in many respects unpopular. Some of their laws were very vexatious; Troubles with the Spaniards. The colony after Oglethorpe's departure.

as, for instance, that which limited the size of a man's farm, and that which prohibited women from inheriting land. After a while there were so many complaints that they gave up their charter; and Georgia became a royal province. The king appointed most of the officers, though there was an Assembly of the people. General Oglethorpe never came back to America, but was always a warm friend to it. He lived to be a very old man, and was distinguished, when almost ninety, by his personal eloquence and courtesy. He was one of the best and noblest men ever connected with the settlement of America.

Scotch Highlanders.

Besides the Moravian settlement, there was a Highland settlement, of Scotch Highlanders, in Georgia, whose affection Oglethorpe had first won by wearing the Highland dress when he went to visit them. These Highlanders, like the Moravians, took a good deal of pains about the education of their children,— a thing much neglected in the rest of the colony. The people cleared the forests, and occupied themselves in agriculture, with the aid of their slaves. Great pains were taken by the English Government to encourage the manufacture of silk, and, for a time, it flourished. Persons skilled in the rearing of the worms, and the winding of the silk, were sent out from England; and this industry was continued in Georgia down to the time of the Revolution. General Oglethorpe took to England the first silk that was produced; and the queen had a dress made of it. Georgia never was thickly settled, and was the youngest and weakest of the colonies at the time when the great war broke out that separated them from the mother-country, and united them all into a nation.

Manufacture of silk.

CHAPTER XV.

THE INDIAN WARS.

SOON after the Pilgrims landed on Plymouth Rock, they saw a few Indians, who ran away. But, in the following spring, an Indian came boldly among them, one day, saying, "Welcome, Englishmen!" This surprised them very much; for they did not know how the stranger could have learned the English language. It turned out that his name was Samoset, and that he lived farther east, along the coast, and had known the English fishermen. Many Indians had made acquaintance with Europeans in this way, and had sometimes been treated badly; so that they were not all as confiding as Samoset. He remained one night with the settlers; and, when he went away, they gave him a knife, a bracelet, and a ring; and he promised to return soon, and bring other Indians with beaver-skins for sale. Ere long he returned, and made the Englishmen acquainted with a chief, called Massasoit, who ruled more men than any one in that region. He soon made a treaty with the colonists in behalf of his tribe; and this treaty lasted more than fifty years. Massasoit was the sachem of the Wampanoags, a tribe that had been very important, though it had just been greatly reduced

Samoset.

Massasoit

by disease; and his friendship was of the greatest value to the Pilgrims.

The Pilgrims visit Massasoit. Once the Pilgrims sent an expedition to Massasoit's lodge to visit him. The messengers carried "a horseman's coat of red cotton" for the king, and beads and jack-knives for his chiefs; and Massasoit put on his red coat, and treated them kindly. At another time, when

"WELCOME, ENGLISHMEN!"

a friendly Indian, named Squanto, was said to have been killed by the Narragansetts, a party of ten colonists marched into the forest, and surrounded the hut where the chief of this tribe was; and, though he had five thousand fighting men at his command, they compelled him to leave Squanto unhurt. The Indians had not yet learned the use of fire-arms; and their arrows did not put them on an equality with the well-armed Englishmen. Afterwards the chief of the Narragansetts sent to Governor Bradford a bundle of arrows wrapped in the skin of a rattlesnake. The governor stuffed the skin with powder and shot, and sent it back; and the Indians were afraid to keep it, and threatened no more. But the Pilgrims paid for all they obtained from the natives; and, when they finally went to war, it was to defend another colony, which had treated the Indians badly. In this war, under Capt. Miles Standish's orders, several Indians were killed; and this caused great regret to good Mr. Robinson, the pastor whom the Pilgrim congregation had left behind at Leyden. "I would you had converted some," said he, "before you had killed any."

Governor Bradford's reply to the Indians.

Both in the Plymouth and the Massachusetts Colonies, it was the rule that no one should take anything from the Indians without paying for it. The year after the Massachusetts Colony was founded (1631), the court decreed thus, in the quaint spelling of those days: "It is ordered, that Josias Plastowe shall (for stealing four baskets of corne from the Indians) returne them eight baskets againe, be fined five pounds, and hereafter be called by the name of Josias & not Mr. as formerly he used to be." This shows how carefully they tried to do justice; though it is very likely that there was often occasion for such punishments as this. Large tracts of land were often obtained for a blanket or a knife; and, though this bargain would now seem to us very unfair, yet we must remember that the knife or the blanket might often be of more value to the Indian than a dozen square miles

Dealings with the Indians.

of forest land, especially as there was a whole continent left for him to occupy. It was only when settlers multiplied, that land began to have any of the value that it now possesses.

The Pequot War. The first Connecticut settlers found fiercer tribes to deal with than the Pilgrims; and they had very early a war with the Pequots, in which all the New England colonists were involved. It would have been much more serious than it was, but that Roger Williams used his influence over the Narragansett tribe to keep them from joining the war. A council of the Indians was being held; and Roger Williams, in order to save the very men who had banished him from Massachusetts, went many miles in a canoe in a severe storm. The Pequots were enraged with Williams for interfering, but, after four days of delay, the Narragansetts refused their aid. The Pequots kept up constant attacks upon the Connecticut settlers; and at last an expedition was sent against them (in 1637), consisting of ninety white men and several hundred Indian allies, under command of Capt. John Mason. Their object of attack was the chief fort of the Pequots, which lay near *Description of Pequot fort.* what is now Stonington, Conn. The fort covered more than an acre, which was enclosed by trunks of trees, about twelve feet high, set firmly in the ground, close together. Within these were some seventy wigwams, covered with matting and thatch, and arranged in two lanes. There were two entrances; and Captain Mason stationed himself at one of these, and the next in command, Captain Underhill, at the other, each having a portion of the colonists with him, while the Indian allies were arranged outside. As they were taking their posi-

tions, a dog barked, and they heard the cry from within,
"*Owanux, Owanux!*" ("Englishmen, Englishmen!")

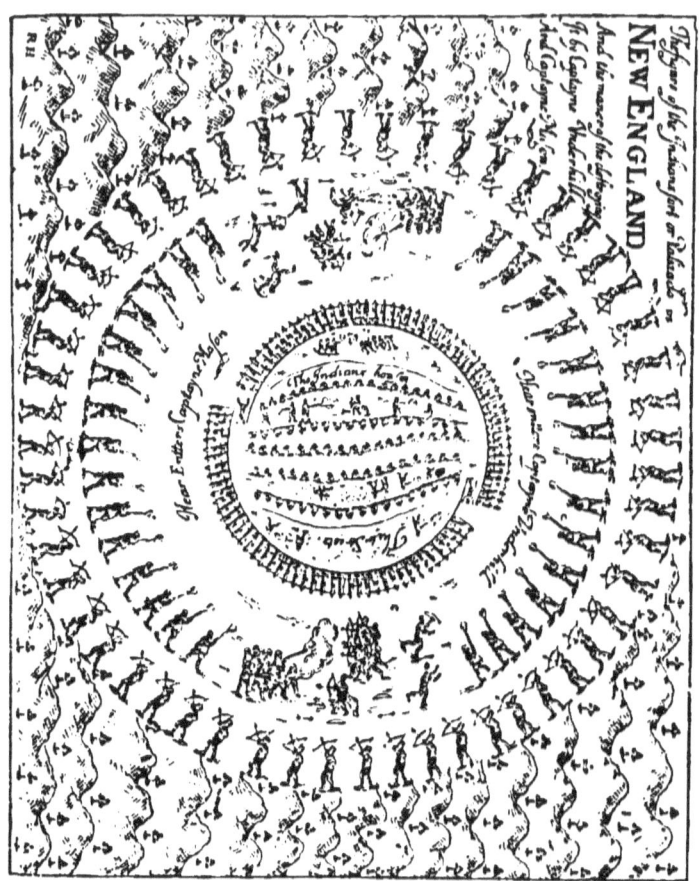

CAPTAIN UNDERHILL'S PICTURE OF THE FIGHT.

Then the attack began. The roofs of the Indian cabins were set on fire, and the greater part of the Indians were killed; while only two white men were slain,

Attack on the fort.

many, however, being wounded. It was the first great blow inflicted by the whites on the Indians; and for forty years after it there was much more peace between the two races in New England.

John Eliot. It is pleasant to know that, while this fighting was going on, there were men among the Puritans who were trying to do good to the Indians and to secure peace in a gentler way. One of the most eminent of the Massachusetts clergymen, Rev. John Eliot, "the apostle Eliot," as he was called, devoted himself to learning their habits and language, and to making for them a translation of the Bible. This translation was printed at Cambridge; and part of the type was set by an Indian compositor. Eliot gathered those who became Christians into a town at Natick, Mass. Other good men imitated him, such as the Mayhews, Cotton, Brainerd, and others; and at last there were thirty churches of "praying Indians" as they were called, under native preachers. Similar churches had been established in Canada by the French Roman Catholic missionaries. Once, during the time when there was bitter hostility between the English and French settlers, *Dreuillettes.* a Jesuit missionary named Dreuillettes, came to the Massachusetts Colony on an embassy, to try to make a league with the English settlers against the Mohawks. It was a time when Jesuits were forbidden, on pain of death, from coming to Massachusetts; but this missionary came, and was kindly received by Eliot, whom he calls "Maistre Heliot," and who invited the supposed Jesuit to pass the winter with him. There were so many quarrels between the French and the English in those early days, and between the Roman Catholics and

THE INDIAN WARS. 137

Protestants, that it is pleasant to see any instances of harmony and toleration.

The severest of the early Indian wars broke out in 1675, and was called "King Philip's War." King Philip was the son of Massasoit, the firm friend of the whites, and he ruled over the Wampanoags. His chief residence was at Mount Hope, nearly opposite what is now called Fall River, Mass. That peninsula had been reserved for the tribe when the rest of their lands were sold. Philip was a brave and thoughtful man. He saw that the white settlements were gradually increasing, and that the Indians were being confined to a smaller and smaller space; and he resolved to unite the tribes in a desperate effort to drive the English from the soil. He went from tribe to tribe, all the way from Maine to Connecticut, and almost every tribe joined the league, even the friendly Narragansetts, whose chief, Miantonomi, had been slain through the treachery of some whites. Philip had laid his plans so well, that the war broke out along a line of two hundred miles, within three weeks. It was peculiarly severe in Western Massachusetts, where town after town was burned. Tradition says that in one village, Hadley, when it was attacked by the Indians, and the settlers were all irresolute for want of a leader, a ven-

King Philip's War.

Destruction of towns in western Massachusetts.

KING PHILIP.

erable man, unknown to all, appeared suddenly in the streets, took command of the people, gave military orders that led to the defeat of the Indians, and then disappeared as suddenly as he came. It was afterwards supposed that this mysterious person was William Goffe, who had been a general in Cromwell's army, and had been compelled to flee from England as a "regicide" for having been one of the judges who sentenced Charles I. to death. Goffe, and his companion Whalley, were long in concealment among the forests and caves of Connecticut. This sudden appearance at Hadley is described in Hawthorne's story of "The Gray Champion," though he has changed the time and place of the event.

Narragansett expedition. To break the power of the Indian league, an expedition of a thousand men, under Captain Winslow, was sent against the Narragansetts in Rhode Island. In the depth of winter the colonists made their way to the Narragansett town. It was in a swamp, surrounded by palisades. At last, after two hours' fighting, the attacking party entered the fort; and the tribe was almost wholly exterminated. Still Philip kept in the field, and is said to have slain one of his warriors for proposing peace. In 1676 a strong Puritan force was sent against him, under Captain Church; and they captured his wife and child. "My heart breaks," said King Philip: "now I am ready to die." The child was a boy of nine, and was the last of the race of Massasoit. The Puritans, who had owed so much to the grandfather, sold the child as a slave to Bermuda. Soon after this King Philip was hunted down and killed; and so ended a war that had lasted two years, and had cost, as was estimated, six hundred lives. Twelve or thirteen towns had been entirely destroyed; and it was estimated that one family in every eleven had been burned out, and that every eleventh soldier had fallen.

While these Indian wars were going on in New England, other colonies had similar troubles. The Dutch in New Amsterdam committed cruel outrages on the Indians, and suffered severely in return. In Virginia the Indians attacked the remoter villages; and the English Government would not let the settlers have arms for their own defence. This led to a sort of rebellion; and a brave man named Nathaniel Bacon procured a supply of arms, and organized a force to fight the Indians. Then Governor Berkeley tried to put him down; and Bacon took the city of Jamestown, and burned it in revenge, beginning with his own house, and destroying the whole town so thoroughly, that scarcely a vestige of it now remains. Soon after this, Bacon died; but there was more peace with the Indians in Virginia for many years after this.

Bacon's Rebellion.

The colony that had least trouble with the Indians in early days was Pennsylvania. This was partly the result of the wise and righteous course pursued by William Penn, the founder. He made a treaty, in the very year of his arrival (1682), with the Delawares and other tribes. Standing under a great elm-tree a Shackamaxon, on the northern edge of Philadelphia, he told the Indians how he meant to treat them. He said to them, "I will not call you children, for parents sometimes chide their children too severely; nor brothers only, for brothers differ. The friendship between

Penn's treaty.

you and me I will not compare to a chain; for that the rains might rust, or the falling tree might break. We are the same as if one man's body were to be divided into two parts; we are all one flesh and blood." To this the Indians replied, "We will live in love with William Penn and his children as long as the sun and moon shall endure." And they fulfilled this treaty. Pennsylvania is said to have been the only colony where the evidence of an Indian was taken in court against that of a white man; and the Indians proved themselves worthy of this just treatment.

The Quakers and the Indians. The Society of Friends, or Quakers, in New Jersey, showed the same generous and just conduct toward the Indians; and the Indians treated them equally well; "You are brothers," said the sachem; "and we will live like brothers with you. We will have a broad path for you and us to walk in. If an Englishman falls asleep in this path, the Indian shall pass him by, and say, 'He is an Englishman, he is asleep: let him alone.'"

It is often said that not a drop of Quaker blood was ever shed by an Indian; and, though this is not quite true, yet it is true that Pennsylvania and New Jersey suffered much less than most of the other colonies. This was partly due to William Penn's policy; but it is also to be remembered that the Indians on whose territory the Quaker colonists settled were a peaceful and humble tribe (the Delawares), who had been conquered by the Iroquois. It is not certain that it would have been as easy to keep the peace with the fierce tribes that then inhabited New England and New York. But Penn's treaty with the Indians has always been very famous; and the great elm-tree under which it was made was so well known, that almost a century afterwards, when the American colonies were fighting for their independence, the commander of an English army placed a sentinel under that tree to protect it from his soldiers, who were cutting down all the surrounding trees for fuel. It stood safely until within a few years, when it was blown down.

The successors of William Penn did not always continue his generous treatment of the Indians. For instance, there was a celebrated purchase of land, called the "Walking Purchase." The proprietors of the soil had a deed from the Indians, granting them as much land in a certain direction as a man could walk over in a day and a half. Of course, it was supposed that the walking would be done by an ordinary man in an ordinary way. Instead of this, the proprietors laid out a smooth road for the whole distance; then chose the most active men they could anywhere find, and put them in training for the walk. Thus they included a great distance in the land walked over, and then required the Indians to remove from it. The Delawares objected; and then the more powerful Iroquois, their previous conquerors, were called in by the English, and forcibly drove the Delawares from the lands. William Penn certainly would not have approved of this mode of dealing. However, the Pennsylvania colonists always suffered less from the Indians than did almost any other colony, down to the terrible period of the "French and Indian wars."

The "Walking Purchase."

The Delawares driven out.

CHAPTER XVI.

THE FRENCH AND INDIAN WARS.

THE terrible "French and Indian wars," in which all the colonies were more or less involved, took place in this way. As the white settlements increased, the native tribes steadily diminished; so that by 1675, when there were fifty-five thousand whites in New England, there were but some thirty thousand Indians, or, as some think, not nearly so many. The Indians' lands had been bought by the new comers, or obtained by treaty, or seized after war, till they were reduced to mere strips of territory here and there. Then the white men were much better armed, even after the natives had learned the use of fire-arms. So the Indians could not cope with the English without some aid; and, unhappily, the French settlers in Canada were very willing to render this aid. For the French had been the first explorers of the interior regions of the continent. They had gone from Canada, along the Great Lakes, and down the Illinois and Ohio and Mississippi Rivers; and they wished to keep the English out of all that region, and not even to let them trade with the Indians. Moreover, the French Roman Catholic missionaries had converted many of the Indians to their form of Christianity; and these converts naturally took the part of their priests against

THE FRENCH AND INDIAN WARS. 143

the English settlers, who were almost all Protestants. Besides all this, the French had treated the Indians with more consideration than the English had shown. The French had adopted the Indian ways when among them; and many had even married Indian wives: so it was natural that the native tribes should have more liking for the French. Yet some of the shrewder men among them did not love either of these nations of foreigners. One of them said to an English visitor, "You and the French are like the two edges of a pair of shears; and we are the cloth which is cut to pieces between you."

All this led to a series of wars which were far worse than the early Indian wars, because the French supplied the native tribes with much better weapons than they had before used, and taught them how to build forts in a stronger way. These wars were called by different names; as, King William's War (1689), Queen Anne's War (1702), King George's War (1744), and, finally, "The Old French and Indian War" (1755 to 1763). This last was the most important; but the whole series made really one long war, sometimes pausing, and then beginning again, the object being to decide whether the French or the English should control the continent. *Their names.*

In these wars the Indians rarely met the whites in open field, but trusted rather to sudden surprises, night-attacks, and swift marches. The chief terrors came upon lonely families and small villages. When the inhabitants were asleep, they were liable to be awakened by the sound of the Indian war-whoop, or the glare of houses in flames. Then the men must get *The mode of warfare* down their loaded muskets; and the women must take the bullet-moulds, and begin melting lead to make bullets; or must load the guns as fast as they were fired. Sometimes, when the lead was gone, they picked the bullets of the Indians from the walls where they had struck, or spread blankets to collect them as they rattled against the chimney, and fell. Or they watched their opportunity to flee to the "block-house," or "garrison-house," that was often placed in or near a village. This was usually a small wooden fort of two stories; the lower story being sunk a few feet into the ground, and the upper projecting a few feet beyond the lower. The first story was made of squared logs, as much as a foot and a half in diameter, though smaller logs were used above. There were loop-holes through which guns could be fired, and gratings in the roof, where smoke could escape. Sometimes these block-houses were held for many days against the Indians; since the attacking-party had no cannon, and could not approach near enough to set the house on fire, without being shot down.

Story of Thomas Duston.

When the Indians attacked by day, they selected houses from which the men were absent. Thus they approached the house of a man named Thomas Duston or Dustin in Haverhill, Mass. He was absent in the fields, and reached the house too late to defend his wife, who was ill in bed, and had her young infant with her. He collected seven of his children, however, and sent them running along the road; then seized his gun, and mounted his horse, with the intention of taking up before him the child he loved best, and defending the others as he could. But he could not possibly decide which child to take: so he hurried the little party along, loading, and firing at the Indians, who fired in vain at him, until he reached a place of safety a mile away. Meanwhile the Indians compelled Mrs. Duston to go with them, together with her baby and nurse and young boy. The baby was soon killed, as being a

DUSTON SAVING HIS CHILDREN.

hindrance to the march; but the others were led for several days through the forest. At last, when they were encamped on an island in the Merrimack River, the prisoners discovered that they were to be put to death with tortures at the end of the journey, and resolved to save themselves. At night, when their captors were asleep, the three prisoners killed with

Escape of the prisoners.

tomahawks ten of the twelve Indians, and escaped to the white settlements.

The attack on Deerfield.
At another time the French and Indians attacked the town of Deerfield, in the western part of Massachusetts. It was in February, 1704. The attacking party came down on snow-shoes from Canada, for the purpose. It consisted of both French and Indians, and was commanded by Hertel de Rouville, a French leader, who was a great terror to the colonists in those days. The people of the village had been warned of their danger, and had built a barricade around their houses, and kept a watch every night. One very cold night the sentinel went to sleep, and the poor people were awakened by the war-whoop. The marks of tomahawks are still to be seen on the door of the old parsonage house, which was attacked. Rev. John Williams, who lived there, was captured with his wife and six children; and they were all carried away to Canada, with nearly a hundred others. It was a terribly cold winter. The Indians took the clothes from some of the captives; and many had only a blanket apiece, and only moccasons on their feet. During all their terrible march, they had scarcely any food except ground-nuts and acorns. Two or three

Cruelty to the captives.
times only they had dog's flesh. They were compelled to walk twenty or thirty miles a day, carrying burdens for their new masters. Sometimes the children were treated kindly by the Indians, and were carried in their arms, or on rude sleds for the purpose; but in other cases, when they lagged behind, they were killed with tomahawks. Mrs. Williams, the minister's wife, was also killed in this way. When the survivors reached

Canada, they were sold to the French as slaves, and were treated with a good deal of kindness by them; and Mr. Williams was redeemed and brought back. He lived to write an account of his adventures, under the name of "The Redeemed Captive." All his children were brought back with him, except one little girl, who had been adopted into a family of Christian Indians, and was not allowed to leave them. She grew up, and married a chief, and returned to Deerfield several times, but would not remain; preferring to go back to her Canadian wigwam and her children.

We can easily imagine how the colonists felt toward the Indians, when such tales as these were talked over by the open fireside, in many a lonely farm-house, where the children lay awake afterwards, listening for the Indians' war-whoop. And they felt quite as bitterly towards the French missionaries in Canada, who were supposed to encourage the Indians in their attacks. Yet these French missionaries often showed humanity to the captives; and, indeed, some tribes, under their influence, ceased to torture their prisoners. These Indian wars were the greatest possible interruption to all other pursuits; for there were times when one-fifth of all those capable of fighting had to be absent from their homes. It is no wonder that the colonists became almost desperate; so that they offered rewards for every Indian killed, — from five to fifty pounds. *Feelings of the colonists toward the French and Indians.*

It was very important to the colonists that the English Government should send expeditions against the French in Canada, to keep them busy in defending themselves. The colonists were always ready to take part in these *Capture of Louisburg.*

expeditions, and sometimes led them. For instance, a party was sent out from Marblehead, Mass., under command of Gen. William Pepperrell, to attack the French fortress of Louisburg, on Cape Breton. This was the most important military enterprise that the colonists had yet undertaken. It was fitted out by the Massachusetts Colony; the men being from Massachusetts, New Hampshire, and Connecticut. Four thousand men took part, leaving their wives and children to plant their fields while they were gone. Louisburg was the strongest fortress on the American continent, — so strong, that it was called "The Gibraltar of North America." The attacking party had but twenty-one field-pieces, and there were a hundred and seven cannon inside the fort; but, after a siege of fifty-days, Louisburg was taken from the French. This was in 1745.

French and English claims.

We must remember that at this time the English colonies occupied only a strip of land along the Atlantic coast, though this strip extended for a thousand miles; while the French held Canada and Nova Scotia, and claimed all the vast interior region, from the St. Lawrence to the mouth of the Mississippi. The Governor of New York wrote home to England, that, if the French were allowed to hold all that they had discovered, the kings of England would not "have a hundred miles from the sea anywhere." Not only did the French claim all this; but they kept busily at work in the interior of the country, establishing trading-posts, building forts, making boats on the lakes, and collecting the materials of war. They would not let the English make so much as a survey of land in the valley of the Ohio. So it was resolved to send a messenger to remonstrate with the French officers and

<small>Washington's mission.</small>

WASHINGTON AMID THE ICE OF THE ALLEGHANY.

agents; and George Washington, then a young man of twenty-one, was appointed by the Governor of Virginia for that purpose. This was in October, 1753.

Washington had to travel through an almost unbroken forest, and to meet many perils; and he accomplished nothing by his appeals. His return was in the dead of winter, and harder and more perilous than his journey westward. Much of the journey was through forests which no white man had ever explored; and he had to pass over rivers on the ice, or else, amidst floating ice, on hastily constructed rafts. As he crossed the Alleghany River in this way, his raft was entirely hemmed in by the ice, his "setting-pole" was whirled from his hand by the swift current, and he himself was thrown into the water. Finally he and his companion left the raft, and took refuge on an island in the river, where they stayed till daylight, soaked with water, and almost frozen. In the morning they succeeded in crossing the ice to the shore, and at last got safely home. After all Washington's efforts, the French went on building forts with as much energy as ever, till they finally had a chain of sixty, stretching from Quebec to New Orleans, and securing to them, as they thought, all the interior of the continent.

It happened very fortunately for the colonists that the powerful Iroquois tribes, who lived west of the Hudson River, had long been their friends, and hostile to the French. These tribes were called the "Five Nations;" they were the Cayugas, Mohawks, Oneidas, Onondagas, and Senecas. After a while they were joined by the Tuscaroras, and were called the "Six Nations." The names of these tribes are likely to be preserved, because some lake or river in New York is named after each of them. And they ought to be remembered with gratitude; for their friendship was of great importance to the English colonists. In 1754 the English Government instructed the governor of the colonies to call a convention of delegates at Albany, to make a treaty with these "Six Nations," and to

THE FRENCH AND INDIAN WARS. 151

form a union for self-defence against the French. There had been several attempts at such union before, but without much success.

Albany was then a little Dutch town of only three hundred houses, protected by the Hudson River on one side, and by a line of picket-fence on the other: it had also a stone fort. At this place the twenty-five delegates from the different colonies met a hundred and fifty Indian chiefs, and made a treaty with them, though the Indians reproached them for not being so warlike as the French, and for not building forts everywhere like them. Then Dr. Benjamin Franklin proposed to the delegates a plan of union. Before he left home, he had printed in his newspaper at Philadelphia a woodcut representing a snake cut into separate pieces to represent the colonies; each piece having upon it the initial letter of the name of some colony, and the inscription appearing beneath, "Unite or die." This design was afterwards used as a flag. Dr. Franklin told the convention that the French, being under one government, were much more powerful than the thirteen English separate colonies, all jealous of one another. Under his lead, the convention agreed upon a plan of union; but the colonies afterwards rejected it. They were not quite ready for union yet. Still they agreed sufficiently to carry on the Old French War with great vigor for nine years; and it ended in accomplishing all they desired.

Meeting of delegates at Albany.

One of the first steps in this war was a very cruel act

There was a French province called Acadia, now Nova Scotia; and this was occupied by the English at the beginning of the war, in 1755. The French inhabitants would not take the oath of allegiance to England; and so the New England soldiers were sent by the English Government to remove the Acadians from their country. In some villages the men were all summoned into the church to hear a royal proclamation. There they found themselves prisoners; and they were then marched to the seashore. Seven thousand people were thus sent from their homes, and scattered through the colonies. To prevent their returning, their houses were burned, and their farms laid waste. In many cases families were separated in the confusion of embarking; and members of the same family were long lost to one another. Longfellow's poem of "Evangeline" is founded upon this sad event.

Meantime, in Virginia, war was beginning in earnest. When Washington went west to remonstrate with the French officers, he selected a place which he thought would be very good for an English fort. It was just where Pittsburg now stands, at the point where the Alleghany and Monongahela unite to form the Ohio. The government sent an expedition, and began to build the fort. It was thought that as there were so many French forts in that region, there should be a few for the English also. But this was just what the French did not wish: so they drove the workmen away, finished the fort themselves, and called it Fort Du Quesne. Washington carried on war against the French and Indians for a time, with the Virginia soldiers who had been placed under his command: but he was not quite strong enough to attack this important post; and so a veteran English army was sent out under General Braddock; and Washington went with him as one of his staff-officers. The English general knew nothing about Indian warfare, and would take advice from no one. He marched slowly through the forests, building roads as he went, and spending several months on the way. As he drew near the fort, Washington urged him to place the American companies in front, for the purpose of clearing the woods of Indians. He explained that these provincial soldiers were used to dealing with Indians, while the red-coats were accustomed only to regular warfare, and to fighting in the open field. Braddock refused to listen to the advice, but marched on in regular military order, with flags flying, music playing, and the men presenting a fine appearance. The army was within seven miles of the fort, when the advanced guard was attacked by Indians in a deep ravine, and was thrown into complete confusion. The Virginia riflemen fought from behind trees; but the regular troops crowded together, and were shot down. The fight lasted three hours. It ended in a disorderly retreat of the British troops, more than seven hundred of whom were killed out of twelve hundred. General Braddock showed great courage, but was at last mortally wounded; and every one of his officers was killed or wounded, except Washington, who had two horses killed under him, and had four balls through his coat. Washington was almost prostrated by illness that day, but took an active part in the battle, and had the command after Braddock fell. An old Indian chief said afterwards, that he and his "young braves" had

Braddock's defeat.

Retreat of the British

fired very often at that tall young American, and had decided that he must bear a charmed life.

Effect of a defeat. Braddock's defeat took place July 9, 1755. It made the greatest excitement throughout the colonies and in England; and its consequences were very important. The French were left in possession, for the time, of all the region west of the Alleghanies; and the Indians began to despise the English, to reverence the French, and to make new attacks upon the colonists. All through the western parts of Virginia, especially, there were scenes of massacre and fire; and family after family had to flee for their lives. Washington, who was in command of the Virginia forces, wrote, that "the supplicating tears of women, and the moving petitions of the men, melted him with deadly sorrow." He had to meet swift and stealthy enemies, who came and went in the night, and were to be tracked only by the ruin they had left behind them.

The Indians were told by their French allies that the time had come to drive the English forever from their settlements. But the colonists resisted desperately; and, three years after, Washington himself was sent against Fort Du Quesne, and took it at last. It was this distinguished military career that fitted Washington to take part in the war of the Revolution, which was fast approaching. Braddock's defeat had, moreover, taught the colonists that the red-coats were not invincible, but would run away as fast as anybody, if met by greater numbers or greater skill.

Capture of Quebec. Several valuable forts were taken from the French during this war, such as Niagara, Ticonderoga, and Crown Point; but the most important event was the famous expedition against Quebec. General Wolfe was sent from England to command this attack, and had eight thousand men with him; for Quebec was one of the strongest fortresses in the world. He was at first repulsed at every point. At last he discovered a steep and narrow path which led up to the Heights of Abraham, above the city; and he resolved to climb it with his men. So he sent Captain Cook (afterwards so famous as a navigator) to make a pretended attack in another place; and Wolfe went with boats to the path he had discovered. As he was rowed along in his boat, he spoke to his officers of Gray's "Elegy in a Country Churchyard," and said that he would rather have written that poem than take Quebec. Then he repeated the lines: —

Scaling the Heights of Abraham.

> "The boast of heraldry, the pomp of power,
> And all that beauty, all that wealth, e'er gave,
> Await alike the inevitable hour:
> The paths of glory lead but to the grave."

Then they landed, climbed the steep: and, in the morning of Sept. 13, 1759, General Montcalm, the French commander, was amazed to see an army above him. If he had even then remained in his fortress, the English could not have taken it; but he chose to come out and fight them on the open ground, and was defeated. The English were victorious: but General Wolfe died in the hour of victory. Hearing the shouts, "They fly; they fly!" he asked, "Who fly?" Hearing it was the French, he said, "Now God be praised: I die happy." General Montcalm was also mortally wounded, and, when told of his condition, said, "So much the better. I shall not live to see the surrender of Quebec."

Death of Wolfe.

YOUNG FOLKS' UNITED STATES.

Quebec was surrendered five days later; and a peace was made in 1763, by which France gave up Canada to England, with all her American possessions east of the Mississippi, except some fishing-stations near Newfoundland. France had just before given up to Spain all her claims to the vast territory west of the Mississippi. It was supposed that all the Indian tribes would at once submit to the English power, and would show the same friendship that they had formerly shown to the French. But unfortunately the Indians were not willing to submit so easily; and the flames of battle were to be rekindled once more before the great series of French and Indian wars ended.

There was an Indian chief named Pontiac, a man of great courage, skill, and influence. He had led the Ottawa tribe at the time of Braddock's defeat, and had seen the red-coats run away before his men. He believed that, if the Indian tribes could be united for one more effort, they might yet expel the English from the interior of the country, at least. The French inhabitants of Canada secretly encouraged these thoughts, and told the Indians that the King of France had been asleep for a time, and that the English had therefore triumphed, but that he would soon wake up, and "drive the intruders from the country of his red children." Pontiac heard all this eagerly. "I am a Frenchman," he said, "and will die a Frenchman!" He sent ambassadors through the country, each with a belt of wampum (red or black beads, signifying war), and a tomahawk stained red. In each village the belt was accepted, the tomahawk taken up, and the chiefs agreed to join in the war. Afterwards a council was held; and they agreed to attack the fort of Detroit, under Pontiac's lead.

This was Pontiac's plan: he would go some day to the fort, with thirty or forty men, and ask leave to come in and show an Indian dance. While they were dancing, a few should stroll about the fort, unnoticed, and observe everything within the walls. Then they would again visit the fort, ask to hold a council, carry weapons under their blankets, and at a given signal strike down the white officers. The first part of the plan succeeded; but the second failed. A warning was given by some Indian women to the English commander; and when Pontiac entered the fort with his fifty warriors, each carrying his gun under his blanket, they found ranks of armed soldiers drawn up within. They saw that their plan had failed, and were glad to be allowed to go out unharmed.

Plan of attack on Detroit.

After this, Pontiac collected his allies, and laid siege to Detroit for many weeks in 1763. It was the longest siege ever conducted by Indians; for they commonly relied on swift and sudden movements; but it failed at last, although several other forts were captured by Indians during this siege. At Michillimackinac, for instance, on a holiday, several hundred unarmed Indians played a game of ball outside the fort, and invited the soldiers out to see them play, while their squaws stood wrapped in their blankets, watching the game. Suddenly the ball was struck so that it fell near the gate of the fort. The warriors pursued it; but, on the way, each snatched one of the hatchets that had been concealed by the women beneath their blankets, then rushed into the fort, and began striking down the gar-

Siege of Detroit.

rison. Scarcely twenty men escaped. Thus, in one way or another, almost every fort in the region of the lakes was retaken by the Indians from the English. Detroit, however, held out with great courage; but the garrison had become almost exhausted by famine, when, at the approach of winter, the Indians gradually scattered, and gave up the siege after five months. Nothing but the remarkable power and energy of Pontiac could have carried it on so long. He was at last compelled to make peace with the English, and was afterwards murdered by another Indian in a drunken frolic. This was the end of the long series of French and Indian wars; and the English colonists were now to have a little rest, until the beginning of their own Revolution.

CHAPTER XVII.

THE BEGINNING OF THE REVOLUTION.

I HAVE thus described the early history of the thirteen original colonies, — "the old thirteen," as they were often called. These were New Hampshire, Massachusetts, Rhode Island, Connecticut, New York, New Jersey, Pennsylvania, Delaware, Maryland, Virginia, North Carolina, South Carolina, and Georgia. All the rest of the present States were made from these, or from territory added to these; so that the history of the country down to the Revolution is the history of these thirteen colonies. *The "Old Thirteen"*

It is easy to see that each of the thirteen had something peculiar in its history to distinguish it from the rest. To begin with, they were established by several different nations. Most of them, it is true, were founded by Englishmen; but New York and New Jersey were settled by the Dutch, and Delaware by the Swedes; while the Carolinas were first explored and named by a French colony. Most of them were founded by small parties of settlers, among whom no great distinctions of rank existed; but two of them, Pennsylvania and Maryland, were founded by a single proprietor in each case, who owned the whole soil; while New York had its "patroons," or large *Peculiar history of each.*

landholders with tenants under them. Most of them were founded by those who fled from religious persecution in Europe; yet one of them, Rhode Island, was made up largely from those persecuted in another colony; and another, Maryland, was founded by Roman Catholics. Some had charter governments; some had royal governments without charters; and others were governed by the original proprietors, or those who represented them.

Points of resemblance. But, however differently the thirteen colonies may have been founded or governed, they were all alike in some things. For instance, they all had something of local self-government; that is, each community, to a greater or less extent, made and administered its own laws. Moreover, they all became subject to Great Britain at last, even if they had not been first settled by Englishmen; and finally they all grew gradually discontented with the British Government, because they thought themselves ill treated. This discontent made them at last separate themselves from England, and form a complete union with one another. But this was not accomplished without a war, — the war commonly called the American Revolution.

Loyalty to England. When we think about the Revolutionary War, we are very apt to suppose that the colonies deliberately came together, and resolved to throw off the yoke of Great Britain. But this was not the case at all. When the troubles began, most of the people supposed themselves to be very loyal; and they were ready to shout "God save King George!" Even after they had raised armies, and had begun to fight, the Continental Congress said, "We have not raised armies with the ambitious design of separating from Great Britain, and establishing independent States." They would have been perfectly satisfied to go on as they were, if the British Government had only treated them in a manner they thought just; that is, if Great Britain either had not taxed them, or had let them send representatives to parliament in return for paying taxes. This wish was considered perfectly reasonable by many of the wisest Englishmen of that day; and these statesmen would have gladly consented to either of these measures. But King George III. and his advisers would not consent; and so they not only lost the opportunity of taxing the American colonies, but finally lost the colonies themselves.

There were some reasons why it seemed just that the Americans should be taxed. The debt of the British Government was very great, and part of this debt had been incurred in defending the American colonies from the French and Indians. So it seemed fair that these colonies should help to pay it; and probably they would not have objected, if they had been represented in the British Government, so that they could at least have had a voice in deciding what their taxes should be. But this was not allowed; and so, when the famous "Stamp Act" was passed, in 1765, the popular indignation was very great. *Reasons for taxation.*

There was nothing very bad about the law called the "Stamp Act," in itself; and Englishmen would not have complained of it at home. This famous act required only that all deeds and receipts, and other legal documents, should be written or printed on stamped paper, and that this paper should be sold by the tax-collectors; *The "Stamp Act."*

the money going to the government. It was such a law as has always existed in England; and, indeed, taxes have since been imposed in a similar way in America. The colonists objected to it only because it involved a principle. No matter how trifling the tax might be, they objected to it. They said the British Government had no right to put this or any other tax upon them, when they were not represented in the government. "No taxation without representation" was a phrase constantly heard in the colonies in those days; and the excitement about the Stamp Act was the real beginning of the Revolutionary War.

Even in the British parliament, when the Stamp Act was being discussed, there were persons who had been in America, and who declared that the imposed law was very unjust. The member to whom the people of America felt most grateful was Colonel Barré, who had fought under General Wolfe at the taking of Quebec. Mr. Charles Townshend had one day said in a speech, "Will these Americans, children planted by our care, nourished by our indulgence, till they are grown up to strength and opulence, and protected by our arms, — will they grudge to contribute their mite to relieve us from the weight of that heavy burden under which we lie?"

"They planted by your care?" replied Colonel Barré. "No, they were planted by your oppression. . . . They nourished by your indulgence? They grew up by your neglect. . . . They protected by your arms? They have nobly taken up arms in your defence. . . . They are, I believe, as truly loyal as any subjects the king has, but a people jealous of their liberties, and

THE BEGINNING OF THE REVOLUTION. 163

who will vindicate them, if ever they should be violated."

This bold speech by Colonel Barré made a great excitement. It was at once sent to America, in a letter, and was reprinted by all the newspapers. Every schoolboy learned to declaim it. Nevertheless, almost everybody in England supposed that the Stamp Act

Its effect.

PATRICK HENRY MAKING HIS GREAT SPEECH.

would go peacefully into effect; and indeed it seemed doubtful, for a time, whether the colonies would not submit. The first sign of opposition was given in Virginia. In the Virginia Assembly, in May, 1765, a young lawyer named Patrick Henry offered resolutions, declaring that no power but the General Assembly of the colony had the right to levy taxes upon it, and that

Patrick Henry.

to allow such power in any other body was to destroy all freedom. In his speech he said, "Cæsar had his Brutus, Charles the First his Cromwell, and George the Third" — "Treason!" cried the speaker of the Assembly, interrupting him; and the cry of "Treason!" rang through the hall. Patrick Henry looked sternly round, and finished his sentence, — "may profit by their example. If that be treason, make the most of it." Then his resolutions were adopted by a small majority; all the younger members being with him. Thus Virginia gave the signal of resistance for the colonies.

This example was quickly followed. In Massachusetts, James Otis proposed that an "American Congress" should be called, which should come together without asking the consent of the British Government. Others took up the plan, and proposed that American liberties should be left "to the watchfulness of a united continent." The Congress met in October, 1765; and though only nine of the thirteen colonies sent delegates, it did great good to their cause. This Congress drew up a "Declaration of Rights," and a petition to the king. All over the country the merchants agreed not to buy British goods; and men and women promised to wear homespun clothes, and go without all imported things, in order to show that they were not dependent on England. One patriotic woman, Mrs. Cushing, wrote to her friends, "I hope there are none of us but would sooner wrap ourselves in sheep and goat skins than buy English goods of a people who have insulted us in such a scandalous manner."

Then there were still more violent proceedings. In Boston, one morning, the people saw an effigy of

Andrew Oliver, the newly appointed agent for stamped paper, hanging on a great elm, afterward called "Liberty Tree." Chief Justice Hutchinson ordered the sheriff to take it down; but the people said, "We will take it down ourselves at evening." In the evening a great crowd collected, took down the image, carried it through the streets, and burnt it before Andrew Oliver's door. Then they grew so excited that they tore down Oliver's house, and destroyed the contents of the house of Chief Justice Hutchinson. In Maryland, also, a mob destroyed the house of the stamp-officer. In Rhode Island they destroyed the houses of two men who had favored the Stamp Act, and they compelled the stamp-officer to resign. In Connecticut nearly a thousand men set off on horseback, and hunted the stamp-officer till they caught him, and made him promise to resign, and to fling up his hat, and cry, "Liberty and Property!" three times. In New York the people burnt the governor in effigy, after dragging the image through the town in one of his own chariots. Similar things happened in other States; so that nobody dared to act as stamp-officer, and the law was never enforced. The news went quickly to England; and, while the king and his ministers were enraged, there were many in parliament to defend the cause of the Americans. The statesman, William Pitt, Earl of Chatham, said, "The gentleman tells us that America is obstinate; America is almost in open rebellion. *I rejoice that America has resisted.*"

By the strong efforts of such men as Lord Chatham, the Stamp Act was repealed in just a year from its passage; although another act was passed, declaring

Stamp officer hung in effigy.

Repeal of the Stamp Act.

that parliament had a perfect right "to bind the colonies in all cases whatsoever." Then there was great rejoicing. In Boston the bells were rung, flags were displayed everywhere, and prisoners for debt were released to share in the general joy. At night the houses were illuminated, and Liberty Tree was covered with lanterns till its boughs could hold no more. For some time nothing more was said about taxes. But, a year or two after this repeal, another act was passed, laying taxes on glass, paper, tea, and other articles. This roused new indignation; and troops were stationed in New York and Boston in the hope to keep the people quiet. But the effect was just the other way. In New York the soldiers cut down the liberty-pole, which had been raised when the Stamp Act was repealed; but the people put it up again, and yet again, the soldiers cutting it down each time.

Another act of taxation.

In Boston the troops made themselves still more unpopular. There was quite a quarrel between them and the boys; for the soldiers used to destroy the snow-slides that the boys had prepared for their sleds. After appealing in vain to the captain, the boys finally went to the British general, and complained. "What!" he said, "have your fathers been teaching you rebellion, and sent you here to exhibit it?" — "Nobody sent us, sir," said one of the boys. "We have never injured nor insulted your troops; but they have been spoiling our snow-slides, so that we cannot use them any more. We complained; and they called us 'young rebels,' and told us to help ourselves if we could. We told the captains of this; and they laughed at us. Yesterday our slides were destroyed once more; and we

Boston boys.

THE BEGINNING OF THE REVOLUTION.

will bear it no longer." The general ordered the damage to be repaired, and told Governor Gage, who said that it was impossible to beat the notion of liberty out of the people, as it was rooted in them from their childhood.

But the British troops in Boston had already got into more serious trouble. The young men of the town

Boston massacre.

THE BRITISH GENERAL AND THE BOSTON BOYS.

used often to insult the red-coated soldiers, calling them "lobsters," "bloody-backs," and such names, and threatening to drive them from the town. On the other hand, the soldiers used to be allowed, by their officers, to stray about the town in the evening, carrying their guns, and without any proper authority to control them. One moonlight evening (March 5,

1770), some soldiers were going about in this way, and got into a quarrel, as they often did. As they were taunting the people, and calling, "Where are they? Where are the cowards?" some boys began to snowball them, crying, "Down with them! Drive them to their barracks!" The noise increased, until the guard was called out, commanded by Captain Preston. He

PEOPLE ATTACKING THE SOLDIERS IN BOSTON.

came roughly through the crowd, with six or eight men, whom he drew up in line. Many of the people fell back: but about a dozen men, some of whom had sticks, advanced to meet the soldiers, and spoke angrily to them; and some, it was said, struck at the muskets with sticks. The noise increased every moment, till at last Captain Preston gave the word, "Fire!" When the smoke had cleared away, there were eleven men stretched upon the ground, of whom eight were wounded, and three killed. Among these last was Crispus Attucks, a mulatto, and the leader of the mob. This affair made an intense excitement; and Captain Preston was tried for murder. But some of the leading lawyers of Boston, who were also eminent patriots, defended him on the ground that he had done his duty as an officer; and he was acquitted. The public indignation was, however, so great over the whole affair, that the two regiments of troops were soon removed to the barracks at Castle William, and were not allowed to stray about the streets. But this bloodshed never was forgotten; and the "Boston Massacre" was another step towards the Revolutionary War.

Very soon another step was taken, on the shores of Narragansett Bay. An armed British schooner, the "Gaspee," had been stationed in that bay to look out for smugglers. The duty was discharged by the commander with needless severity; and he and his vessel became very unpopular. It was believed that they went far beyond any authority the law gave them. One day (June 10, 1772), a packet-boat left Newport for Providence, without notifying Lieutenant Dudingston of the "Gaspee;" and he pursued the packet more than twenty miles, and then ran hard aground on Namquit Point, about seven miles below Providence. The news soon spread through town that the hated vessel was aground near by, and that she must lie there until high tide, which would be early in the morning. Soon a drummer went through the streets, calling all men who would help destroy the "Gaspee"

Destruction of the "Gaspee"

to meet at a certain tavern after sunset. At half-past
nine, eight large boats filled with men, whose oars
were muffled, were seen gliding down the bay. They
approached the "Gaspee" at midnight. It was very
dark; and the alarm was hardly given, when the
Rhode Island men had boarded the schooner, over-
powered the crew, and tied their hands. They were put

DESTRUCTION OF THE "GASPEE."

on shore; and the schooner was set on fire, and utterly
destroyed. The boats went home in broad daylight.
Almost every one in Providence knew what had happened; and yet, though a reward of a thousand
pounds was offered to anybody who would give information against the offenders, no information was
ever given, and nobody was ever brought to trial.

Meantime the news went through all the colonies that the "Gaspee" was destroyed; that the British Government pronounced its destruction an act of high treason; and yet, that, with all its power, it could not reach one of the offenders. Through all the colonies the excitement went on increasing; and men felt more and more disposed to resist what they thought the unlawful acts of King George and his ministry.

Meanwhile the people everywhere were learning to go without those articles on which taxes were laid. They wore homespun clothes, instead of importing the goods. They also tried various experiments in making tea; using raspberry-leaves for that purpose, and sage, and other plants, some of which still bear the names of "Jersey tea" and "Labrador tea." So strong was the popular feeling, that the British Government finally decided to abandon all the other taxes, but to insist on that laid upon tea. Some large shiploads of it were therefore sent, in hopes that the people would everywhere be induced to pay the tax. "The king," said Lord North proudly, "means to try the question with America." But the people seemed determined to try the question with England also; for they were resolved that the tea should not be landed. In Boston, when the tea-ships had arrived, the "Committee of Correspondence" set a guard over them as they lay at the wharf; and people from all parts of the country promised to sustain the Bostonians, and implored them "to stand by the liberties of America." They hoped to get the tea sent peaceably back to London; and, when this proved impossible, a meeting of seven thousand people, the largest ever held up to that time in

Patriotism of the people.

Boston, took place in Faneuil Hall, and then adjourned to the Old South Church in order to have more room. The owner of one of the tea-ships was sent to the royal governor, Hutchinson, to ask his leave to send the vessels back to England with their cargoes;

FANEUIL HALL IN 1763.

and, when he returned with the answer that the governor refused the request, Samuel Adams rose, and said, "This meeting can do nothing more to save the country." Then a war-whoop was heard at the porch: a body of forty or fifty men, disguised as Indians, went by to the wharf, took possession of the three tea-ships, and threw three hundred and forty chests of tea into the water. Then they quietly dispersed, and did no other mischief whatever. This was called "the Boston tea-party;" and it took place Dec. 16, 1773.

SAMUEL ADAMS.

THE BEGINNING OF THE REVOLUTION.

New York and Philadelphia followed the example of Boston; but they did not have occasion to throw the tea into the water, for the captains of the ships readily consented to return to London immediately. In Charleston the tea was landed: but no one would take it for sale, or pay the duty; and meanwhile it was stored in damp cellars, where it was spoiled. In Annapolis the tea was burned. All these things excited the people very much, and made the colonies more and more ready to unite in resisting England. The first Continental Congress had met before this, and there was soon to be another. Meanwhile in Massachusetts, which seemed in greater danger of attack than any other State, there was also a Provincial Congress created; and under its direction military stores were collected at various points. There were also "minute-men" drilling under old soldiers who had fought in the "French and Indian War." There were also organizations called "Sons of Liberty," in Massachusetts and several other colonies; and in Rhode Island there were associations of women called "Daughters of Liberty." *The tea sent to other cities. Steps taken in Massachusetts.*

In the mean time King George and his ministers grew very angry at the conduct of the Americans, and especially of the people of Massachusetts. So they passed several severe laws, abolished the Boston town-meetings, placed troops in the town, and ordered that all persons accused of any offence should be taken elsewhere for trial. But the severest of these measures was the Boston Port Bill, of which one speaker in parliament said that it ought to be called "A Bill to enslave America." This law closed the port of Boston; that is, it forbade all vessels from going in or *The Boston Port-Bill.*

out, unless they brought wood or provisions. Any vessels bringing these things to Boston must sail first to Marblehead (then thirty miles from Boston by the high-road); must be entered at the custom-house, and take on board an officer, who would come to Boston in the vessel. This cut off all the water-communication of the country towns with Boston, unless it went round by way of Marblehead. Not a stick of wood could be brought in from any of the islands in the harbor; nor could a barrel of flour be brought in a row-boat from Cambridge; nor could even a shingle or a brick be taken from one wharf to another in a skiff or a scow. As commerce was then the chief business of the Bostonians, this stopped a large part of the industry of the place.

Of course, the sympathy of other towns, and even of the other colonies, was at once excited. So a great variety of gifts began to be sent into the suffering town, — grain from Groton, and salt fish from Marblehead, and a flock of two hundred and fifty sheep from Windham, Conn. The southern colonies sent flour and rice; and the middle colonies sent corn and iron; and many towns sent money for the poor; so that the effect of the Boston Port Bill was entirely different from what the British Government expected. They thought that it would probably frighten the colonies, and make them fall apart. Instead of this, it made them unite more firmly, and take up the cause of Boston as their own.

This was just what the wisest men in the British parliament, such as Edmund Burke and Charles James Fox, had predicted. They had warned the government that the American people would be driven into open rebellion by such measures. But King George was a very obstinate man, and used all his influence in parliament to push such laws through. The result was as Burke and Fox had said. The Boston Port Bill helped to make the scattered colonies into a nation. The day when the law took effect (June 1, 1774) was observed in Hartford, Conn., as a day of public mourning. The town-house was hung with black; a copy of the bill was posted on it; and the bells were tolled all day. Even so far off as Virginia, the legislature, or "House of Burgesses," attended a solemn religious service on the occasion, and heard a patriotic sermon from the chaplain.

If we could have entered Boston during the summer of 1774, we should have found ourselves on a peninsula much smaller than the present Boston, and protected by earthworks across the "Neck," where a guard was stationed. We should have seen the wharves almost deserted, and only British men-of-war lying in the harbor. We should have found the laborers of the town mainly idle, or at work on the street-pavements or the public brick-yards. We should have seen the poorer families fed by contributions sent from other towns or colonies. We should have observed cannon mounted on the heights, tents pitched on the Common, and companies of red-coated soldiers marching through the streets. We should have heard of private meetings of patriotic citizens, under the name of "clubs," almost every night. In these meetings, usually held in garrets and lofts, we should have seen plenty of tobacco-smoke, and people drinking punch or flip, perhaps,

Boston in 1774.

after the fashion of those times, and discussing plans of resistance, and news from other parts of the country; for in those days every man who had an important letter from any other colony, or from the Continental Congress, then in session at Philadelphia, would bring it to the meeting to read aloud. One would rise up, and say, "John Adams writes that there is a great spirit in the Congress, and that we must furnish ourselves with artillery and arms and ammunition, but avoid war, if possible, if possible!" Another would say, "The great Virginia orator, Patrick Henry, on being told that Major Hawley of Northampton said, 'We must fight,' answered, 'I am of that man's mind.'" Then another man would call out that he had been to see the British fortifications on the Neck, with some old soldiers who had fought at Louisburg, and that they had laughed at these earthworks, and said that "they would care for them no more than for a beaver-dam." Then we can imagine what shouts of laughter there would be in the old smoky room, and what cheers would be given for Patrick Henry and John Adams and the old Louisburg soldiers.

Then we must remember that there were other men, and often good men, too, who felt very sad about all this, and who thought that it was very wrong to resist King George, and that it would ruin the colonies even to attempt such a thing; and who tried, with tears in their eyes, to persuade the patriots to listen to reason. These were generally the rich and prosperous men, and those who held offices under the British Government; in short, the people who had most to lose by war in any case. These men were called Tories in those days, and grew more and more unpopular. ✗Some of them afterwards changed their opinions and became patriots: others left the United Colonies and went to those British Provinces which had refused to take part in the Revolution, especially to Nova Scotia. Some finally fought against their country in the royal armies. But for a time they only discouraged the revolutionists by pointing out all the evils that would follow their "mad attempt," as they called it. The Tories said, and with truth, that King George would not change his policy, and that more and more troops would be sent from England. They pointed out that these would be trained troops, and that the colonies had only raw militiamen to put against them.

To this the colonists answered, that there were now two million Americans, perhaps three millions, and that one-fifth were fighting-men. They said that many of these were trained in Indian warfare, and some had helped take Louisburg and Quebec. Moreover, in Braddock's expedition, they had seen the red-coats run for their lives before the French and Indians, when the Virginia riflemen stood their ground; each man taking to a tree, and exchanging shot for shot. As for officers, did King George suppose that General Putnam, who had been tied to a tree by Indians, and had seen the fire blaze up around him, without flinching, was likely to flinch before English muskets? Had not young Colonel Washington saved Braddock's army from total destruction, and afterwards taken Fort Du Quesne, which Braddock could not take? This is the way the patriots talked in those days; perhaps ending with the words of the brave Dr. Warren, "The contest may be severe: the end will be glorious."

CHAPTER XVIII.

CONCORD, LEXINGTON, AND BUNKER HILL.

Provincial Congress.

IN the midst of all this excitement, General Gage, the royal governor, called the legislature of Massachusetts together, and then, changing his mind, dissolved it, before it had met, by a proclamation dated Sept. 28, 1774. Upon this, all the members elected to the legislature came together, by agreement, without asking his leave, and organized themselves as a Provincial Congress. They at once began to get the militia into good working-order; and a quarter of the militiamen were called "minute-men," and were bound to assemble at the very shortest notice. Then the Provincial Congress saw to the collecting of arms and ammunition, and stored these at Concord and Worcester; and, in short, the governor found himself in more trouble than if he had allowed the legislature to meet. Meanwhile British troops kept arriving in Boston; and General Gage kept sending out spies in disguise, to find where the military stores of the patriots were deposited; and they, in turn watched him. By and by he sent a body of soldiers to Salem (Feb. 26, 1775) to seize such stores, but so many minute-men gathered at once for resistance that the troops retreated. The patriots kept close watch at Charlestown, agreeing that if any large

Watchfulness of the colonists.

force of troops were ordered out by night in Boston, a lantern should be hung from the North Church.

One night the watchers on the Charlestown side of Charles River saw the lantern gleaming in the steeple. Instantly all were in motion; and messengers went riding in all directions. Other messengers had meanwhile been sent across in boats from Boston; and one of these, named Paul Revere, mounted a horse immediately after landing, and galloped out through Medford, to a house where the patriotic leaders, John Hancock and Samuel Adams, were sleeping. *Paul Revere.*

"Do not make so much noise," said the soldier on guard before the house.

"Noise!" said Paul Revere. "You'll have noise enough before long. The regulars are coming out." So he galloped on from house to house, awakening all the principal farmers; and we may well suppose that there was no more sleep in any house that night after Paul Revere had passed by.

Meantime some eight hundred British soldiers, embarking in boats at the foot of Boston Common, crossed to what is now East Cambridge. They marched silently along the marshes; when suddenly the bells of the country towns began to ring, and it was plain that the alarm had been given. Paul Revere and the other scouts had done their work well. The commanding officer of the British then sent back for more troops; and Major Pitcairn was sent forward with two or three hundred infantry, having orders to secure the two bridges at Concord. But when Pitcairn passed through Lexington, at four in the morning, April 19, 1775, he found sixty or seventy militia collected on the green, commanded by Capt. John Parker. *Battle of Lexington*

"Ye villains, ye rebels, disperse!" cried the English officer. "Why don't ye lay down your arms?"

Then the British soldiers fired; and the Americans fired in return, but did little damage. Eight of the Americans were killed and ten wounded; and this was the first blood shed in the Revolutionary War.

After this the British, or "regulars," marched on towards Concord, giving three huzzas. By this time the main body had come up, and joined them. While this went on, the Concord people were removing their military stores to the woods for safety. Then the minutemen, who had been hurrying towards Concord, — to the number of about four hundred and fifty in all, — took up a position on the high ground near what is called the "North Bridge," which is just out of the village. They could see the British soldiers moving about the streets, destroying military stores and provisions, cutting down the liberty-pole, and setting the courthouse on fire. Then the officers of the minute-men decided to march down to the bridge, and at least drive away the British soldiers who were stationed there. Capt. Isaac Davis of Acton said proudly, "I have n't a man that is afraid to go;" and he and his company marched at the head.

When they reached the bridge, the British soldiers fired; and Davis fell dead. Then Major Buttrick called, "Fire! for God's sake, fire!" Then the Americans fired; and the regulars retreated in great disorder, one man being killed, and several wounded. But the Americans knew that they were too few to attack the main body, until it should have set out on its return.

When the British troops had destroyed all the military stores they could find at Concord, they prepared to return, carrying with them their wounded. They were now sixteen miles from Boston, and they were not to go back as easily as they came. The guns and bells had roused the whole country round; and men came hurrying from all directions, commonly in their shirt-sleeves, without order or discipline, but with guns in

The retreat of the British.

RETREAT OF THE BRITISH FROM CONCORD.

their hands; and every man was ready to shelter himself behind a stone wall or a tree. A British officer wrote afterwards, that it seemed as if men had dropped from the clouds. Sometimes there were companies of minute-men, and at other times only single farmers. Every mile that the tired English soldiers marched from Concord to Lexington, they had more and more opponents, who kept firing from behind walls and trees; so that men were constantly falling, wounded or killed. At last the British soldiers fairly ran. There was great confusion. Their ammunition was almost gone; and they would have had to surrender, had not Lord Percy marched out to meet them with reinforcements, and formed his troops into a hollow square at Lexington. Into this square the tired fugitives ran, and were safe at last.

The retreat.

"They had to lie down for rest on the ground," an English historian says, "their tongues hanging out of their mouths, like dogs after a chase."

Lord Percy had now eighteen hundred men under him, and he retreated more slowly for the rest of the way; but he was pursued to Boston by greater and greater numbers, and was constantly fired upon; and his troops were glad, at sunset, to get under protection of the guns of the men-of-war. The British had suffered nearly three times as much, in "killed, wounded, and missing," as the Americans.

The effect of the retreat.

Great was the excitement produced throughout all the colonies, and great was the wonder in England, over this astonishing retreat of regular officers before provincials. The American farmers, the English said, had been called "too cowardly to face the regulars;" and yet the affair had turned out a flight of the English; and "Lord Percy's activity was in running away." This was very unjust to Lord Percy, who was a brave officer; but it shows the feeling that existed in England. And in America, this day was the real beginning of the Revolution. Samuel Adams, when he heard the guns at Lexington, exclaimed, "Oh, what a glorious morning is this!" for he knew that the contest would end in the freedom of the colonies. President Jefferson said afterwards, "Before the 19th of April, 1775, I never had heard a whisper of a disposition to separate from Great Britain."

Soon after this (May 10, 1775), Ethan Allen, with a few men, captured Fort Ticonderoga, on Lake Champlain, "in the name of the great Jehovah and the Continental Congress," as he said. Meanwhile the Massachusetts Committee of Safety sent out appeals for troops, and fifteen thousand men were soon collected. General Ward commanded those from Massachusetts; General Stark, those from New Hampshire; General Greene, those from Rhode Island; and Generals Spencer and Putnam, those from Connecticut. The army was not at all disciplined; it had few cannon, and little ammunition; the men came and went very much as they wished. But they were strong enough to keep the British army of five thousand shut up in Boston; and General Gage sent most of the families of the patriotic party out of town; so that there was very little intercourse between those within and those without.

It was found that there were two ranges of hills that commanded Boston on two sides, — Dorchester Heights on the south, and Bunker Hill and Breed's Hill on the north-west. It was of importance to both sides to get the control of these hills; and the Americans had reason to know that General Gage was planning to extend his lines, and include Bunker Hill. So a force of a thousand men was sent, one night, under command of Colonel Prescott, to erect some earthworks for its protection. His men were mostly farmers: they had no

Capture of Ticonderoga.

The gathering of the troops

The fortifying of Bunker Hill.

uniforms, and carried fowling-pieces without bayonets. They formed on Cambridge Common, and, after a prayer by the president of Harvard College, marched at 9, P.M., June 16, 1775. They marched so silently that they were not heard; and the bells of Boston had struck twelve before they turned a sod. It was finally decided to fortify Breed's Hill, as being nearer to Boston, instead of Bunker Hill. The work was soon begun. As they worked, they could hear the sentinels from the British men-of-war cry, " All 's well ! " As day dawned, the newly-made earthworks were seen from the ships, which began to fire on them, as did a battery in Boston. But the Americans went on completing their fortifications. General Gage with his telescope watched Colonel Prescott as he moved about the works. " Will he fight ? " asked he. " To the last drop of his blood," said an American loyalist who stood near. Soon the British general made up his mind to lose no time, but to attack the works that day.

Preparation for the attack. It was now the 17th of June. The day was intensely hot. Three thousand British soldiers were embarked in boats, and sent across to Charlestown; and more followed. Prescott placed his men behind the half-finished mounds; and a detachment was stationed at a rail fence, on the edge of Bunker Hill, to keep the British troops from flanking the redoubt. This rail fence was afterwards filled in with new-mown hay, to screen better those behind it. Without food, without water, and with very little ammunition, the Americans awaited their opponents. There were from two to three thousand behind the breastworks, and four thousand British to attack them; and the Americans were almost without drill or discipline, while the British troops were veteran regiments. On the other hand, the British were obliged to advance in open field, while the Americans were behind their earthworks,—a far safer position. There they waited as quietly as they could, while Putnam, Prescott, and others moved about among them, saying, "Aim low." "Wait till you can see the whites of their eyes."

The British soldiers marched forward slowly; for they were oppressed with the heat, and were burdened with their knapsacks of provisions. But they marched with great regularity and entire confidence. They fired as they went; but only a few scattering shots were fired in return. On, on, they came, till they were within some ten rods of the redoubt. Then the word, "Fire!" was given; and, when the smoke cleared away, the ground was strewed with the British soldiers, and the survivors had already begun to retreat. A great cheer went up from the forts; and the shout was echoed from the rail fence. The Americans behind the fence were next attacked by the right wing of the British. The Americans withheld their fire till the last moment; and three-fourths of the advancing soldiers fell, and the rest faltered. Twice the British advanced, and twice they were driven backwards; while very few of the Americans were hurt. Then a third attack was made upon the main fort. The British officers were seen threatening the soldiers, and even striking and pricking them, to make them advance; but they were very unwilling. Putnam passed round the ranks, telling his men, that, if the British were once more driven back, they could not rally again; and his men shouted, "We are ready

The Battle

186   YOUNG FOLKS' UNITED STATES.

for the red-coats again." But Putnam knew that their powder was almost gone, and told them to reserve their fire till the British were within twenty yards. Once more they awaited the assailants, who now advanced with fixed bayonets, without firing, and under the protection of batteries of artillery. Most of the Americans had but one round of ammunition left, and few had more

DEATH OF GENERAL WARREN.

than three. Scarcely any had bayonets. Their last shots were soon fired; and there was nothing for them but to retreat as they best could. They fell back slowly, one by one, losing far more men in the retreat than in the battle. Among their losses was the brave General Warren, eminent as a physician and as a patriot. He was president of the Provincial Congress,

Death of General Warren.

and was there only as a volunteer, not in command. The British general, Howe, on hearing of his death, said that it was equal to the loss of five hundred men to the Americans.

Howe's estimate of Warren.

CHAPTER XIX.

WASHINGTON TAKES COMMAND.

Effect of the battle of Bunker Hill.

THE battle of Bunker Hill was of the greatest importance to the colonies. First, it settled the question that there was to be a war, which many people had not before believed. Secondly, it showed that inexperienced American soldiers could resist regular troops. It is said that when Washington heard of it, he only asked, "Did the militia stand fire?" And when he was told that they did, and that they reserved their own till their opponents were within eight rods, he said, "The liberties of the country are safe." The battle was not claimed as a victory by the Americans; and yet it roused their enthusiasm very much. The ranks of the Continental army were filled up, and the troops were in high spirits. On the other hand, the greatest surprise was felt in England at the courage shown by the Americans in this contest, and the great number of

The severe loss of the British.

killed and wounded among the British troops. By the official accounts, the British loss in killed and wounded was more than a thousand (1,054), including an unusually large proportion of officers; being one in four of the whole force engaged. The Americans lost less than half as many, — not more than four hundred and fifty. People in England complained that none of their regiments had ever returned so diminished in numbers from any battle. One came back, for instance, with only twenty-five men. And it was said that "no history could produce a parallel" to the courage shown by the British in advancing beneath such a murderous fire. "So large a proportion of a detachment," it was said, "was never killed or wounded in Germany," where the British armies had lately been engaged.

Even before the battle of Bunker Hill, the Continental Congress had voted to adopt the army besieging Boston, as the national army, and to raise additional troops in other States. At the recommendation of the New England delegates, George Washington was unanimously chosen general-in-chief, with four major-generals, — Artemas Ward, Charles Lee, Philip Schuyler, and Israel Putnam. It was thought best that the general-in-chief should not be from New England, because it was wished that all the colonies should join in the war; and, besides, there was no man in America who could claim to equal Washington in military reputation. So he came on from Virginia, arriving July 2, 1775, and the next day stood under the great elm in Cambridge (still known as the Washington Elm) to take command of the Continental army. No doubt there was great curiosity to see this famous officer; and we can imagine with what eagerness the soldiers looked at him. When they looked, they saw a man forty-three years old, more than six feet tall, broad and vigorous, with large hands and feet, rather clumsy in his movements, yet with great dignity of bearing, and with a noble and commanding countenance at all times. He was dressed in a blue coat with buff facings, buff small-

Condition of the Continental army.

clothes, an epaulet on each shoulder, and a black cockade in his hat.

And when Washington looked, in turn, upon his army, he saw, to use his own words, "a mixed multitude of people, under very little discipline, order, or government." They were armed with fowling-pieces or muskets, hardly any two of which were of the same calibre.

WASHINGTON TAKING COMMAND OF THE ARMY AT CAMBRIDGE.

Few of the regiments had any uniform: they were collections of men in their old coats or their shirt-sleeves, and many of them wearing leather small-clothes. Those who came from a distance had usually some similarity of dress, to distinguish them on the march; and many of the riflemen who soon arrived from Virginia wore hunting-shirts of brown Holland, "double caped over the shoulder, in imitation of the Indians;" and having embroidered on the breast, in capital letters, "Liberty, or death." But, in general, the aspect of the Revolutionary army was not at all that of disciplined soldiers. And when General Washington went round among the camps and forts, which spread from Cambridge to Charlestown, he found anything but military regularity and neatness. Some of the troops, especially those from Rhode Island, had regular lines of tents; while others lived in little huts, made of boards, or stones, or turf, put in any place where shelter could be found, and sometimes protected at the doors and windows by basket-work. The food was rough and often scanty; and, worst of all, there was a great scarcity of powder. At first there were only seven cartridges to a man. Washington wrote to Congress, "Our situation in the article of powder is much more alarming than I had the faintest idea of." Another officer wrote, "The word 'powder' in a letter sets us all on tiptoe." Another wrote, speaking of General Putnam, "The bay is open: everything thaws here, except old Put. He is still as hard as ever crying out for 'powder, powder! Ye Gods, give us powder!'"

Scarcity of powder.

By degrees, the army was supplied with many necessary equipments from the store-ships taken as prizes by the Americans, who sent out privateers, and who, after retaking Castle William, put up a British flag there to decoy in the English vessels. But powder was always scarce; and this was the chief reason why General Washington had to be content for many months with keeping the British army besieged in Boston, without trying to take the city. Meanwhile the British troops in Boston be-

British troops in Boston.

gan to suffer from small-pox and also for want of food and fuel. They had to pull down old houses to burn, and had to send hundreds of the inhabitants out of the town, because they could not be fed. Some of the churches were turned into barracks; and the "Old South," into a riding-school; and Faneuil Hall, into a theatre. Sometimes the British used to send out play-bills to Washington and his generals. Once, in this theatre, the British officers were acting a play called "The Blockade of Boston," in which a figure intended to burlesque Washington was just coming in, wearing a large wig and a long rusty sword, and attended by a countryman with a rusty gun. Suddenly a sergeant appeared on the stage, and cried, " The Yankees are attacking our works on Bunker Hill!" At first this was taken for a part of the play; but when General Howe rose, and called out, "Officers, to your posts!" the people dispersed hastily, amid the shrieking and fainting of women. The attack at Charlestown, thus announced, did not amount to much; but General Washington at last succeeded in erecting a battery at Dorchester Heights, which so effectually assailed the British, that General Howe finally embarked his army, and quitted Boston forever, March 17, 1776. Nearly twelve hundred American loyalists went with the fleet to Halifax; and most of these never returned.

Evacuation of Boston.

Determination of the British government.

But, because the British army evacuated Boston, we must not suppose that they meant to give up the contest. After the British Government heard of the battle of Bunker Hill, it was resolved to subdue the American colonies, no matter at what cost. All trade and intercourse with the colonies were prohibited; and their property on the ocean might be seized by any one. Sixteen thousand Hessians (or Germans) were employed in the British army ; and the whole force destined for America amounted to fifty thousand men. Against this, the whole American army included as yet but some twelve thousand. Yet the only effect of all this was to make the Americans feel that they had gone too far to retreat, and must persevere. *Strength of the American Army.*

CHAPTER XX.

THE DECLARATION OF INDEPENDENCE.

The work of Congress.

WE must remember that the most important responsibilities of the Revolution were not taken by the farmers who fought at Lexington or Bunker Hill, but by the Continental Congress at Philadelphia. For, even after one or two fights, the Americans might have drawn back, and made peace again, but after the Congress had solemnly declared that the "United Colonies are and of right ought to be free and independent States," there was no going back, and they must take the consequences. Moreover, the soldiers had only to fight; but the Congress had to take all the difficult work of raising soldiers, appointing officers, collecting and expending money, and negotiating with foreign governments to get, if possible, their aid. It looked like a very desperate undertaking.

Ideas of the people concerning Independence.

To be sure, when the patriots in Congress looked back upon the few battles that had yet taken place, they could feel that the Americans had begun well. Dr. Franklin, who was always cheerful and hopeful, described their situation in this way, in a letter to a friend in England: "Britain, at the expense of three millions, has killed a hundred and fifty Yankees in this campaign, which is twenty thousand pounds a head; and at Bunker Hill she gained a mile of ground, half of which she lost again by our taking post on Ploughed Hill. During the same time, sixty thousand children have been born in America. From these *data*, Dr. Price's mathematical head will easily calculate the time and expense necessary to kill us all, and conquer our whole territory." This remark was printed in all the American papers, and was very encouraging. But Dr. Franklin and all the wise men knew in their hearts that the Americans were unaccustomed to military discipline, that there was great jealousy between the different colonies, and that many of the richest and most influential men were entirely opposed to separating from the mother-country. Washington himself said, "When I first took command of the army, I abhorred the idea of independence; but I am fully convinced that nothing else will save us." That was the feeling with which the Continental Congress came together to consider whether independence should be declared. And the people at large were becoming gradually prepared to support such a declaration, especially those who had read a book called "Common Sense," by Thomas Paine, which had been circulated very widely through the country, and undoubtedly did more than any other book toward convincing the Americans that the time for separation had come.

The leading colony at that time was Virginia; while Massachusetts and Pennsylvania came next in order. So it was thought best that the first proposal of independence should come from Virginia, and that it should be seconded from Massachusetts. On the 7th of June, 1776, Richard Henry Lee, of Virginia, moved these resolutions: — *The resolutions*

"That these united colonies are, and of right ought to be, free and independent States; that they are absolved from all allegiance to the British crown; and that all political connection between them and the State of Great Britain is and ought to be totally dissolved.

"That it is expedient forthwith to take the most effectual measures for forming foreign alliances.

"That a plan of confederation be prepared, and transmitted to the respective colonies for their consideration and approbation."

Unanimity of feeling among the colonies. They were seconded by John Adams of Massachusetts. The first discussion of them showed that, though the members generally were in favor of independence, yet there were some who thought the nation not ready for it. So it was decided to postpone further discussion to the 1st of July. By that time, it was thought, the people of the colonies would show whether they were ready for independence or not. And this was just what happened. Before the end of that month, the people of every colony but one had either held meetings, and voted that they wished for independence, or else had instructed their delegates to vote for it; and, when the subject came up on the appointed day, New York was the only colony that did not vote to declare independence; and even New York did not vote against it.

The Declaration of Independence. During this time of delay, a committee had been appointed to draw up a declaration of independence to be used, if necessary. This committee consisted of Thomas Jefferson of Virginia, John Adams of Massachusetts, Benjamin Franklin of Pennsylvania, Roger Sherman of Connecticut, and Robert R. Livingston of

THE DECLARATION OF INDEPENDENCE. 197

New York. The Declaration was written by Thomas Jefferson; though a very few verbal changes were made by Adams and Franklin, which may still be seen, in their handwriting, on the original document. There was a long discussion in the Congress; and the Declaration was debated and criticised, word by word, and sometimes very severely attacked. During this attack, John Adams was its chief defender; while Jefferson, who had written it, did not say a word. He says in his journal, "During the debate I was sitting by Dr. Franklin, who observed that I was writhing a little under the acrimonious criticism of some of its parts; and it was on that occasion, that, by way of comfort, he told me the story of John Thompson the hatter, and his new sign." This was a story — told, also, by Dr. Franklin in his Autobiography — in regard to a man who was about opening a shop for hats, and who proposed to have a sign-board with a hat painted on it, and the inscription, "John Thompson, hatter, makes and sells hats." But almost every word of this inscription met with objection from somebody, as being unnecessary; and at last it was reduced to "John Thompson," with the figure of a hat. It was thus that Franklin amused Jefferson during the anxious hours when this most important measure was under discussion.

The Declaration of Independence was adopted July 4, 1776, though it was not signed until some weeks later. When the members of Congress came up to sign, Dr. Franklin was still ready with his cheerful wit. John Hancock, who headed it, said to the others, "We must be unanimous: there must be no pulling different ways: we must all hang together."—"Yes," said Franklin, "we must all hang together, or else we shall all hang

Signing the Declaration.

separately." We can imagine how they all may have laughed at this. But it was really a dangerous responsibility that they were taking; and no doubt there were some anxious hearts even among those who laughed.

The Declaration adopted. But at last the great Declaration was adopted, without being much altered. The principal change was in striking out a passage which condemned the king of England, more severely than some of the Southern members approved, for his support of the slave-trade.

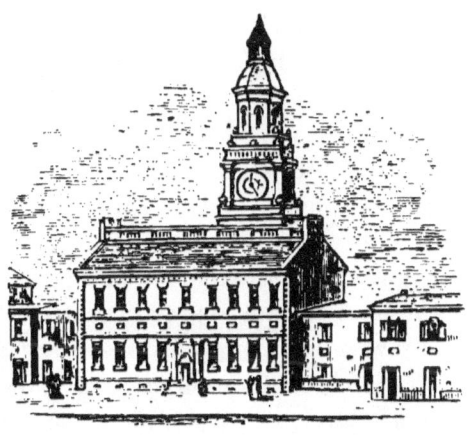

OLD STATE HOUSE, PHILADELPHIA.

Rejoicings. In its final form it was adopted by twelve colonies; New York still declining to vote. It had been privately resolved that, when it was passed, the bell of the old State House should be rung. This was a bell which had been put up some twenty years before, and which bore the inscription, "Proclaim liberty throughout the land to all the inhabitants thereof." So the old bell ringer placed his little boy at the hall-door to await the signal of the door-keeper; and, when independence was declared at last, the door-keeper gave the signal, and the boy ran out, exclaiming, "Ring, ring, ring!" Then the bell rang out joyfully, proclaiming liberty to all the land. There were rejoicings everywhere; and the Declaration was read to each brigade in the army. This is the way the "Pennsylvania Journal" described the excitement: —

"This afternoon (July 10) the Declaration of Independence was read at the head of each brigade of the Continental Army posted at and in the vicinity of New York. It was received everywhere with loud huzzas, and the utmost demonstrations of joy; and to-night the equestrian statue of George III., which Tory pride and folly raised in the year 1770, has, by the Sons of Freedom, been laid prostrate in the dirt, — the just desert of an ungrateful tyrant."

This was the courageous feeling with which the Declaration of Independence was received. Yet at this very time the enterprise seemed so daring, and the condition of the American army was so poor, that Adjutant-General Reed, who, from his position, knew the state of military affairs better than any one else, had written thus a few days before: —"Every man, from the general to the private, acquainted with our true situation, is exceedingly discouraged. Had I known the true position of affairs, no consideration would have tempted me to take an active part in this scene."

The boldness of the step.

After the Declaration of Independence had been adopted, it was thought to be time that the "United States" should have a flag of its own, as being an independent nation. At the opening of the war a variety of flags had been used. That carried by the first war-vessels commissioned by Washington was called "the

The national flag

pine-tree flag," and originated with the Massachusetts Colony. It had a white ground, a tree in the middle, and the motto, "Appeal to Heaven." This is the way the English papers describe the flag taken from a colonial vessel in 1776; and a map of Boston was published in Paris that same year, which represented this flag. The American troops still sometimes used the British flag, considering themselves still a part of the British nation. While Washington was in command at Cambridge, he unfurled before the army a new flag, which had thirteen stripes of red and white, as now, but had upon its corner the red and white cross which then marked the British flag. This was the flag carried by the American troops into Boston when the royal troops marched out; but Congress voted, June 17, 1777, "that the flag of the thirteen United States be thirteen stripes, alternate red and white, and the union be thirteen white stars in the blue field.

Adoption of a national flag.

The first person to hoist this new flag over an American ship-of-war was Capt. Paul Jones, afterwards famous in fight. It is said that the flag was first made and given to him by some patriotic ladies in Philadelphia, and that he procured a small boat, and sailed up and down the Schuylkill River, with the colors unfurled, to show the assembled people what their national ensign was to be. This is the flag that now waves over every United States vessel, or camp, or building, except that, for every State added to the Union, a new star has been placed on the flag; while the thirteen stripes still remind us of the "old thirteen" colonies that won their independence.

The "old flag."

CHAPTER XXI.

THE REMAINDER OF THE WAR.

Capture of New York by the British. UP to the time of the Declaration of Independence, almost the whole fighting had been about Boston, although the British had made an unsuccessful attack on Charleston, S.C., and the Americans had tried, with equal ill-success, to overrun Canada, and take Quebec. But Washington foresaw that an attempt would be soon made by the royal generals to occupy New York: so he sent General Lee from Cambridge to defend it; and he himself soon followed, after the evacuation of Boston. Sir William Howe also took thither the British soldiers who had been withdrawn from Boston; and his brother, Admiral Lord Howe, went thither with re-enforcements to meet him; and General Clinton came from the South with additional troops. So there were some twenty-four thousand British and Hessian troops to be met, and only about half that number of Americans yet enlisted.

Lord Howe offers terms of peace. Lord Howe had orders from King George to offer terms of peace; but he did not know exactly to whom to offer them. First he wrote a letter to the royal governors: but there were no royal governors left; and the letter came into Washington's hands, and proved to contain nothing satisfactory. Then Lord Howe wrote a letter addressed to "George Washington, Esq.;" and

THE REMAINDER OF THE WAR.

his brother wrote another addressed to "George Washington, &c.:" but Washington declined to receive any that were not addressed to him in his true character as general commanding the United States army. So Lord Howe wrote no more letters, but prepared to fight. He won an important victory over General Putnam on Long Island (Aug. 27, 1776), and Washington with his main army had to leave New York to the British troops, and to retreat gradually through New Jersey, followed by Lord Cornwallis, who reached one side of the Delaware River just as Washington and his army had landed on the other. This retreat naturally encouraged the British very much, and discouraged the Americans. Washington had hardly three thousand men in Pennsylvania; and many of these had neither shoes nor decent clothing. Washington was defeated at White Plains (Oct. 28) and the British captured Fort Washington (Nov. 16). *Washington's retreat.*

All this made it particularly desirable, as Washington thought, that he should strike some daring blow. He knew that there was a body of about a thousand Hessian troops at Trenton. These Hessians were hired troops from the Province of Hesse-Cassel in Germany; and Washington knew the ways of the Germans. He was quite sure that on Christmas Day (1776), they would have a great celebration, and would be particularly off their guard. So he waited until the evening of that day, crossed the Delaware, and marched all night through storm and sleet, taking them by surprise at daylight. Some loyalist had written a note to the German commander, warning him; but he had paid no attention to it. He was killed in the fight, while all his soldiers were taken prisoners. *Battle of Trenton*

Battle of Princeton.

Soon after this, Washington gained a victory at Princeton, through a surprise. These successes encouraged the Americans very much; and, though they had now nearly fifty thousand soldiers against them, they all wished to persevere. Additional troops were raised. Washington fought the battle of Brandywine (Sept. 11, 1777) in the effort to save Philadelphia, but he was defeated by Howe, who entered that city Sept. 27.

At Germantown (Oct. 4) Washington attacked Howe's

WASHINGTON CROSSING THE DELAWARE.

army and was nearly successful. He finally went into winter quarters (1777–78) with his army at Valley Forge.

Winter at Valley Forge.

If we could see in imagination the camp of Washington at Valley Forge, we should understand better the sacrifice made to secure our liberty. The American army had diminished one-half, through desertion and illness. From forty-five thousand men it had shrunk to twenty thousand. At Valley Forge the soldiers slept without blankets; and many had to sit up all night by their fires. At one time there were more than a thousand without shoes; and you might track them in the snow by their bleeding feet. Even the sick often had to lie on the bare ground for want of straw. They had scarcely any horses; and the soldiers made little carts to draw their wood and provisions to their huts. Officers on parade sometimes wore old blankets or faded bedquilts to cover them. The troops were hardly ever paid; and the money in which they were paid had almost lost its value. Food was scarce; and the gloomy saying was, "No bread, no soldier." There were foreign officers in the camp, who had come to aid the cause of liberty, — La Fayette, De Kalb, Kosciusko, Pulaski, Steuben. They were men accustomed to courts and luxury; and the buildings where they lived were "no gayer than a dungeon," La Fayette said. During all this hard time Washington behaved most nobly. He was obliged to conceal, as far as possible, the wretched condition and small numbers of his army; and at the same time he was constantly censured by members of Congress, and even by other generals, for not making these poor starved soldiers into "an irresistible body of men." Meanwhile the British army lived in comfort in Philadelphia, and their officers enjoyed every luxury.

General Burgoyne, with a part of the British army, invaded the New England States, through Canada, early in 1777, issuing a proclamation, inviting the Indians to join him. He passed along Lake Champlain, took Fort Ticonderoga, and afterwards sent a large detachment to destroy military stores at Bennington. It was attacked, near that town, by General Stark, with

Burgoyne's invasion.

militia-men from Vermont, New Hampshire, and Massachusetts. Stark had been at Bunker Hill, and had satisfied himself that the American troops could be trusted to attack as well as to resist. He is said to have called out to his men, before the battle, "There are the red-coats! Before night we must conquer them, or Molly Stark is a widow." The Americans carried the day; and when, a little later, another force of Hessians came up, Stark attacked and defeated them also. This success helped to encourage the Americans; and a still greater event followed. Burgoyne, with his whole army, encamped at Saratoga, and was followed thither by General Gates with an American force. Two battles were fought at Stillwater, without decided results; but after this the British army retreated. They were, however, hemmed in by the army of General Gates. And on Oct. 17, 1777, General Burgoyne, with his whole army of more than five thousand men, surrendered as prisoners to the Americans, at Saratoga.

Treaty with France. This was an event of the greatest possible importance to the Americans. It encouraged the suffering army of Washington at Valley Forge; and it startled the friends of America in Europe, who had not hoped for any success so great. This was especially the case in France, where much sympathy had already been felt for America, so that young Frenchmen had volunteered in our army; and yet the French Government had steadily refused to make a treaty with the American colonies. But, after the surrender of Burgoyne, Dr. Franklin and the other commissioners succeeded in obtaining not only a treaty, but many promises of substantial aid, from France. This was Feb. 6, 1778. This treaty again alarmed the English Government, and parliament passed bills, and sent over commissioners, to conciliate America. But it was now too late; for the Americans had grown accustomed to the thought of entire independence, and would take nothing less. However, the commissioners came, and tried to influence Congress, and offered large bribes to leading patriots, to aid their efforts. For instance, a sum of ten thousand pounds was offered to Gen. Joseph Reed; and he replied, " I am not worth purchasing; but such as I am, the king of Great Britain is not rich enough to buy me."

But the direct aid from France proved less than was expected. Fleets were sent out by the French Government, to be sure; but they did little good, and were unsuccessful in all their enterprises. The Revolutionary War dragged slowly on for three years more, with varying success. Sometimes the Americans were brilliantly successful; as once at Stony Point, on the Hudson, in 1779. where Gen. Anthony Wayne — " Mad Anthony " as he was often called — took a strong fortification on a steep hill, by making his men charge up the hill in two columns, with fixed bayonets, and without firing a gun. At other times the Americans were beaten, as when Sir Henry Clinton besieged and took Charleston, S. C. The battle of Monmouth (June 28, 1778) was first a defeat for the Americans, and then a victory, Lee's troops being driven back and then rallied by Washington. There were cruel massacres, as when in 1778 a band of Tories (or American loyalists) employed the service of Indians to murder men, women, and children at Wyoming, Penn. Then there were sea-fights, in the course of which Paul Jones

Last three years of the war.

was made famous by one contest between his ship, the "Bonhomme Richard," and the British frigate "Serapis." The ships were lashed side by side; and they fought for three hours, chiefly from the rigging and tops, both ships taking fire again and again, until the British vessel yielded. This was in 1779. Then there were very daring deeds in the way of what is called par-

THE "BONHOMME RICHARD" AND "SERAPIS."

Marion and Sumter. tisan warfare, especially by Marion and Sumter, in the forests of South Carolina. These brave men threaded the woods by paths known only to themselves, and made long journeys at night to attack the various posts of the British troops, who then held Charleston and its neighborhood. Marion was called the Swamp-Fox; and the British officers complained of him for not coming

out into the open field "to fight like an officer and a
gentleman." But he proved just as brave in the open
field, at the battle of Eutaw Springs, S. C. (1780). Gen.
Nathanael Greene commanded the Americans in this
fight, defeating the British severely: and Greene's whole
campaign in the South was so successful, that he afterward ranked second only to Washington as a general.

There was one great act of treason committed during the war by one of the most distinguished officers of the American army, — Gen. Benedict Arnold. He had taken part in the war from its very beginning, and had distinguished himself by marching a party of troops through the forests of Maine to attack Quebec, and by commanding a naval force in a severe battle on Lake Champlain, and in various other ways. Nevertheless, he had the reputation of being selfish and revengeful, had not the full confidence of his brother-officers, and had seen others promoted above him. For a year and a half, as it afterwards proved, he had been in secret correspondence with the British commander-in-chief, Sir Henry Clinton, the letters passing under feigned names; so that Sir Henry himself did not know, for a long time, with whom he was corresponding. In the course of this, Arnold got himself appointed to the command of the Hudson River, with his headquarters at West Point. This was then considered the most strongly fortified point in the colonies, and was called the "American Gibraltar." It was called "the key of communication between the Eastern and the Southern States;" so that it would have been almost ruinous to the colonial cause if it had been transferred to the English. This was what Arnold proposed to surrender; *Arnold's treason.*

The American Gibraltar.

and he would have succeeded, but for the capture of the British officer who carried on the negotiations.

One day some young Americans who were out among the hills in what was called the neutral ground, between the lines of the two armies, saw a man advancing along the road, stopped him, and questioned him. Supposing them to be loyalists, of whom there were many in that

Capture of André.

CAPTURE OF MAJOR ANDRÉ

region, he indiscreetly told them that he was a British officer. He proved to be Major André, aid-de-camp to the commander-in-chief. They then searched him, and found papers concealed in his boots, giving full information, received from Arnold, in regard to the garrison and defences of West Point, and the plan of its surrender. Major André offered them large sums for his release; but they refused to accept them, and took him to the nearest military station. This was on the 23d of September, 1780. He was afterwards tried by court-martial, and hanged as a spy. Much sympathy was felt for André; but it was remembered that a brave young American officer, Captain Nathan Hale, had been hanged as a spy by the British, four years before (Sept 22, 1776). Arnold afterwards escaped to the British lines, and finally joined the British army. He aided in fighting against his own countrymen, was made a brigadier-general, and had a large reward in money; but he was generally despised, avoided, and insulted.

Hanging of André.

The friendship of France had been a great help and encouragement to the Americans; but the French army had not done much direct service thus far, though Count Rochambeau had landed at Newport, R.I., in 1780, with six thousand men. But the war closed with one great victory, in which the French played a very important part. It was at Yorktown, Va., where General Cornwallis had made his headquarters. General Washington was there with American troops, and Count Rochambeau with a corps of French soldiers, while Admiral de

LORD CORNWALLIS.

Grasse blockaded York River. After ten days' siege, when some of his most important works had been destroyed by the American artillery, Lord Cornwallis planned to leave Yorktown at night, to cross York River, and retreat to New York. A storm prevented; and he surrendered to Washington.

Surrender at Yorktown.

On Oct. 19, 1781, the allied armies, French and American, were drawn up in two columns outside Yorktown, with Washington and Rochambeau, on horseback, at their head; and between them the conquered troops marched out, and laid down their arms. There were about seven thousand British troops, and some sixteen thousand French and American. Even now, in some country militia musters, the soldiers go through the forms of that surrender, and call the military performance "a Cornwallis." Great was the joy which followed: and those who were awake that night in Philadelphia heard the watchman cry, "Past two o'clock, and Cornwallis is taken!" On hearing the news, Congress recommended a day of thanksgiving to be observed throughout the States; and Washington ordered the liberation of all persons under arrest for any offence, that all might share in the general joy.

Cost of the war.

Well might the Americans rejoice; for all men felt that the surrender of Cornwallis decided the result of the war. It was a war that had lasted nearly seven years, and cost Great Britain a hundred million pounds sterling, and fifty thousand lives, besides depriving that nation of the very colonies for whose taxation the war was waged. It was a war, in the words of the great English statesman, Mr. Pitt, "which was conceived in injustice, nurtured in folly, and whose footsteps were marked with slaughter and devastation." It had also cost the Americans untold suffering; but they knew that the end was worth the sacrifice. There was more fighting, here and there, after the surrender of Cornwallis; and the British held, for nearly two years more, the cities of New York, Charleston, and Savannah. But no extensive campaign took place; and at last, on Sept. 3, 1783, a treaty was made at Paris, between the English and American commissioners, by which was established all that the Declaration of Independence had proclaimed; and the new nation, called "The United States of America," took its place among the governments of the earth.

_{Treaty of Paris.}

CHAPTER XXII.

AFTER THE WAR.

Poverty of the colonies.

ON the 3d of November, 1783, the Revolutionary army was disbanded. At the end of the long struggle, the American Colonies were left very poor; and their money had so declined in value, that it took a hundred paper dollars to buy a pair of shoes. The discharged soldiers of the army were so destitute and so dissatisfied that it needed all General Washington's influence to quiet them. People had to be taxed to pay the expenses of the government; and yet many had not money to pay their taxes; and a rebellion broke out in Massachusetts, called "Shays' Rebellion," composed of men who thought that no taxes or debts ought to be paid at such a time. All this was very alarming, and convinced the Americans that they needed a stronger government than the mere league which they had formed in 1777, and which had carried

Defects of the old confederation.

them through the war. The trouble with the government had been, all along, that the colonies were jealous of each other, and especially the smaller of the larger; and so they had all wished to give the "Confederation," as it had been called, just as little power as they could. They were so afraid that their government would be tyrannical, that they had hardly given Congress any means of action. Congress was not authorized to raise money by taxes, or to fix the rates of duties on foreign goods imported, or to compel obedience to any law. It was found that foreign countries did not like to make treaties with such a loose and feeble government. Washington said, "We are one nation to-day, and thirteen to-morrow: who will treat with us on these terms?"

It was perceived that this would never do; and so a convention of delegates was called, to meet in the State House at Philadelphia, in order to decide upon a new constitution, and make, if possible, a stronger government, without doing harm to the liberties of the people. There was a long discussion, lasting many weeks, in this convention; but at last, on Sept. 17, 1787, the present Constitution was adopted. It had still to be accepted by the different States, and there was a good deal of opposition to it; while it was very strongly urged by Alexander Hamilton and others, in a celebrated series of papers, called "The Federalist." However, ten of the thirteen States agreed to it almost immediately; so that it went into effect in 1788. Of the three which remained, New York accepted the Constitution in time to take part in the first presidential election, that same year. North Carolina accepted it during the year following; and Rhode Island, last of all, in the year after that (1790). Thus the old "Confederation" ended, and the new "Union" began. The Confederation had changed the Colonies into independent States; and the Union now united these States into a single nation. The nation has governed itself, ever since, under the Constitution then adopted,

The Constitution.

The Union

although some amendments have been made to it from time to time.

Celebration at Philadelphia. There were great celebrations over all the country when the new Constitution went into effect, and the new nation began to exist. In Philadelphia, for instance, there was a procession of five thousand people, representing all trades and pursuits. Such a procession of trades was then quite a new thing; and it was thought to show the difference between republican and monarchical government; because in Europe, at that time, all triumphal processions were almost wholly military in their character. In the procession there were figures in emblematical costumes, representing the Declaration of Independence, the French Alliance, the Treaty of Peace, and so on. The Constitution was represented by a lofty car, in the shape of an eagle, drawn by six horses. The judges of the Supreme Court sat in this car, bearing the Constitution, framed, and fixed upon a staff, which was crowned with the cap of liberty, and was inscribed in gold letters "The People." Then a carriage, drawn by ten white horses, supported the model of a building representing the Federal Government; its roof being upheld by thirteen columns. Three of these were left unfinished, to represent the States that had not yet ratified the Constitution; and ten were finished, to represent the States that had already joined. There were also ten ships along the river, with flags and gilt inscriptions, in honor of these ten States. The clergy of the city walked in the procession; and the Jewish rabbi went between two Christian ministers, to show that the new Republic was founded on religious toleration.

George Washington was chosen the first President of the Republic, and John Adams the Vice-President. New York was to be the seat of government; and as Washington travelled thither from his home in Virginia, he had enthusiastic greetings everywhere. At Trenton, for instance, where he had formerly fought several battles, he found a triumphal arch thrown across a bridge

Our first president.

His journey to New York.

RECEPTION OF WASHINGTON AT TRENTON.

which he was to pass. It was the very bridge over which he had once retreated before the army of Cornwallis. The arch was supported on thirteen pillars, was wreathed with flowers, and bore the inscription, "The Defender of the Mothers will be the Preserver of the Daughters." Beneath this arch stood a party of young girls, with baskets of flowers in their hands; and they sang this song as Washington drew near: —

> "Welcome, mighty chief, once more,
> Welcome to this grateful shore:
> Now no mercenary foe
> Aims again the fatal blow, —
> Aims at thee the fatal blow.
>
> Virgins fair, and matrons grave,
> Those thy conquering arm did save,
> Build for thee triumphal bowers:
> Strew, ye fair, his way with flowers!—
> Strew your hero's way with flowers!"

Suiting the action to the word, they strewed before him the flowers from their baskets.

His reception at New York. As he approached New York, a delegation was sent out to meet him. A barge was provided with a crew of thirteen, wearing white uniforms, this number being chosen to represent the thirteen colonies; and many other boats joined in procession, with flags flying. The governor of the State and many others were in waiting at the wharf, and escorted Washington, amid great enthusiasm, to his quarters. Carriages were provided, but he preferred to walk; and the procession passed through the streets, while handkerchiefs were waved, and flowers were strewed in the way. *The Inauguration.* Some days after, the ceremony of inauguration took place on the balcony of what was then **the senate-chamber**. It was a building called "**Federal Hall**," which stood at the meeting of four streets; and these streets were so crowded, that, as an eye-witness said, "It seemed as if one might literally walk on the heads of the people." When Washington came forth upon the balcony, the chancellor of New York read the inaugural oath to him, and he repeated it. After the oath was administered, there was a cry of " Long live George Washington, President of the United States!" to which the assembled crowd replied with shouts of enthusiasm. Then a flag was raised on the cupola of the hall, and there was a general discharge of artillery, and pealing of bells. Thus was the new Republic fully organized at last, with a chief magistrate who had the respect and love of the whole people. This was April 30, 1789.

The new Republic fully organized

CHAPTER XXIII.

WASHINGTON AND ADAMS.

Condition of the country.

BUT Washington and those who aided him in the American Government had need of all their wisdom, and of all the public confidence, amid the duties that were to be done. The affairs of the United States were found to be in most alarming condition. The nation was very much in debt; people were very unwilling to pay taxes; the Indians were hostile; the pirates of the Barbary States often attacked American ships; and the relations of the new government with England, France, and Spain, were all very unsatisfactory. But within a few years all was changed. The money-matters were put on a sound basis; the rioters and the Indians were subdued; and treaties were made with Algiers, Spain, and England. This last treaty was made in 1794, by John Jay, and was very much opposed by many people, because it was thought to be too favorable to England; but it was at length ratified, and there was a period of peace between the two nations.

Relations with France.

During all this prosperity the affairs of France still gave the United States a great deal of trouble. There had been in France a great revolution, which the success of the American struggle had helped to bring about. The old French monarchy had been overthrown; and an attempt had been made to set up a republic in its place. Unhappily this attempt had led to terrible violence and bloodshed. All this made much excitement in the United States, because France had been the great ally of America during the Revolutionary War; and, moreover, the French seemed to be trying to do just what the Americans had done, though the attempt ended very differently in the two cases. So there was in the United States a very strong party which sympathized heartily with the French Revolution; and, on the other hand, there was another strong party, composed of those who were afraid of French example and French influence, and who wished the United States Government to resemble the English Government as much as possible. These admirers of England were commonly called "Federalists" in those days; while those who sympathized with France were called "Republicans," and afterwards "Democrats." Washington, Hamilton, and John Adams were considered Federalists; while Jefferson and Samuel Adams were Democrats. *The two parties.*

This difference between the two parties showed itself even in regard to the forms and ceremonies of the government, and the style of living among public officers. The Federalists were afraid that the national government would not command respect enough; and they wished to see a good deal of formality, and even of elegance. On the other hand, the Democrats feared that the national government would become too powerful; that it would destroy the rights of the States; and that it would become too costly and aristocratic, as in European nations. President Washington's way of *Further differences between the two parties.*

living was complained of as too showy and expensive; and it certainly would seem so to us, although, in those days, the habits of society were different, and these things attracted less attention. When, for instance, it was doubted by what official name the president should be called, Washington was himself in favor of the words, "High Mightiness," — the words used to describe the Stadtholder of Holland; that State being then a republic. This phrase was, however, rejected; and the more moderate title, "Excellency," was substituted. Again: when Washington drove to the sessions of Congress, he went in a state-coach, of which the body was in the shape of a hemisphere, cream-colored. bordered with flowers round the panels, and ornamented with figures representing cupids, and supporting festoons. On great occasions the coach was drawn by six horses; on ordinary occasions, by four; and on Sundays, by two only. The driver and postilions wore liveries of white and scarlet.

The title of the President.

The state-coach.

Levees.

President Washington held levees, or receptions, once a fortnight, in his own house. At precisely three in the afternoon the doors of the great dining-room were thrown open; and the guests who were admitted saw the president standing before the fireplace. with members of his cabinet or other eminent men around him. On these occasions he was usually dressed in black velvet, with white or pearl-colored waistcoat, yellow gloves, and silver knee-buckles and shoe-buckles. His hair was powdered, and gathered into a silk bag behind. He carried a cocked hat in his hand, and wore a long sword with a scabbard of polished white leather. He never shook hands with his guests, but bowed to each when introduced, and afterwards had a little conversation with each. Mrs. Washington, also, had evening levees, at which every one appeared in full dress. The birthday of the President was celebrated by dinners and public meetings in all the large towns of the nation, as the birthday of the king of England had been before celebrated; and on these occasions odes were often addressed to Washington by poets. All these things were believed by many people to have an important influence in adding dignity and decorum to the young Republic. Others, however, thought that harm was done by this imitation of the customs prevailing in monarchies; and such persons accused Washington of too much etiquette and ostentation. *The birthday of the President.*

It must be remembered that in all classes of society there was then more formality than now, and that the display of elegant costumes was much greater. The judges of the Supreme Court in winter wore robes of scarlet faced with velvet, and in summer wore very full black silk robes, as is still their practice. Clergymen wore wigs, with gown and bands, in the pulpit, and cocked hats in the street. In private life, there was much the same style of dress after the Revolution as before, although, for a time, people were poorer. Ladies wore those beautiful silks and brocades which are still preserved as heirlooms in many American families; and their hair was dressed with powder and pomatum, and often built up to a great height above the head. The hair-dressers were kept so busy on the day of any fashionable entertainment, that ladies sometimes had to employ their services at four or five in the morning, and had to sit upright all the rest of the day, *Costume.*

in order to avoid disturbing the head-dress. Gentlemen had a great variety of color in their clothes, and employed a richness of material such as only ladies now display. "If a gentleman went abroad, he appeared in his wig, white stock, white satin embroidered vest, black satin small-clothes with white silk stockings, and fine broadcloth or velvet coat: if at home, a velvet cap, sometimes with a fine linen one under it, took the place of a wig; while a gown, frequently of colored damask, lined with silk, was substituted for the coat, and the feet were covered with leather slippers of some fancy color." Gentlemen took snuff almost universally in those days; and a great deal of expense and beauty was often lavished on a snuff-box. To take snuff with one another was as much a matter of courtesy as the lifting of the hat.

The snuff-box.

The theatre was only just beginning to be publicly tolerated; but private theatricals sometimes took place; and Washington occasionally had them at his own house. Concerts of music were allowed; and balls were sometimes given on a very large scale, especially by foreign ambassadors. At one of these, given in Philadelphia by the French Ambassador, a building was erected on purpose for the entertainment. There were seven hundred guests, and ten thousand spectators were collected in the street outside. In those days ladies and gentlemen went to balls in sedan-chairs, carried by men; and guests were expected to arrive between seven and eight. The dances were chiefly minuets and contra-dances; quadrilles being only just introduced. At the first Inauguration Ball, a quantity of fans, ordered from Paris for the purpose, were dis-

Entertainments.

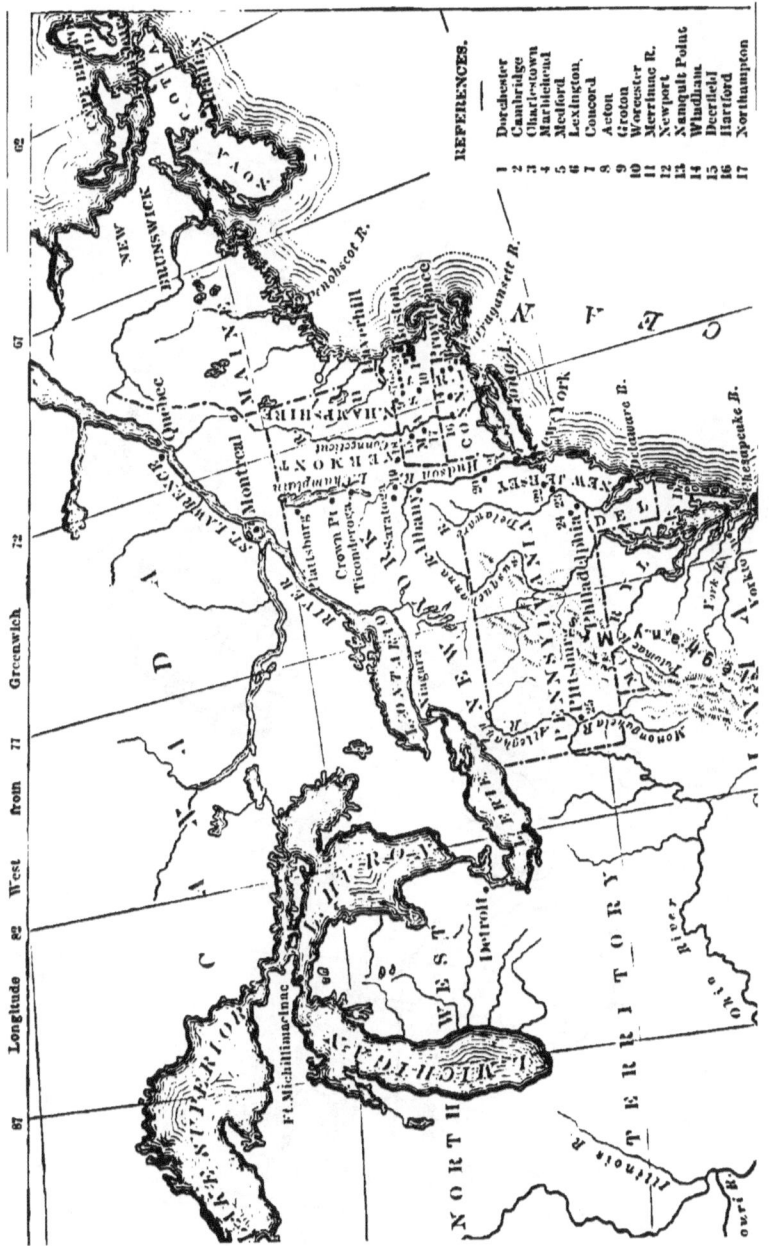

tributed among the ladies. These fans were of ivory and paper; and each bore a medallion portrait of General Washington.

While this was the way of living among the more fashionable classes of society, the people at large were gradually recovering from the losses of war, and were engaging in various branches of industry. War is apt to unsettle the habits of a people; but most of the discharged soldiers of the Revolution went willingly back to their farms and workshops, and were proud of having established a republic where there was liberty and also law. Many were for a time very poor; but there were few beggars to be seen, — so few as to surprise foreign travellers. The chief occupations of the people were agriculture and commerce, together with hunting and fishing. There were as yet neither cotton-mills nor woollen-mills; and very few of the varied modern mechanical inventions had yet been introduced. In the country, people still had great open fires of wood, still burned tallow candles of their own making, and wore homespun garments. Even people in the cities were not far from the wilderness; and the gun and fishing-rod were to be found in most houses, even in the Eastern States; while at the South there were hardly any large towns at all, and the Far West was as yet unexplored by the English colonists, and was only known by the Canadian French.

The people at large

Primitive customs

During the administration of Washington, a most important invention was made, which was destined to have great influence on American history. When the first European explorers came to the American Continent, they found growing wild, in its southern parts, a plant called cotton. It had already been used in other parts of the world; its fine fibre, or down, being spun into cloth. It was easy enough to raise cotton; but the great trouble was to separate the seed from the fibre, which was called "ginning" it. It had to be done by hand, and it took a whole day to gin a pound. Finally an ingenious young man from Massachusetts, named Eli Whitney, who had just graduated at Yale College, went to Georgia to teach school; and the widow of General Greene, in whose family he was living, and who had seen how skilfully he made toys for her children, begged him to invent a machine for ginning cotton. He had never even seen the cotton-seed; but he walked to Savannah, got some of the seed, and tried experiments in machinery. He could not even buy tools or wire in that region, but had to make them for himself. This was in 1792. At last, with great difficulty, he made a rude machine, and showed it to his friend, Mrs. Greene, who invited the leading cotton-planters to examine it. All saw at once that it was to be successful; but, before it could be finished, the building in which he worked was broken open by night, and the machine was carried off. Other machines were made from it; and it was long before the inventor could get any compensation for his labor. After this invention was perfected, the cultivation and manufacture of cotton at once grew up to immense importance; and American cotton supplied the world, which never could have been the case but for some such invention as that of Eli Whitney.

Invention of the cotton-gin.

Soon after Washington became president, one of the most distinguished of Americans died, — one of those

Benjamin Franklin.

who had rendered the greatest services to the liberty of their country. This was Dr. Benjamin Franklin. He was born in Boston, in 1706, and was the son of a poor tallow-chandler. When a boy he learned the printer's trade; and at seventeen left home, and established himself in Philadelphia. He and a young partner began business with no capital, and felt very grateful to a friend whom they met in the street, who, gave them a five-shilling job. Then they set up a newspaper, and published an almanac, called "Poor Richard's Almanack," which had a great circulation. They also dealt in all sorts of small wares,— rags, ink, soap, feathers, coffee.

BENJAMIN FRANKLIN.

Franklin was a great reader, and a great student of the sciences, especially of electricity; and he formed the theory that lightning and the electrical fluid were the same thing. This he said in a pamphlet; and some readers thought it a very absurd view. Then he resolved to prove it; and he and his young son made a great kite of a silk handkerchief, fastened a piece of

<small>Franklin's theory of electricity</small>

sharpened wire to the stick, and went out to fly the kite in a thunder-storm. As the low thunder-cloud passed, the electric fluid came down the string of the kite; and, when Franklin touched a key that he had fastened to the string, his knuckles drew sparks from it and proved that electricity was there. This soon led him to invent the lightning-rod which is now in such universal use, and draws down the electricity from the cloud, on the same principle. This discovery at once made him very famous in Europe, as well as in America. He was afterwards sent to England on a public mission, and remained there till the outbreak of the Revolution. Returning to America, he was one of the framers and signers of the Declaration of Independence. Afterwards he was sent ambassador to France, and aided in making the treaty with France which secured the independence of the American Colonies. He was a

Franklin's character. man of the greatest activity, public spirit, and wit. He had a most important influence in all public affairs, and founded more good institutions and benevolent enterprises than any American of his time. His last public act was to sign a memorial to Congress, in behalf of the Philadelphia Antislavery Society, of which he was president, asking the abolition of slavery. He lived to be eighty-four, dying April 17, 1790. The whole nation mourned when he died; and Mirabeau, then the leader of the French Assembly, called him "the sage whom two worlds claim as their own," and proposed that the Assembly should wear mourning on the arm for him, during three days, which was done. It was said of him by a celebrated Frenchman, Turgot, that "he snatched the lightning from the sky, and the sceptre from tyrants."

During Washington's administration several new States were added to the original thirteen. The first of these was Vermont, in 1791. Vermont had been first settled by pioneers, to whom the governor of New Hampshire had granted lands, — hardy men, who lived by cutting down the forests, and by establishing iron-furnaces. After a time New York claimed this territory, and tried to drive out the settlers. They resisted, and sent Ethan Allen, their leader, to remonstrate with the New York legislature. The legislature treated the demands of the settlers with contempt; upon which Ethan Allen went away, defying them, and said in the words of the Bible, "Our gods are gods of the hills: therefore they are stronger than yours." Then New York sent officers to drive out the settlers; but the "Green Mountain Boys," as they began to be called, resisted. If any one attempted to eject them from their settlements, he was seized, tied to a tree, and whipped with beechen rods; which process they called "applying the beech seal." Large rewards were offered for the arrest of Ethan Allen, Seth Warner, and others, but to no avail. When the Revolution broke out, the "Green Mountain Boys" wished to join the Provincial Congress; but New York objected to this, and they were excluded. However, they distinguished themselves very much during the Revolution, and were admitted soon after the Union had been formed; taking for their settlement the name of Vermont, which signifies "Green Mountain." *Vermont admitted.*

Then Kentucky came into the Union in 1792. This region was at first considered as a part of Virginia, and was only explored a short time before the *Kentucky admitted.*

American Revolution. The first explorer was Daniel Boone, a famous hunter and pioneer. He used to penetrate the wildest regions with small parties of men, to hunt and trap wild animals for the furs, and to make salt at the famous "Salt Licks," or springs. He built forts, and sometimes held them for several days, with his few men, against much larger bodies of Indians. Once he was carried away a prisoner, and adopted into an Indian family, but at last made his escape. After his adventures were made known, settlers rapidly flocked in, coming mostly from the lower parts of Virginia, and bringing their slaves with them. They were stoutly resisted by the Indians; and a long series of conflicts followed, from which came the name by which that region was long known, "The Dark and Bloody Ground." The Spanish Government tried at one time to induce the Kentuckians to declare themselves independent of the Union, and then to join Louisiana, which still belonged to Spain. But all these efforts failed, and the "Dark and Bloody Ground" became one of the United States. The name Kentucky is said to mean "Long River."

Tennessee admitted.

Tennessee came into the Union next, in 1796. This part of the country had been explored much earlier than Kentucky, and had, probably, been visited by De Soto long before the settlement of the more eastern States. De Soto was probably the first European to conduct a party of men to the Mississippi River, or the "Hidden River," or "Inland Sea," as it was then often called; and he had marched with his troops and cannon, for weeks, through wildernesses before unexplored. When he died of fever at last, in 1542, his

WASHINGTON AND ADAMS.

soldiers wished to secure his remains against the Indians: so they hollowed the trunk of an old tree, placed his body in it, and sunk it in a deep part of the Mississippi River. But, for a long time afterwards, that part of the country was almost unvisited by white men, and the land was occupied more slowly than in Kentucky. The settlers came chiefly from North Carolina; and for a time their settlements were considered a part of that colony. At one time the people became dissatisfied, and tried to establish a separate State, under the name of Franklin; but the project was given up, and, after various changes, that whole region was admitted as one of the United States under the name of Tennessee; this being the Indian name for the principal river that flows through it. The settlers had brought their slaves with them; so that Tennessee, also, was a slave State.

Thus, at the end of Washington's administration, there were sixteen States in the Union. There was also the "North-west Territory," as it was called, not yet organized into States,—the whole wide region between the Ohio and Mississippi Rivers, from which slavery had been forever excluded by a law passed by Congress in 1787. The first census of the nation was taken in 1790; and the population was about four millions (3,929,214). *The North-West Territory. The first census, 1790.*

Washington served two terms, or eight years, and then declined a re-election. John Adams of Massachusetts, who had been vice-president, was the second president of the United States (1797–1801). He was what was called a Federalist, and was chosen by a small majority over Thomas Jefferson, who belonged to the opposite party. It was the law in those days that the candidate *The second President.*

who came second in the presidential election should be made vice-president; and so Mr. Jefferson was assigned to that office under Mr. Adams, though they differed a great deal in their politics. President Adams had been one of the foremost of the patriots from the outbreak of the Revolution. He had afterwards assisted in framing the Declaration of Independence; and he had been one of the ambassadors to make the treaty with France at the close of the Revolution. He was inaugurated president at Philadelphia, to which city the seat of government had been removed. Under his administration it was removed thence to Washington, to a site which President Washington himself had selected.

JOHN ADAMS.

Removal of the seat of government.

Troubles with France. After President Adams came into power, the troubles with France went on increasing. Ambassadors had been sent there from the United States; but the French Government would not receive them. Then it was hinted to the ambassadors that a payment of money would reconcile France; and one of them answered, "Millions for defence, not a cent for tribute." It was Charles C. Pinckney of South Carolina who said this; and the sentiment was repeated everywhere through the United States. There seemed to be great prospect of another war; and General Washington was called from his quiet home in Virginia, to take command of the army. There were some sea-fights between French and American vessels; but, when Napoleon Bonaparte came into power, President Adams succeeded in making a treaty with him, in 1800; and after this there was peace with France.

But there had to be an increase of taxation to meet the expense of these preparations for war; and this made the administration of President Adams unpopular with many people. Some laws had also been passed, called "Alien and Sedition Laws," which were very much disliked, because they gave the president authority to arrest any foreigner, and to send him out of the country without a trial; and also gave unusual power to the president in other ways. Great as President Adams's public services had been, he was made very unpopular by these laws; and he was not re-elected for a second term, as Washington had been. The popular vote was so divided, that there was no choice; and the House of Representatives, which had in such cases the right of deciding, chose Mr. Jefferson as president, in Mr. Adams's place. *Unpopularity of Adams.*

It was during the administration of President Adams, that General Washington died, Dec. 14, 1799. There had been much party bitterness during the latter part of Washington's administration; but when he died the whole nation mourned. All felt how much the new American Republic had owed to his courage, *Death of Washington.*

foresight, truthfulness, and disinterestedness. The resolutions passed by the House of Representatives declared that he was "first in war, first in peace, and first in the hearts of his countrymen." This was very true; and the phrase has become almost a proverb in speaking of Washington.

<small>A new territory organized.</small> No new States were admitted into the Union in President Adams's time; but the region between Georgia and the Mississippi River was organized into a "territory," and began to be settled. It comprised what is now included by the States of Mississippi and Alabama. None of the vast region west of the Mississippi yet belonged to the United States, nor did <small>The second census, 1800.</small> Florida. Another census of the nation was taken in 1800; and the population had risen to nearly five millions and a half (5,308,483).

CHAPTER XXIV.

JEFFERSON'S ADMINISTRATION.

THOMAS JEFFERSON of Virginia was the third president of the United States, and served two terms (1801-1809). He was well known as having been the framer of the Declaration of Independence, and as having been vice-president under John Adams. He represented the Republican party, as it was then called, or Democratic party, as it was afterwards called, — the party which sympathized with France rather than with England in the war that was going on between those nations. American politics turned very much on

The third President

THOMAS JEFFERSON.

this war, because it put the United States in a very difficult position. Both France and England had issued orders, each nation forbidding all trade with the other, and claiming the right to confiscate all vessels engaged in such trade. Thus every American vessel on the ocean was liable to capture by the one or the other of these two nations; and, whether an American shipmaster saw the English or the French flag, he tried equally hard to keep out of the way, for fear of having his vessel seized, and his crew perhaps imprisoned.

Commercial troubles.

Besides this, the English claimed the right to search American vessels to see if there were any English seamen on board, and to take any such, if found; and several hundred men were thus seized in the course of a single year. It even happened, once or twice, that the whole crew of a ship was taken, and the vessel was left with nobody to man it. Once the British man-of-war "Leopard" attempted to search the American frigate "Chesapeake," for deserters, within sight of Fortress Monroe in Virginia; and, when the American commander refused to submit, his ship was fired upon, and compelled to surrender; and four men were carried away, one of whom was hanged. All this caused the greatest injury to American commerce, and much angry feeling against Great Britain. Then Congress, wishing to punish England by ceasing to trade with her, laid, in 1807, an "embargo," as it was called, or prohibition, forbidding American shipping from leaving American ports. But this hurt the United States, in the end, much more than it hurt England. It completed the injury that other causes had begun; and it made President Jefferson very unpopular, for a time, with American merchants.

The right of search.

The Embargo.

JEFFERSON'S ADMINISTRATION.

There was also much trouble with the Barbary States, along the Mediterranean Sea. These States subsisted by piracy, and by claiming as slaves the crews and passengers of all vessels that they took. It was a common thing, at that time, for notices to be read in American churches of the captivity of members of the church in Tripoli or Algiers. Then a sum of money was usually raised for the ransom of each, — as much as four thousand dollars for a captain or a passenger. Sometimes these sums were paid by subscription, and sometimes by the government. Thousands of Americans were thus held in captivity; and millions of dollars were spent for ransom. A treaty was made with these Barbary States, by which it was agreed that the United States should pay a certain

Troubles with the Barbary States.

amount of money for the protection of the national commerce. Then a dispute arose about the terms of this treaty; and President Jefferson resolved to bear this humiliation no longer. The American navy consisted, at that time, of but six vessels; and he sent four of them to the Mediterranean. One of these, the frigate "Philadelphia," under Captain Bainbridge, ran aground

LIEUTENANT DECATUR.

in the harbor of Tripoli, and was captured; and the crew were made slaves. A young lieutenant, named Decatur, proposed to the commander of the fleet to take command of a Tripolitan vessel that had just been captured, put an American crew on board, enter the harbor by night, and rescue or burn the "Philadelphia."

Burning the "Philadelphia." This was successfully done. The little Tripolitan ves-

DECATUR BURNING THE "PHILADELPHIA."

sel came quietly in beside the captured frigate; and Decatur and his men recaptured her in ten minutes. But it was impossible to move her; and in a few minutes the "Philadelphia" was in flames, and the little vessel of Decatur was sailing out of the harbor again, without the loss of a man. This was on Feb. 15, 1804. Decatur afterwards distinguished himself in some desperate contests with the Tripolitans; and many years later, at the head of a squadron, he so intimidated all the Barbary States, that they never afterwards demanded tribute of Americans, or claimed the right to hold them as slaves.

Jefferson's administration was conducted on a system very different, in some respects, from those of Washington and Adams. His personal habits were very simple, and so were his views of government. Instead of going in a coach-and-six to the Capitol, as Washington had done, Jefferson rode thither on horseback, on the day of his inauguration, dismounted, tied his horse to a post, and read his address. Afterwards he did not do even this, but sent a "message" to Congress by a secretary, as has been the practice ever since. He abolished the weekly levees, but, on New Year's Day and the Fourth of July, threw open his doors to the whole people. He would not have his birthday celebrated, as had been the previous custom; but concealed the day in order to prevent this. He reduced the expenses of the government as far as possible, and paid off thirty-three millions of debt. He believed strongly in universal suffrage, at least for all persons of the male sex. He thought that all men had a natural right to vote for their own rulers, and his party sustained him in this; while the Federal party looked with great distrust on the system of government by popular vote, and believed that suffrage should be very carefully limited. We must remember that in those days a republican government seemed, even to many patriotic Americans, a very doubtful experiment; while Jefferson had a very hearty faith in it, and so did a great deal

Jefferson's personal habits and views of government.

for its success. But party spirit ran very high then; and there has been a great division of opinion, ever since, as to the wisdom of much that was done by Jefferson.

Prohibition of the African slave trade. One important event that happened during Jefferson's administration was the passage of a law forbidding the African slave-trade. This trade had existed ever since 1619, when the first slaves were brought into Virginia; and it was agreed, when the Constitution was formed, that there should be no interference with the slave-trade until Jan. 1, 1808. More than a year before that time, President Jefferson called the attention of Congress to the subject, and congratulated the members that they would soon be able to forbid a traffic, "which," he said, "the morality, the reputation, and the best interests of the country, have long been eager to proscribe." Then arose a very exciting debate in Congress. No one was in favor of continuing the slave-trade, but there were great differences of opinion as to the way of putting it down; and it was, moreover, pointed out, that, if it was right to hold slaves at all, it could not be wrong to import them. At last, under the lead of Josiah Quincy of Massachusetts, and others, a law was passed, forbidding the importation of slaves from any foreign country into the United States, after the year 1807. In spite of the law, however, slaves were secretly imported for many years, until treaties were made with other maritime countries, by which the slave-trade was declared to be piracy, and the navies of different nations united to break it up. But the slave-trade between the States of the American Union, not being prohibited by law, lasted till American slavery itself was abolished by the war of the Rebellion.

THE FIRST STEAMBOAT.

The most important invention made in America during Jefferson's administration was that of the steamboat. The first person to propose it was Thomas Paine, in 1778, during the Revolution. James Ramsey in 1784 built a vessel which reached a speed of three or four miles an hour, against the stream, on the Potomac. John Fitch built one, soon after, that was employed on the Delaware; and he predicted, moreover, that steamships would one day cross the Atlantic. But these steamboats were not at all like those now built; their engines being made upon a different principle. The first boat constructed on the present plan was launched upon the Hudson, by Robert Fulton, in 1807. While the vessel was being built, it was called "Fulton's Folly," and every one laughed at it. He himself wrote that no one had ever made to him a single encouraging remark about it. But, before the boat had gone a quarter of a mile, unbelievers were converted; and the people who had collected to see the experiment began to shout with applause. The vessel was named the "Clermont," and made the trip from New York to Albany, at the rate of five miles an hour, against the wind and tide. As it moved, it sent

ROBERT FULTON.

showers of sparks into the air. The noise of machinery and paddles was very great; and, when it passed other vessels, their sailors sometimes hid themselves below the deck, and knelt, praying for protection from this horrible monster. From this time forward, steamboats rapidly multiplied, were greatly improved, and were soon in general use; though it was not generally supposed, for a long time after, that they could safely cross the ocean.

THE "CLERMONT."

Aaron Burr.

The vice-president under President Jefferson, at his first election, was Aaron Burr, who was one of the most brilliant men of that period. He and Jefferson had precisely the same number of votes for president; so that the House of Representatives had to decide between them, as was the rule; and, after a great many ballotings, Jefferson was chosen president, and Burr vice-president. Burr had distinguished himself as a soldier and as a statesman; but he lost most of his popularity, after he had killed, in a duel, his political rival, Alexander Hamilton, who was much more beloved than himself, and who had performed an important part in establishing the government. Through

SETTLEMENT OF OHIO.

this unpopularity, Burr failed to be re-elected vice-president in Jefferson's second term; and he was afterwards generally believed to have formed a plan to invade Mexico, and to separate several States from the Union. He was tried for treason on this charge, but was acquitted; yet he never again was respected or trusted by the people.

During Jefferson's administration, the State of Ohio was organized and admitted into the Union, in 1802, making the seventeenth State of the Union. The Ohio Valley had been visited by the French as early as 1680; and it has already been told how they and the English had contended for its possession through the period of "French and Indian Wars." It was abandoned by the French in 1763, together with all their American possessions; and, after the American Revolution, the question came up whether the Ohio Valley belonged to certain States which claimed it, or to the United States Government. Finally it was agreed that it should be surrendered to the United States, except certain small portions which were reserved by different States; and the main part was then called "the North-west Territory." Even after this, there were frequent wars with the Indians; so that the Ohio Valley was slowly settled. When it was at last organized into a State, it still retained the name of the river, "the beautiful river," as the early French explorer had called it.

Ohio admitted.

The State of Ohio had seemed very far west, down to the time of Jefferson; and a man who had seen Lake Michigan or the mouth of the Missouri River was considered in those days a great traveller. But

The far west at that time.

an event soon happened which opened the eyes of people to the vast extent of the American Continent and to the prospects of the American Union. This was the purchase of a vast and unexplored region, stretching west from the Mississippi River to the Rocky Mountains, if not farther, and called by the name of Louisiana.

<small>The discovery of the Mississippi River.</small> The history of the discovery of the Mississippi River is like a romance. It was first reached in 1541, as has been already told, by the Spaniards who had marched through the forests with De Soto. That great leader died, and was buried beneath its waters; and for a century the river was almost forgotten. It hardly appeared on the Spanish maps; and, when men spoke of it, they called it "The Unknown River." A hundred years after, the French explorers from Canada reached the rivers that flow into the Mississippi. La Salle, the most daring of them all, after trying again and again, — often setting off on his expeditions in the dead of winter, travelling on snow-shoes, living on buffalo-meat and the flesh of alligators, sometimes almost drowned amid floating ice, at other times almost killed by starvation and Indian cruelty, — at last descended the Illinois to the Mississippi, and floated down that stream to the Gulf of Mexico. There, at the mouth of the river, in the year 1682, he took possession of that whole region in the name of the French king, Louis XIV.; named it Louisiana, after him; and set up a column, on which the name of the king was inscribed, with the lilies, which were the arms of France.

Almost a hundred years after that (in 1762), the

French gave up Louisiana to the Spaniards; and they, forty years after, gave it up to Napoleon Bonaparte, who sold it during the year 1803, even before he had taken possession of it, to President Jefferson, for the United States Government. The price paid was fifteen million dollars. What is now the State of Louisiana was but a little part of the vast territory which then bore that name; for this territory extended from the Mississippi to the Rocky Mountains, if not actually to the Pacific Ocean, and from the British Possessions on the north, to Mexico on the south. The new purchase comprised nearly nine hundred thousand square miles (899,579), whereas the whole domain of the original thirteen colonies was not much more than eight hundred thousand square miles (820,680). Thus the purchase of what was called Louisiana more than doubled the area of the national territory.

Purchase of Louisiana.

When we consider how little explored, even to this day, is much of this great territory west of the Mississippi, we can imagine what an unknown world it must have seemed, seventy years ago, when only its outskirts had been visited by white men. But when President Jefferson had once secured it for the American nation, he was much too energetic to leave it unexplored. He desired to know what the formation of the country was, what great rivers watered it, what its animals and plants and minerals were, and, above all, what tribes of Indians were to be found there, — whether they were disposed to be warlike or peaceful, and whether they would sell the title to their lands. So the president sent out his private secretary, Capt. Meriwether Lewis, together with Capt. William Clark,

The unexplored region west of the Mississippi.

Exploring expedition to the Rocky Mountains. to conduct an exploring expedition to the Rocky Mountains. There were thirty men in all; and they carried with them provisions, camp-equipage, fire-arms, and presents for the Indian tribes. They left St. Louis, which was then a mere trading-post, in the autumn of 1803, and were gone between two and three years, encamping three winters in the wilderness. They ascended the Missouri River in boats to the great falls, which no white man had then visited; then traced the river to its sources in what were then called the Stony Mountains; and there, finding a rivulet flowing toward the west, they followed it until they reached the Pacific Ocean. The river they descended was one whose mouth had before been visited by a Boston trader, Capt. Robert Gray; and he had named it, after one of his vessels, the "Columbia." This Captain Gray was the first man to carry the American flag round the world by water, as Lewis and Clark were the first to carry it across the continent by land.

The return of the explorers. After reaching the Pacific, the party returned, ascending the Columbia River, and crossing the mountains once more. President Jefferson wrote, in regard to their return, "Never did a similar event excite more joy throughout the United States. The humblest of its citizens had taken a lively interest in the issue of the journey, and looked forward with impatience for *Their report.* the information it would furnish." And indeed the travellers could tell of many wonders, when their narrative was published. They told of finding the buffalo so abundant, that, in one case, a herd occupied the whole breadth of a river a mile wide, and the party had to stop for an hour to see the animals pass by. They described Indian tribes before unknown, — the Mandans, Shoshones, and others. They reported some of these tribes as being wretchedly poor and destitute, and others as having good houses, excellent guns, and such a plenty of horses, that a traveller could at any time buy one for a few beads. These Indians knew so little of civilized habits, that one chief was very grateful for some dried squashes, and said that they made the best food he had ever tasted, except sugar, of which he had once eaten a single lump. He said that he should be very happy if he lived in a country that produced so many nice things. The white explorers learned that, by trading with the Indians, they could obtain a great supply of valuable furs; and a New York merchant, named John Jacob Astor, soon established a trading-post, called Astoria, at the mouth of Columbia River. But this post was afterwards sold to one of the British fur-companies; and it was not till many years later that any part of the Pacific slope was distinctly claimed as being actually a part of the United States.

Asto-ia

CHAPTER XXV.

MADISON AND MONROE, THE WAR OF 1812, AND THE ERA OF GOOD FEELING.

The fourth President.

THE next president was James Madison, of Virginia. He had been a member of the convention that had framed the Constitution; and he served as president for two terms, or eight years, — from 1809 to 1817. When he was inaugurated, he found the nation involved in disputes with the British Government, about the right of searching American vessels, and the restrictions laid on American commerce. These disputes remained unsettled; and at last, June 18, 1812, the Congress of the United States, by a large majority, declared war against England.

JAMES MADISON.

Cause of of the war of 1812.

There was a great deal of opposition to the war, as it was thought by many to be quite unnecessary; and many even thought that the offences committed by England were not so great as those of France. This increased the hostility between the Democrats, who favored France, and the Federalists, who liked England better; and at one time some members of this last party held a convention at Hartford, Conn., in order to oppose the prolongation of the war. *Opposition to the war.*

But the war went on, though at first the American troops were quite unsuccessful. There was an attempt to conquer Canada; but General Hull had finally to surrender Detroit to the British troops; and General Van Rensselaer was also defeated. The Indians took an important part against the Americans in this war, under a chief named Tecumseh, who formed a plan to unite the various Indian tribes against the whites, as had been attempted by Pontiac half a century before. Even before the war with England, Tecumseh had led his Indians against the Americans, and had been defeated by General Harrison at Tippecanoe; and this made him strive more desperately to unite the Indian tribes with the English troops. He took an active part in many battles, but was killed at last. *The defeats of our army.*

But while the United States army was rather unsuccessful, the navy obtained great honor in the War of 1812. The frigate "Constitution," under Captain Hull, took the British frigate "Guerrière;" and there were other important American successes. On the other hand, the British frigate "Shannon" captured the United States frigate "Chesapeake," at the mouth of Boston harbor; and the brave Captain Lawrence, the *The successes of our navy.*

The Chesa-peake and Shannon. commander of the "Chesapeake," was killed, exclaiming as he died, "Don't give up the ship!" Afterwards, on Lake Erie, there was a contest (Sept. 10, 1813) between a British squadron of six vessels, and an American squadron of nine; these last being under command of Lieut. O. H. Perry. His flagship was named the "Lawrence," after the brave captain of the "Chesapeake"; and his flag had inscribed upon it the dying words of Lawrence. But this ship was almost destroyed in the fight; and Perry, getting into an open boat, transferred his flag to a second ship, and gained the victory. When the British ships surrendered, Perry wrote to his commanding officer, on the back of an old letter, "We have met the enemy, and they are ours." This is said to have been the first instance in the history of the British navy of the surrender of an entire squadron. Later in the war, Capt. David Porter fought the "Essex" against two British vessels, for two hours and a half, and only surrendered when his frigate was burning under him.

LIEUTENANT PERRY.

Perry's victory.

The war lasted nearly three years; and in the last

BATTLE OF NEW ORLEANS.

year (1814), the British troops took and plundered many towns on the southern coast, and finally burned the Capitol, and the president's house at Washington. They also attacked New Orleans, which was defended by Gen. Andrew Jackson, with a much smaller force than that brought against it. He built breastworks of cotton-bales, and fought from behind them, repulsing *The third year of the war.*

PERRY'S VICTORY.

the attacking army of twelve thousand, with the loss of but seven Americans killed. This happened Jan. 8, 1815, and was the last battle of the war; indeed, the treaty of Ghent had been signed a fortnight before the battle (Dec. 24, 1814); making peace between the two nations, though the news of this peace had not yet reached the armies at New Orleans. It is a remark- *Treaty of Ghent.*

able fact, that the treaty of Ghent said not a word in regard to the right of search on board of American vessels, the very thing about which the war had been chiefly waged. But the bravery and success of the United States navy had virtually settled that dispute; and no further trouble ever arose about it. Thus ended the "War of 1812," sometimes called the "Late War," between the United States and Great Britain. Since that time, in spite of some temporary disagreements, there has been peace between the two great English-speaking nations; and it is to be hoped that it will always continue.

Thirty years of peace. For a long time after this, the United States seemed very peaceful and prosperous. For thirty years there was no war; and the feeling of hostility between political parties gradually diminished. The population of the country in 1810 was more than seven millions, *The third census, 1810.* (7,239,881); and after this it went on increasing more rapidly. The new States and Territories of the West were being opened for settlement. A great national road had been built from Cumberland, Md., to Wheeling, Va.; and along this road a perpetual stream of wagons poured into Ohio, Indiana, and Kentucky. *Emigration westward.* Other emigrants went westward and southward by the new steamboats just introduced on the Ohio and Mississippi. Others went on rafts and barges, carrying all their household goods with them. The forests still covered all Ohio; and there were almost no roads, so that water-communication was the chief dependence. A whole neighborhood would unite and build a flatboat to send their produce to New Orleans; the boatmen perhaps walking home again. Other emigrants

MONROE'S ADMINISTRATION. 253

went round by sea to the distant mouth of the Columbia River, on the Pacific, where John Jacob Astor had established his trading-post. Then more and more people arrived from Europe. More than twenty-two thousand came in 1817, the last year of Madison's administration, — twice as many as had arrived during the previous year. It seemed an enormous number then, though it would seem but a small number now. Thus the whole nation was in a state of activity and growth. Two new States, Louisiana (1812) and Indiana (1816), were added to the Union during Madison's administration; these making nineteen in all. Louisiana was formed out of the southern part of the great territory purchased from France a few years before. This southern part had previously been called "The Territory of Orleans;" but the name of Louisiana was the old name that the French had given it in honor of Louis, king of France. The name of Indiana came from the Indians, who still inhabited that region. *Immigration from Europe. Louisiana and Indiana admitted.*

The next president was James Monroe of Virginia (1817-1825), who had fought in the Revolutionary War, and had been Secretary of State under Madison. His administration was often called "the era of good feeling," because party strife, as well as war, for a time had died away. There was, however, much trouble with the Seminole Indians in Florida; for, though Florida was not yet a part of the United States, it lay just beyond the border of Georgia; and the Indians of Florida, many of whom had married fugitive slaves, were often committing depredations on the frontier. General Jackson in vain endeavored to subdue them, and, in the effort to do it, marched his troops into *The fifth president. The "era of good feeling." Purchase of Florida*

Florida, though it was still a Spanish colony. This led to a dispute with Spain, which was finally settled by a treaty made in 1819, giving Florida to the United States, five million dollars being paid for it. This made another addition of nearly sixty-seven thousand square miles (66,900) to the area of the United States, though Florida was not admitted as a separate State for many years.

Hostility between the free and the slave States.

But in this era of good feeling there was arising a cause of trouble far greater than any that had afflicted the young nation before. That source of difficulty was slavery. Ever since the first shipload of slaves had been brought to Virginia, in 1619, slavery had become more and more thoroughly the settled system of the Southern States of the Union; and the Northern States had been more and more disposed to regard it as an evil. When the Constitution was formed, it was supposed that slavery was a thing that would soon die out, and that the main source of dispute would be a jealousy between the large and small States of the Union. But this proved to be a great mistake; and the hostility that arose was between the free and the slave States. During Monroe's administration, new States were rapidly formed out of the vast unsettled region of the West; and it became a matter of much importance whether they should come in with slavery or without.

Free States and slave States admitted alternately.

For a time it happened that free States and slave States came in alternately; since the "Ordinance of 1787" excluded slavery from the Northwestern Territory, while the South-western Territories had introduced it. Thus, after Indiana, came Mississippi (in 1817), a free State and a slave State; after

Illinois (1818), came Alabama (1819), a free State and a slave State; after Maine (1820), came Missouri (1821), a free State and a slave State; all these being admitted during Mr. Monroe's administration. But there came a struggle over the admission of this last State, Missouri, showing that the era of good feeling had come to an end. The Northern members of Congress declared that it was wrong and unwise that there should be another slave State in the Union. The Southern members declared, that as there were many such States already, and the Constitution protected them, so there must be more of them to preserve the balance of power; and they claimed, that, whenever a free State was admitted, a slave State ought properly to come in also. Between these two opinions there arose a great and angry contest. *The struggle over the admission of Missouri.*

Thus the era of good feeling under Monroe proved to be only a calm between two storms. The old political disputes were at an end; and a new contest about slavery was beginning, — a contest that was destined to convulse the land for nearly half a century. All the arguments for and against slavery were brought up in the Missouri discussion. It was said that slavery was inhuman; that no man could rightfully hold property in his brother-man; that the relation between master and slave was demoralizing to both; that it was a cruel wrong to sell people at auction, and to break up families; and that the founders of the Republic, as Washington and Jefferson, had opposed slavery, and had wished to get rid of it. On the other hand, the friends of slavery said, that, even if Washington and Jefferson were opposed to it in theory, they, neverthe *The "era of good feeling" ended.* *The arguments for and against slavery.*

less, kept their own slaves; that the Constitution recognized and defended slavery; that it was the best condition for the colored people; that white men could not work out of doors in hot climates; and that cotton and sugar could be raised in no other way. There was great excitement over the dispute; and finally it ended in a compromise. It was agreed by Congress that Missouri should come in as a slave State, but that slavery should be elsewhere prohibited in new States north of 36° 30′ north latitude; this being the line of the southern border of Missouri. South of this, the people of each new State might have slavery or not, as they might prefer. This was the famous "Missouri Compromise" of 1820. Like compromises of principle generally, it only postponed the evil day. At the time of that agreement, slavery was comparatively weak, and might have been abolished, or at least restricted by the nation. By letting it grow, it was allowed to reach such power, that it required for its abolition a great civil war, and the lives of many thousand men.

The Missouri compromise.

Still it was supposed, for a time, that the slavery question had been finally settled by this compromise; and there were other questions, about tariffs and banks, that were generally considered much more important. When General La Fayette came from France to revisit the young nation for whose freedom he had fought, everybody greeted him with enthusiasm; and the nation seemed quiet and at peace. This was just before Mr. Monroe retired from office.

Visit of La Fayette.

He left the nation with five new States added to the Union, as has already been said. Of these, Illinois had been previously a part of Indiana; and the word

The five States admitted.

"Illinois" was the name of an Indian tribe, and meant "The Men." Mississippi and Alabama were both made out of the old Mississippi Territory, which also took its name from a river; the Indian word meaning "The Great River." The words "Alabama" and "Missouri" were both taken from rivers; the latter name meaning "Muddy Waters." All these States had been originally explored and settled by the French. As for the State of Maine, it was formed out of Massachusetts, of which it had been a district; and it is generally supposed to have been named in honor of Henrietta Maria, queen of Charles I., who owned the province of Maine, in France. Others think that this name was given because it was the mainland, as distinguished from the numerous islands along the coast. These new States made the number twenty-four in all, — almost twice as many as "the old thirteen." At the census taken in 1820, the population of the United States was about nine and a half millions (9,638,453).

GENERAL LA FAYETTE.

The fourth census,

The "Monroe doctrine." Monroe's administration had expressed great sympathy for the new republics formed in South America, and had announced the opinion that the United States should thenceforward never allow any European government to plant a colony on the soil of North or South America, or to interfere in American affairs, but that the people of the different parts of the continent should govern themselves. This has always been called "the Monroe doctrine," and is considered one of the most important results of this president's administration.

CHAPTER XXVI.

ADAMS AND JACKSON. — INTERNAL IMPROVEMENTS. — NULLIFICATION AND THE ANTISLAVERY MOVEMENT.

JOHN QUINCY ADAMS of Massachusetts was the next president, serving one term, — from 1825 to 1829. All the previous presidents had taken part in the Revolutionary War, or in founding the government; but John Quincy Adams belonged to a younger generation, and had been but nine years old when his father had signed the Declaration of Independence, and when he himself had heard it read from the State House in Boston. Since then, the young nation had freed and established itself, had widened its bounds, and was now at peace. During the administration of Mr. Adams, much was done to open

The sixth President

JOHN QUINCY ADAMS.

Opening of the interior of the country for settlement. the interior of the country for settlement. Almost all the Indian tribes had been removed west of the Mississippi; and their lands had been bought by the government. A great system of canals had been begun, affording better means of communication than any that had before existed. Chief among these was the Erie Canal, which connected Lake Erie with the harbor of New York. It was completed in 1825; and Gov. De Witt Clinton of New York, who had planned it, and had himself dug the first spadeful of earth, was conveyed the whole distance in a barge, amid the ringing of bells and the discharge of cannon. After this, population poured rapidly into the interior of New York State; and, wherever canals were built, towns and villages grew up.

The first railroad in America. It was during Mr. Adams's presidency, moreover, that the first railroad in America was built, in 1827, —

EARLY RAILROAD TRAIN.

a road of three miles only, leading from the granite quarries to the wharves at Quincy, Mass. The cars were drawn by horses; and the first locomotive engine was not used until two years later, when it was imported from England, where such engines had only just been introduced. This first engine only averaged about fourteen miles an hour, and was regarded as a great curiosity. Many people predicted in America, as they had in

England, that it would never be able to move its own weight, but that the wheels would spin round and round upon the rail. Others thought, that, if it succeeded, it would destroy the value of farming-lands by frightening all the animals, and would stop the raising of sheep, because their wool would be so blackened by the smoke. They were very much surprised when they saw locomotives running peaceably, and without causing any of these disasters.

During John Quincy Adams's administration, his father, Ex-President John Adams, died ; and Ex-President Jefferson died on the same day. As they had grown older, these two eminent statesmen had become friends, and had outlived all the disputes between Federalist and Democrat. They used constantly to write friendly letters to each other; and, by a singular coincidence, the day on which they died was July 4, 1826, the fiftieth anniversary of the Declaration of Independence, which they both had signed. The last words said by Jefferson were, " Is this the Fourth ? " and the last words of Adams were thought to be, " Thomas Jefferson still lives." A patriotic celebration was being held in the village where Mr. Adams lived ; and he had sent to it a toast : " Independence forever." As he lay dying, at sunset time, those who watched by his bed could hear the distant shouting at the village, when the people had heard the old man's last message. *Death of Adams and of Jefferson.*

One public question, about which there was great difference of opinion at that time, was in regard to the amount of duty to be placed on goods imported from foreign countries. Such a system of duties is called a "tariff;" and there is a difference of opinion in *Protective tariff.*

America to this day about it. There are those who think that a high tariff, or duty, should be put on certain manufactured goods, in order to keep out foreign goods, and protect American manufactures. There are others who think that trade should be entirely free, and that there should be no duties or custom-houses at all. Between these, there are people of all shades of opinion, even now, as there were in Mr. Adams's time. But he favored a higher tariff than his opponent; and this was one chief reason why he failed of re-election after his first term of office.

The seventh President. Andrew Jackson, of Tennessee, was the next president, serving two terms, — from 1829 to 1837. He had been well known as an army officer, from the time when he built up the cotton breastworks at New Orleans, and repulsed the British army by firing from behind them. He was a man of great courage, honesty, and energy, though somewhat narrow and violent. While he was president, there grew up much discontent in the

ANDREW JACKSON.

Nullification. Southern States with regard to the tariff. In South Carolina especially, it was thought that the duties imposed

NULLIFICATION IN SOUTH CAROLINA.

were altogether too favorable to Northern manufacturers; and finally a convention was held in the State, in 1832, to plan secession from the Union. It was decided that no duties should be paid in South Carolina after a certain day; and that, if the United States Government attempted to enforce such payment, South Carolina should organize a separate government. At the head of this organization was to be placed Mr. Calhoun, the vice-president of the United States. Medals were made with the inscription, "John C. Calhoun, First President of the Southern Confederacy." Blue cockades were worn in the streets, with a button in the centre, bearing a palmetto, a symbol chosen for the new nation. All this was called "nullification." Preparation for armed resistance was also made. But President Jackson issued a proclamation announcing, "to say that any State may at pleasure secede from the Union is to say that the United States are not a nation." At the same time, additional troops and vessels of war were quickly sent to South Carolina, and placed under the command of Gen. Winfield Scott; and, soon after, Congress passed a law for a gradual reduction of the duties of which South Carolina complained. After this the threats of South Carolina were withdrawn; and the danger of civil war for that time passed by. *Convention in South Carolina.*

During President Jackson's term of office, several of the remaining Indian tribes were removed west of the Mississippi, including the Sacs and Foxes, the Chickasaws and Choctaws. But the Seminoles in Florida refused to remove; and a war was carried on with them for a long time in the swamps of that region, — the "Everglades" as they are called. Many fugitive *Seminole war.*

slaves had escaped to these swamps, and had intermarried with the Indians. These slaves and their children were called Maroons. The principal Indian chief, a half-breed named Osceola, had a Maroon wife, born in the Everglades; and once, when she went with him to one of the United States forts, she was seized as a slave by the former owner of her mother. Osceola was placed in irons while she was taken away into captivity: and, after his release, he pledged himself to vengeance against the whites. He was accordingly the leader of the Indians in war, till he was treacherously seized under a flag of truce; and he was then confined in a fort until his death. The war was continued for many years, at a great cost of money and life, until the tribe was almost extinct; but the expense of the contest had been more than three times as much as had been paid to the Spanish Government for the whole of Florida.

Antislavery publications. This Florida war, having been waged largely against fugitive slaves, only increased the excitement on the question of slavery. During General Jackson's administration, a man named Benjamin Lundy, a Quaker, began a newspaper, called "The Genius of Universal Emancipation," urging that the slaves should be gradually freed. This did not attract much attention; but in 1831 a young man named William Lloyd Garrison, who had been Lundy's assistant editor, established a weekly paper in Boston, called "The Liberator," whose open aim was immediate, unconditional emancipation. This made a great excitement all over the country. The legislature of Georgia offered five thousand dollars for the head of Garrison; and the governor of Massachusetts (Edward Everett) expressed in his annual message the opinion that the abolitionists might be prosecuted in the courts. Mr. Garrison had, however, said, in his paper, "I will not equivocate; I will not excuse; I will not retreat a single inch; and I will be heard." The excitement was much increased by an insurrection that took place in Virginia, headed by a slave named Nat Turner, who, with a band of associates, went from house to house, putting whole families to death. Mr. Garrison was opposed to this, and to all war and to all bloodshed; but the insurrection was, nevertheless, attributed to his teachings. Turner was at last arrested, tried, and executed. After this, the New England Antislavery Society, which was founded by Garrison in 1832, exerted more and more influence. Other societies were founded in different parts of the country. To resist all such agitation, President Jackson urged Congress to pass a law excluding antislavery publications from the mails; but the bill was finally defeated. *Slave insurrection in Virginia. New England Antislavery Society.*

President Jackson was made popular with many people by the energy and firmness he had shown in several cases, especially in his first dealings with South Carolina, and in preventing, by his veto, the establishment of a national bank, to which his party was much opposed. He was, however, much disliked by many, for these same acts; and there was much party excitement while he was in power. He also made himself unpopular by removing from office, in many cases, those opposed to his administration, and appointing his political supporters to the places thus left vacant. This practice had never before existed on any large scale; but it has, unfortunately, continued ever since. The nation was, however, *Popular and unpopular acts of Jackson* prosperous, and out of debt; and indeed there was a surplus of revenue, so that there was a sum of money to be distributed among the States. The census taken in 1830, under Jackson's administration, showed a population of nearly thirteen millions (12,866,020), — more than three times what it had been during the presidency of Washington. Under Jackson, moreover, two new States were added to the Union,— Arkansas (1836), formed from a portion of the great Louisiana purchase, and named for a tribe of Indians now extinct; and Michigan (1837), named from Indian words meaning "great lake." Michigan was formed from a part of the old North-west Territory, early explored and settled by the French; and, as slavery had been prohibited in all that territory by the "Ordinance of 1787," Michigan came in as a free State; but Arkansas came in as a slave State.

CHAPTER XXVII.

VAN BUREN, HARRISON, TYLER, AND THE ANNEXATION OF TEXAS.

THE next President was Martin Van Buren of New York (1837-1841). Like General Jackson before him, he was the candidate of the Democratic party, which differed from the Whig party, as the opposition party was now called, mainly in insisting more on the rights of the separate States, and less on those of the General Government. During Mr. Van Buren's administration there was great excitement on the Canadian frontier, because of a rebellion against the British Government in Canada. Many people in the States bordering on Canada sympathized with this rebellion; but the American Government discouraged all active assistance, as being contrary to international law. The rebellion was finally subdued.

MARTIN VAN BUREN.

The eighth President.

Canadian rebellion.

Anti-slavery agitation. But there was an excitement which kept on increasing in the United States during all President Van Buren's time, and was far more important than the Canadian rebellion. This was the antislavery agitation, which grew steadily greater, and was often resisted by mobs and violence, even in the free States. A slave child named Med, who had been brought by her master into Boston, was declared free by the Supreme Court of the State, as not being a fugitive; and several similar triumphs were obtained. On the other hand, a meeting of the Boston Female Antislavery Society was broken up by a mob, while the mayor declared himself unable to protect it; and Mr. Garrison, who had attempted to address the society, was dragged through the streets with a rope round his body, and was finally saved by the police, who lodged him in jail for protection. A public hall in Philadelphia, called Pennsylvania Hall, where the national convention of antislavery women had met, was burned. Schools for colored children in New Hampshire and Connecticut were broken up. At Alton, Ill., Rev. Elijah P. Lovejoy, who edited an antislavery newspaper, was killed by a mob. In **Proposition to annex Texas.** Congress, a plan was brought forward for the annexation of Texas, then an independent Republic; and, as it was seen that this measure would have the effect of strengthening slavery, petitions were poured into Congress by the thousand, many of them signed by women, against it. Great efforts were made to exclude these petitions; and Ex-President John Quincy Adams spoke an hour a day, for twelve days, amid constant interruptions, in behalf of the petitioners. The annexation of Texas was for the time defeated; but a rule was adopted by Congress, and for ten years remained in force, excluding all petitions on any subject pertaining to slavery.

While Mr. Van Buren was president, there was great commercial distress, and there were many failures among men of business; and this was one great reason why he was not re-elected, but was defeated after his first term. No new States were added during his administration; but when the census was taken (in 1840) it was found that the population of the country had increased to seventeen millions (17,069,453), — more than four times the population of Washington's time. *Crisis of 1837.* *The sixth census, 1840.*

The general discontent of the nation over business troubles, during Mr. Van Buren's administration, led to a great excitement as to the choice of his successor. Gen. William Henry Harrison, of Ohio, who had fought Tecumseh and his Indians bravely thirty years before, was nominated for president by the Whigs. As he came from what was then the Far West, some one gave him the name of "The Log-Cabin Candidate;" and all over the country log-cabins were soon built for political meetings; and there were political celebrations, at which cider was the only beverage, this being a favorite drink among farmers. There were many songs composed and sung at these gatherings, — songs about "the hero of Tippecanoe" and about "Tippecanoe and Tyler too;" John Tyler being the candidate for vice-president. In short, it was the liveliest political campaign that had ever been known; and the end of it was the election, by an overwhelming vote, of General Harrison, who was inaugurated president in 1841. *The ninth president.*

The tenth president.

The Northeastern boundary question.

The "Dorr War."

Anti-rent troubles.

The Mormons.

General Harrison lived precisely a month after his inauguration; and Vice-President John Tyler, of Virginia, became president for the remainder of the four years (1841–1845). During his administration, the nation was at peace with foreign countries, though war was at one time threatened between the United States and Great Britain, because of a dispute about the boundary-line between Maine and New Brunswick. A treaty was at last made (in 1842), by Lord Ashburton in behalf of England, and by Daniel Webster for America; and this settled the question of the boundary. Then there were internal troubles in several of the States. In Rhode Island (in 1842), there was a revolt against the old colonial charter under which the State had always been governed; and, after a brief military contest known as the "Dorr War," the rebellion was defeated, though a new constitution was adopted at last, in consequence of it. In New York, along the Hudson River, where the estates of the old Dutch "patroons" lay, the tenants who occupied these estates grew unwilling to pay rent to the descendants of the early proprietors, and there was armed resistance for a time. There was also much disturbance in Illinois, where the religious sect called the "Mormons," or "Latter-Day Saints," who had built a city named Nauvoo, were assailed repeatedly by mobs. The Mormon sect had been founded fourteen years before, by a man named Joseph Smith, who claimed to have discovered a book, called "The Book of Mormon," written on gold plates that were found buried in the earth. The Mormons first established themselves in Missouri, were driven thence by mob violence to Illinois, and thence to the Territory of Utah, where they made for themselves a settlement in the wilderness, and still remain.

One new State was admitted into the Union during Mr. Tyler's administration, — Florida. As has already been told, Florida contained older European settlements than any part of the nation to which it was annexed; St. Augustine even dating back to the early Spanish colony of 1565. Florida had been alternately claimed by the Spaniards, the French, and the English, and had been finally ceded by Spain to the United States in 1819. For many years it was governed only as a Territory; but in 1845 it was admitted as a State. Its name came from the day on which it was first explored, Easter Sunday, called by the Spaniards Pascua Florida, or Flowery Easter.

Florida admitted

But Mr. Tyler's administration will be chiefly remembered as having brought about the annexation to the United States of a foreign State, — the State of Texas. Texas had been first explored by La Salle in 1684. when looking for the mouth of the Mississippi. From that time forth, it had been almost constantly the scene of war between hostile claimants. First the Spaniards and French contested for it, and established rival "missions," or religions settlements. Then the large province of Texas revolted from Mexico, and declared itself an independent State. Many Americans took part in obtaining the independence of Texas; for several large American colonies had been established there, and these Americans had carried their slaves with them; whereas Mexico had before abolished slavery. Thus there was much sympathy for Texas in the South-western States of the American Union; and

Early history of Texas.

Sympathy for Texas in the south-western States.

there was a strong desire to annex it to the United States. On the other hand, the free States were generally much opposed to its admission, as it was frankly admitted by Mr. Calhoun, the great leader of the pro-slavery party, that the object of the measure was "to uphold the interests of slavery, extend its influence, and secure its permanent duration." This seemed very likely to prove true, because Texas was an immense region, including three hundred and eighteen thousand square miles, and being thus one-third as large as the original thirteen States combined, forty times as large as Massachusetts, and more than twice as large as the great States of New York, Pennsylvania, and Ohio put together. If, now, all this were to be admitted as slave territory, it seemed as if freedom would be entirely outvoted in the government forever. This accounts for the great opposition that was made to the annexation of Texas, which, however, finally took place at the end of Mr. Tyler's administration. A joint resolution for this purpose passed the United States House of Representatives Feb. 25, 1845, and the United States Senate March 1: and it was approved by the president on the very day it passed the Senate, — three days before he went out of office. A great territory was thus added to the nation, in return for which the United States assumed the Texas debt of seven and a half million dollars. This seemed to many people at that time to be a great sum to pay for a very doubtful advantage; and it was often said that the word "Texas" was only "Taxes" with the letters differently arranged.

Opposition to the annexation.

The annexation.

CHAPTER XXVIII.

POLK AND THE MEXICAN WAR.

JAMES K. POLK of Tennessee was President of the United States for the next four years (1845-1849); and the report of his nomination was the first news ever transmitted by telegraph in America, being sent on the new line which Professor Morse had just completed between Washington and Baltimore. Mr. Polk was the canditate of the Democratic party; and he was opposed by the Whig party and the new party called the "Liberty" party, which was formed to resist the influence of slavery. Mr. Polk's election turned mainly on the question of the annexation of Texas, though this was finally settled just before he came into power. There was also a question, which, for a time, caused much anxiety, as to the possession of Oregon. *The eleventh President.*

The American Government had made claim to Oregon, because an American captain had discovered the Columbia River, and an American expedition, Lewis and Clark's, had explored it. But that whole region had been practically under control of the British fur companies; and, though many Americans had settled there, it had always been disputed territory. In 1846, however, under President Polk, a treaty was made which divided this great region. The United *The northwestern boundary question.*

273

States had claimed as far north as 54° 40′ north latitude; and "Fifty-four forty, or fight," was a favorite electioneering motto in the presidential campaign. But it was finally agreed that the line should be drawn at 49°. All north of this was given to Great Britain; and all south, including more than three hundred thousand (308,052) square miles, to the United States. Thus the western boundary question was peacefully settled, as the north-eastern boundary question had been settled just before; and this did much credit to Mr. Polk's administration, and gave satisfaction to almost all.

Outbreak of the Mexican War. But the other great event of Mr. Polk's administration was something about which people were not at all agreed, and which many, especially in the Northern States, regarded as a great calamity,— the Mexican War. When the United States had annexed Texas, the nation found that it had still another question of boundary on its hands. Texas claimed that its western boundary was the Rio Grande, and Mexico claimed that it was the River Nueces; and, as these rivers were a hundred miles apart, there was a wide range of disputed territory between. The United States took up the cause of Texas; and General Taylor was sent to the disputed ground with a small army. The Mexicans, also, sent troops thither; and fighting soon began, first in a small way, then in some larger battles, at Palo Alto and Resaca de la Palma, in which the Americans were successful. Then General Taylor crossed the Rio Grande, and took Matamoras, which was within undisputed Mexican territory.

Action of Congress. There was much excitement in Washington on hearing this news. Congress voted thus, May 11, 1846:

THE MEXICAN WAR.

"By the act of the Republic of Mexico, war exists between that government and the United States;" though the Whig members declared that the war was not really begun by Mexico, but by General Taylor. Congress also voted ten million dollars for the war, and resolved to raise fifty thousand volunteers. There was not much sympathy for the war in the Eastern States; but the South-western States, which were nearest the scene of excitement, sent many volunteers to the aid of General Taylor. At last his army reached nearly seven thousand men; and with this he took, in three days, the fortified town of Monterey, garrisoned by ten thousand Mexicans. Then General Santa Anna, who had formerly been President of Mexico, and was regarded as the best soldier of that Republic, took command of the Mexican army, but was beaten by General Taylor, with a much smaller force, at Buena Vista. Then General Scott was sent, with an additional army, to attack the principal port and fortress of Mexico, Vera Cruz, with the hope of thus penetrating to

Taylor's campaign.

GENERAL SCOTT.

Scott's campaign

Bombardment of Vera Cruz. the capital of the country, and "conquering a peace." He accordingly, with twelve thousand men, bombarded Vera Cruz; and it was surrendered, with the fortress of San Juan d'Ulloa, the strongest fortress on the continent, except that of Quebec. A fleet under Commodore Matthew C. Perry also assisted in this attack. Then the American army advanced toward the capital, over-

BATTLE OF BUENA VISTA — REPULSE OF MEXICAN LANCERS.

coming all difficulties, and winning a series of daring victories on the way, always against great superiority of numbers. Among these battles were those of Cerro Gordo, Churubusco, El Molino del Rey, and Chapultepec; and the Americans finally took possession of **Occupation of the city of Mexico.** the city of Mexico, Sept. 14, 1847. It was a city of a hundred and forty thousand inhabitants; and the army that entered it consisted of less than six thousand men.

Meanwhile the Mexican provinces were being attacked in several different directions. Gen. Stephen Kearney marched into New Mexico, and Colonel Doniphan, into Chihuahua; and their small forces took possession of those provinces. Capt. J. C. Fremont, who was exploring California with only sixty men, had formed a plan of making California into an independent State, such as Texas had been, and had induced the American settlers in the Sacramento Valley to join him in this effort. He had raised over his troops a flag, bearing the figure of a bear, to represent independent California; but, on hearing that an American fleet had taken Monterey, on the seacoast, he raised the American flag instead. After a series of fights with Mexican troops, and with the aid of Commodore Stockton and a naval force, he took possession of California in order that it might become a part of the United States. At last a treaty was made with Mexico, by which Mexico gave up New Mexico and Upper California to the United States, and agreed to accept the Rio Grande as the boundary between herself and Texas. The territory thus added to the United States was more than half a million (522,955) square miles. In return, the United States agreed to pay Mexico fifteen millions of dollars, and to assume the debts due citizens of the United States from Mexico, amounting to three and a half millions besides. The treaty by which all this was accomplished was called the "Treaty of Guadalupe Hidalgo," from the city where it was made. It was signed Feb. 2, 1848, and was ratified by Congress

Attack on Mexican provinces.

Treaty of Guadalupe Hidalgo.

March 10 of the same year. Thus the Mexican War closed in two years from its beginning.

Discovery of gold in California. Nobody knew, when this treaty was made, how great was the value of the territory thus gained. California had been known only as a distant region, whither men went by sea, around Cape Horn, to buy hides and furs. But in 1848 there came rumors to the Eastern States of gold mines on the Sacramento River, in California, which promised to be richer than any in the world. It was said that a laborer in the employ of Captain Sutter, a Swiss settler in the Sacramento Valley, had found in the sand some glittering particles, which turned out to be gold. Then there was a sudden and eager emigration to that region from all parts of the Union; and in the very first year the mines yielded four million dollars' worth of gold. Within two years San Francisco contained fifteen thousand inhabitants. The name of California is supposed to have been taken from an old Spanish romance, in which the name was given to an imaginary island filled with gold; and the early explorer, Cortes, when he visited the western coast of the continent, applied that name to the whole region long before any gold was actually found there.

Texas, Iowa, and Wisconsin admitted. During Mr. Polk's administration three more States were admitted to the American Union, making thirty in all. These were Texas, Iowa, and Wisconsin; the names of all three being taken from Indian tribes or rivers. Texas was admitted as a State in 1845; and the same antislavery feeling that had resisted its annexation was revived to resist its admission as a State, but unsuccessfully. Then came Iowa (1846), which was made out of a part of the great Louisiana purchase, and Wisconsin (1848), which had been a part of the old "North-west territory" originally belonging to the United States. Both these last were free States; and it became plainer and plainer that the multitude of foreign immigrants would always prefer free territory to slave territory, and that the free States would inevitably grow faster than the others. This made the slaveholding States still more desirous to secure more States of their own description, wherever it was possible; and when, at the close of the Mexican War, a great extent of new territory was acquired, great efforts were made on both sides to secure control of it. For this purpose Mr. Wilmot of Pennsylvania introduced into Congress a measure, commonly called the "Wilmot Proviso," absolutely excluding slavery from the whole of the new acquisitions. It was long discussed, and finally defeated; but the agitation led to the formation of a new party, whose object was to oppose the extension of slavery. It was called the "Freesoil" party, and took the place of the old Liberty party. Under its new name it took an active part in the next presidential election, and at a later period, under the name of the "Republican" party, obtained the control of the government.

The Wilmot proviso.

The "Freesoil" party.

CHAPTER XXIX.

THE APPROACH OF THE CIVIL WAR.

TAYLOR, FILLMORE, AND PIERCE.

The twelfth president.

AT the next presidential election, the Whig party, which had opposed the Mexican War, thought it best to nominate for president the most successful general of the war, Zachary Taylor, of Louisiana. He had been popular with his soldiers, and had been named by them "Old Rough and Ready." He was opposed by the Democratic party and by the new "Freesoil" party, but was elected, and was inaugurated March 5, 1849. He died a little more than a year afterwards, July 9, 1850; and Vice-President Millard Fillmore, of New York, became president for the remainder of that presidential term, 1850-1853.

The thirteenth president.

Clay's "Omnibus Bill."

The antislavery struggle had now risen to be the chief question before Congress; and an attempt was made by Henry Clay, of Kentucky, a very eloquent and persuasive orator, to settle it forever by a series of what were called "Compromise Measures." One of the principal measures was the admission of California as a free State. Another was the abolition of the slave-trade in the District of Columbia. These were adopted, and were regarded as concessions in favor of freedom. On the other hand, to balance these, a bill was introduced, called the Fugitive Slave Law, giving the owners of slaves the opportunity to recapture their escaped slaves in any part of the free States, and to carry them back without trial by jury. This was considered by many to be unconstitutional, as well as inhuman. It was opposed and denounced by the leading antislavery orators, such as Charles Sumner, Horace Mann, Wendell Phillips, and Theodore Parker; but it was supported by leading Northern statesmen, such as Daniel Webster; and it became a law, Sept. 18, 1850.

This law produced more excitement than anything that had before happened during the antislavery agitation. In Syracuse, N. Y., a fugitive named Jerry was rescued by force from the government officers: in Boston one named Shadrach was rescued; and an attempt was made to rescue another, named Anthony Burns. One man was killed in this last attempt; and troops were ordered out to aid in the surrender of the alleged slave. In Ohio a fugitive woman, named Margaret Garner, killed two of her own children to save them from being carried into slavery. In several of the States, laws were framed to restrict or defeat the operation of the Fugitive Slave Law, and to secure at least a jury trial for those claimed as slaves. *Opposition to the fugitive slave law.*

These compromise measures formed the most important feature of Mr. Fillmore's administration. In other respects his term of office was a peaceful one. One new State was admitted during this time: it was formed, in 1850, out of the territory purchased at the close of the Mexican War, and was named California; *California admitted.*

YOUNG FOLKS' UNITED STATES.

Two new territories organized. thus perpetuating the old Spanish name. The two Territories of New Mexico and Utah were also organized out of the same purchase. New Mexico was inhabited chiefly by a population of Spanish origin; and Utah had been settled by the religious sect called Mormons, whose leader, Brigham Young, was commissioned by *Census of 1850.* the president as governor of the Territory. By the census of 1850 the population of the whole nation was about twenty-three millions (23,191,876).

The fourteenth president. Mr. Fillmore had been elected as a Whig; though the antislavery agitation was fast destroying old party lines. His successor, Franklin Pierce, of New Hamp- *The Kansas-Nebraska Bill overthrows the Missouri Compromise.* shire (1853-1857), was a Democrat. During his term the same agitation was further increased by the efforts of the friends of slavery to overthrow the Missouri Compromise, as it was called; a law which had been passed in 1820, prohibiting slavery north of a certain line in that great domain which had been bought under the name of Louisiana. It was now proposed to organize out of that region, from which slavery had been thus excluded, two new Territories, to be named Kansas and Nebraska, and to let the inhabitants determine for themselves whether they should establish slavery or freedom. This change of policy was strongly resisted by the antislavery party, and more than three thousand of the New England clergy petitioned Congress against it; but it was finally passed, May 30, 1854.

Emigration to Kansas. As this law left it to the settlers to decide upon their institutions, it was considered important both by the friends and the opponents of slavery to encourage emigration to the new Territories. Parties were therefore organized for this purpose in various parts of the Union.

Those from the free States generally went as permanent settlers, with their families; but many went in from the slave States, merely to take part in the disturbances, and aid in establishing slavery. This was especially the case with a class of Missourians, who could at any time cross the Kansas border, commit depredations, vote at elections, and then retreat across the border, undisturbed. These invaders were commonly called "Border Ruffians." At one time they stopped the navigation of the Missouri River for all free State settlers, compelling all these to take a tedious overland journey

The border ruffians.

EMIGRANTS CROSSING THE PLAINS.

through Iowa. The United States officials supported, sometimes the one party, and sometimes the other, finally inclining towards the slaveholders; while governor after governor were sent from Washington, and resigned in despair. Two separate governments were organized by the settlers, and two separate codes of law adopted. Actual fighting began at last. The free State military leaders — Lane, Montgomery, and others — organized bands to defend their settlements; and Capt. John Brown took an especially daring part in the defence. At Ossawattomie, for instance, he defended himself, with sixteen men, against several

The struggle in Kansas.

hundred marauders from Missouri; his little band killing and wounding more than four times their own number, and losing but two men. The same invaders sacked and burned the flourishing village of Lawrence, lately settled by men from Massachusetts. Many families in Kansas were reduced to poverty during this period, or lived by taking horses and cattle belonging to those of the other party ; so that men would speak of a proslavery horse or an antislavery cow, according as the owner of these animals belonged to either side. At last the establishment of freedom was secured in Nebraska and Kansas, but at a great cost of suffering and hatred.

The Gadsden purchase. A more peaceful event of President Pierce's administration was a purchase of territory called the "Gadsden Purchase," from the name of the minister who negotiated it. When the treaty of Guadalupe Hidalgo was made, at the close of the Mexican War, it was founded on an inaccurate map; and this afterwards led to a dispute about the New Mexican boundary. To settle the dispute, the United States bought of Mexico (Dec. 30, 1853) a part of the Territories now known as Arizona and New Mexico, for ten million dollars. This purchase included about forty-five thousand square miles, and brought the whole territorial extent of the United States (in 1854) up to nearly three million square miles (2,981,701). This was nearly four times the area of the original thirteen States, and far larger than that of the famous Roman empire in its greatest days.

Treaty of Japan. Another important event that occurred in the time of President Pierce was a treaty with Japan, negotiated March 21, 1854, by Commodore Matthew C. Perry, brother of the hero of Lake Erie. Before this time Japan had rigidly excluded from its ports all foreigners, except about a dozen Dutch traders, and had allowed shipwrecked seamen to be treated with the greatest cruelty. Commodore Perry with an American squadron compelled the Japanese to show more consideration for foreigners in distress; and his treaty secured the removal of almost all restrictions on commerce with Japan.

The new party opposed to the extension of slavery had now reached such strength, that the Whig party had gradually disappeared; and the next presidential election lay mainly between the Republican party, as the new organization styled itself, and the old Democratic party. There was, however, a temporary party, composed of those who called themselves "Know Nothings," and aimed mainly to oppose foreign influence in national legislation. This party carried but one State, Maryland; and the Democratic candidate, James Buchanan of Pennsylvania, was elected president. His administration (1857-1861) will always be remembered as that in which the great civil war, or "War of the Rebellion," arose.

The election of the fifteenth president.

CHAPTER XXX.

THE OPENING OF THE CIVIL WAR. — BUCHANAN.

The Dred Scott decision.

MR. BUCHANAN'S inauguration took place on March 4, 1857, and that very year the Supreme Court pronounced a decision called the "Dred Scott Decision," declaring the right of slaveholders to take their slaves with them into any part of the country. This made a great excitement throughout the free States; and something else soon happened, which excited the slave States almost as much. This was what is commonly called "John Brown's Raid." Capt. John Brown's name has been already mentioned in describing the resistance of the "Free State" settlers of Kansas to the "Border Ruffians" of Missouri. After order was restored in Kansas, John Brown resolved to fulfil a plan he had long formed for resisting slavery in the slave States themselves. In his youth he had been familiar with the mountains of Virginia, and had there visited places which, as he used to say, had evidently been created to be the stronghold for fugitive slaves. General Washington, long before him, had formed a plan to take the American army into these mountains, should the colonies be defeated; and John Brown proposed to do the same with an army of blacks. So, having collected a small body of men near Harper's

John Brown in Virginia.

John Brown's raid.

Ferry, Va., he entered and took possession of the town, Oct. 16, 1859. He at once seized the United States Arsenal, intending thus to secure arms for the fugitive slaves whom he meant to summon to his side.

He seizes the United States arsenal.

He frankly announced his object to be the freedom of the slaves; and he promised safety to all property, except slave-property. He had in all but twenty-two

HARPER'S FERRY.

men; but so great was the alarm produced by these, that several eye-witnesses reported the number to be three hundred; and this estimate was at once telegraphed to all parts of the Union. With this small number he took many of the chief inhabitants of the town as hostages for the safety of those under his command. Wishing to spare all unnecessary alarm to the families of these hostages, he stayed at Harper's Ferry too long for his safety; so that militia companies had time to assemble, and finally a detachment of United States marines appeared upon the scene. Fifteen hundred militiamen were gradually collected in the town; but Brown's little force defended the arsenal until nearly every man was killed or wounded, and they then surrendered to the United States troops. Colonel Washington, one of his prisoners, said that Captain Brown was "the coolest and firmest man he ever saw in defying danger and death. With one son dead by his side, and another shot through, he felt the pulse of his dying son with one hand, and held his rifle with the other, and commanded his men with the utmost composure, encouraging them to be firm." He fell at last with six wounds, and was thought to be dying. Ten of the party were killed, and four wounded.

The trial of John Brown. John Brown himself was put on trial before a Virginia court, where he conducted himself in such a manner as to win the admiration even of his enemies. Governor Wise of Virginia said of him, "They are themselves mistaken who take him for a madman. . . . He is a man of clear head, of courage, fortitude, and simple ingenuousness. . . . He inspired me with great confidence in his integrity as a man of truth." He was condemned and executed on the gallows Dec. 2, 1859, at Charlestown, Va.; his last act being to kiss the forehead of a little slave-child, on the way to the place of execution. *His comrades.* Six of his comrades were executed at a later day. A few others, who were on duty outside the town, escaped to the mountains, and thence, with great peril and hardship, to the free States. One of John Brown's

MAP 5.

ILLUSTRATING THE

MEXICAN WAR.

sons was the leader of this party, and has written a thrilling narrative of their escape.

These events brought the agitation on the subject of slavery to its highest point, during President Buchanan's administration. When the time drew near for the election of a new president, the old parties were so broken up, that there were four candidates in the field, though Mr. Buchanan himself was not one of them Out of these four, Abraham Lincoln, of Illinois, was elected, he having been nominated by the Republican party; this being an enlarged form of the Freesoil party, which had itself succeeeded the Liberty party. Mr. Lincoln was a man of very moderate opinions in regard to slavery, and was not disposed to interfere with it where it was already established by law. But his election was regarded by many in the slave States as very dangerous to the interests of slavery; and these men resolved to dissolve the Union. They maintained that the United States consisted of a copartnership of entirely independent governments; and that any State could withdraw from it at will. This was the doctrine called "State Rights," which had long been popular in the Southern States, and especially in South Carolina. It was therefore very natural that South Carolina should take the lead in withdrawing from the Union; and a convention was accordingly called in that State, and adopted (Dec. 20, 1860) an ordinance of secession. Within six weeks similar conventions had been held, and similar votes passed, in the States of Mississippi, Florida, Alabama, Georgia, Louisiana, and Texas. These States then formed themselves into what was called the "Southern Confederacy," and

The election of Abraham Lincoln.

His views about slavery.

The doctrine of State rights.

Secession.

The Southern Confederacy.

elected (Feb. 8, 1861) Jefferson Davis, of Mississippi, as president, and Alexander H. Stephens, of Georgia, as vice-president. The new confederacy maintained the righteousness of slavery as a permanent institution, and it openly aimed to establish a slave-holding nation in the Southern States.

<small>Attack on Fort Sumter.</small>

The authorities of South Carolina at once claimed

ATTACK ON FORT SUMTER.

possession of all national property in the State. Seeing this, Major Robert Anderson, who commanded the garrison of a small fort called Fort Moultrie in Charleston harbor, withdrew his force to Fort Sumter, a stronger position, and sent for re-enforcements from Washington. A steamer called the "Star of the West," carrying two hundred and fifty men, was sent to Charleston in January, but was fired upon from Fort Moultrie, where the insurgents had placed a garrison. Then batteries were erected on the shore; and at last (April 11) General Beauregard, in command of the Confederate troops, demanded the surrender of Fort Sumter; and, this being refused, the batteries opened fire upon the fort early the next morning. For two days the fire continued; and at midnight of the second day Major Anderson surrendered the fort, his eighty men being wholly exhausted, his barracks on fire, and his gunpowder almost gone. He stipulated that he should be allowed to march out with drums beating and colors flying, and to bring away company and private property. This he did on Sunday, April 14, firing away his remaining powder in saluting the United States flag with fifty guns.

The first gun fired at Fort Sumter aroused and excited the whole nation; and many who had before expressed much sympathy for the supporters of slavery now took sides with those who wished to preserve the Union. The event also produced a great impression at the South; and acts of secession were passed in North Carolina, Virginia, Arkansas, and Tennessee. In all these States the colored population took sides unanimously with the Union; but, being composed almost wholly of unarmed and ignorant slaves, they counted at first for little. There were also, in some of these States, many white citizens who opposed disunion; but they were, in most cases, gradually silenced or driven away. Meanwhile President Buchanan showed no decision of character in dealing with the Rebellion; and amid the rising tumult he went out of office.

Effect of the attack on Fort Sumter.

Minnesota, Oregon, and Kansas admitted.

During his administration, three new States had been added to the Union, — Minnesota (1858), Oregon (1859), and Kansas (1861). Of these, Minnesota and Kansas were both formed mainly from the territory gained by the Louisiana purchase; and both bear the Indian names of rivers flowing through them. Oregon was formed out of the territory secured to the United States by the boundary treaty of 1846; and the name is said to come from the word "Oregano," meaning wild rice, which grows profusely on the Pacific coast.

Census of 1860.

By the census of 1860, taken during Mr. Buchanan's administration, the whole population of the country was nearly thirty-one and a half millions (31,443,321).

CHAPTER XXXI.

THE CIVIL WAR. — LINCOLN.

NO one who was not in the midst of it can imagine the excitement that arose in all the Northern States when it was heard that Fort Sumter had been attacked. Up to that moment there had been a great division of feeling at the North; and there were many who thought that, by patient efforts, those who wished to secede from the Union could be brought back again. Few really believed that there was to be any serious fighting. While the white population of the South had been preparing for war, the Northern people *The North taken by surprise.*

ABRAHAM LINCOLN.

ple had gone about their usual employments; and, when the attack came, they were quite taken by surprise. Although, three months before, the Confederates in Louisiana had seized upon the fort at the mouth of the Mississippi, and upon the United States Arsenal at Baton Rouge the Northern people could not convince themselves that actual war would take place. So they were still unprepared.

The first call for troops.

When President Lincoln was inaugurated (March 4, 1861), the regular army was very small, and very much scattered; but, on the 15th of April, he issued a call for seventy-five thousand volunteers for three months only. A few regiments of militia were hastily summoned from the different States for the defence of Washington. One of these, the Sixth Massachusetts,

SIXTH MASSACHUSETTS REGIMENT ATTACKED BY A MOB.

Baltimore riot.

was attacked by a mob in passing through Baltimore; and, after three men had been killed by stones and clubs, one company fired on the mob in return, killing nine men, and wounding many. This took place on April 19, 1861, the anniversary of the Battle of Lexington. It produced almost as much excitement as the attack on Fort Sumter, not that the Baltimore affair was a deliberate act of organized rebellion, but that it showed the feeling of hostility to the government wherever slavery existed.

When it was necessary to send the next troops through Maryland, they were not marched through Baltimore, but through Annapolis. General Butler, with regiments of militia from Massachusetts and New York, passed along the line of railway from Annapolis to Washington; the soldiers repairing it as they went. Finding a wrecked locomotive by the roadside, the general asked if there was any one in the ranks who could repair it. "I can," said a soldier who had been examining the engine; "for I built it." In truth, these troops were made up of men of all occupations, just taken from the daily pursuits of life; and there were few trades which were not represented in every regiment. After a while, troops were sent through Baltimore again; and it became, almost of necessity, a loyal city. But at first the thing most essential was to reach Washington without delay, and make it secure. *Troops sent through Annapolis.*

When the first alarm about the safety of Washington was relieved, it became necessary to create an army. Recruits were gathered in all the States, under the president's proclamation, and were organized into regiments by the governors of the States. But all the materials of war had to be collected by the United States Government. Mr. Buchanan's secretary of war, himself a secessionist, had sent several hundred thousand muskets to Southern arsenals, and left the Northern arsenals almost bare. It was the same with cannon and ammunition. All these, therefore, had to be bought, or manufactured by the government, at very short *Preparations for war at the North.*

notice. It was necessary to have uniforms made for the soldiers, to organize a supply of horses and army-wagons, camp-equipage, medicines, and provisions, and to provide for the proper distribution of these to the troops in such way that there should be no waste or want. This all had to be begun at once, and to be completed as quickly as possible. President Lincoln also issued a proclamation, announcing that the Southern ports were blockaded, and forbidding vessels to enter or leave them.

The blockade.

On the 24th of May, troops were sent from Washington into Virginia, some being ordered to Alexandria, some to Arlington Heights near Washington. Colonel Ellsworth, the youthful commander of a part of these troops, seeing a Confederate flag flying from a hotel, entered the house to take it down, and was shot by the proprietor. He was well known in the Northern cities; and his death produced much indignation. Fighting soon began in both Eastern and Western Virginia. In Western Virginia there was a strong Union party; and the troops of the other party were finally driven out in a series of engagements in which General McClellan was the chief commander. In Eastern Virginia there was an engagement at Big Bethel, in which the Union troops were defeated; but there was no general engagement till July. Then Lieutenant-General Scott, the commander-in-chief, made an attempt to advance on Richmond; and his troops, under General McDowell, were defeated at Bull Run. This was on July 21; some thirty thousand troops being engaged on each side. The result of the battle had seemed very doubtful until three o'clock in the afternoon, when re-enforcements arrived for the Confederate troops;

Death of Col. Ellsworth.

The war in Virginia.

The first advance on Richmond.

and the result was a total rout of the Union forces, which retreated in great disorder to Washington.

Later in the year there was a smaller battle at Ball's Bluff, in which the Union troops were also unsuccessful. Thus the war opened badly in Eastern Virginia. On the other hand, the Confederates were successfully driven out of Northern Missouri by General Lyon; and some important expeditions were sent to different points on the Southern coast, such as Fort Hatteras in North Carolina, and Port Royal in South Carolina. This last was especially important, as the Confederates at once abandoned most of the posts they had seized along the South Atlantic coast, and never afterwards regained them. All this was accomplished in 1861. Towards the end of that year, Lieut.-Gen. Winfield Scott retired from the command of the armies of the United States, and was succeeded by Major-Gen. George B. McClellan.

During the first year of the war the navy of the United States had to be greatly enlarged. At the outset, there were but four ships available for service at home, with less than three hundred sailors; yet it was necessary to have a force large enough to blockade all the ports of the seceded States. The Confederates sent out privateers to prey upon American commerce; and these privateers were protected and refitted in foreign ports, especially those of England. That nation, with France, Spain, and Portugal, recognized the seceded States as having the rights of belligerents; thus putting the Confederacy, as a war power, on the same footing with the National Government. War with England was narrowly avoided, at the time when Messrs.

Mason and Slidell, Confederate commissioners, were captured by a United States vessel from an English mail-steamer, Nov. 8, 1861. This act, being found to be contrary to the law of nations, was promptly disowned by the American Government; and peaceful relations were restored. But the hopes of the secessionists were sustained throughout the war by the expectation of being recognized and assisted by foreign governments.

<small>Peninsular campaign.</small>

<small>Second advance on Richmond.</small>

At the beginning of the year 1862 the whole Union army amounted to more than five hundred thousand men, almost all of these being volunteers. General McClellan, in command of the Army of the Potomac, marched up the peninsula formed by the James and York Rivers, to attack Richmond, the capital of the Confederate Government; and he even crossed the Chickahominy River. When his advanced guard, under General Casey, was at Fair Oaks, within six miles of Richmond, it was attacked (May 31, 1862), and driven back, but was afterwards re-enforced, and drove the opposing army into Richmond. Some eighty thousand men were engaged in this battle. McClellan, after remaining two months in camp, decided it to be necessary to withdraw his force, and change his base of operations to the James River. This led to a series of attacks from the Confederate forces, called "the Seven-Days' Battles of the Peninsula;" the battle at Malvern Hill (July 1, 1862) being the severest, and resulting in the defeat of the Confederates. In these battles nearly a hundred thousand men were engaged on each side; each losing more than fifteen thousand. The army of General Banks was ordered from the Shenandoah Valley to cover the change of position on the part of McClellan.

INVASION OF MARYLAND.

There were battles at Cedar Mountain and Bull Run. General Lee led the Confederate army across the Potomac into Maryland, capturing Harper's Ferry and Frederick City. Whittier's fine poem, "Barbara Frietchie," describes an incident that is said to have taken place at the capture of this city. Finally McClellan encountered Lee at Antietam, Md. (Sept. 17, 1862), in

Lee's first invasion.

Antietam.

BARBARA FRIETCHIE.

one of the severest battles of the war. One hundred and fifty thousand men were engaged in it, including both armies. The Union loss in this battle and in that of South Mountain, which took place just before, was more than fourteen thousand; and that on the other side more than twelve thousand. The Union army was victorious; and, during the following night, General

The third advance on Richmond. Lee withdrew his troops across the Potomac. Great dissatisfaction was felt with General McClellan for permitting this retreat; and, as there had been similar dissatisfaction after Fair Oaks and Malvern, he was removed from command in November, and Gen. Ambrose E. Burnside was put in his place, at the head of the Army of the Potomac. Burnside crossed the Rappahannock, and took Fredericksburg, but was obliged to retreat again with heavy losses.

Monitor and Merrimack. Thus the second year of the war brought little progress towards the immediate aim of the contest, — the capture of the Confederate capital. But a naval contest in Virginia waters meanwhile attracted the attention of the whole nation, and, indeed, of the civilized world. The Union officers, early in the war, had abandoned the navy-yard at Norfolk, and destroyed most of the vessels; but some ships had escaped destruction, and among them the "Merrimack." The secessionists had covered this vessel with railroad iron and heavy timber, and had furnished her with a bow of steel. With this she attacked the Union squadron at Hampton Roads. The wooden frigates assailed her in vain. The balls struck and glanced upward, "having no more effect than peas from a pop-gun;" and at the end of the day the Union frigate "Cumberland" had gone down, her brave commander ordering one more broadside as she sank; the "Congress" was burned to the water's edge, and the "Minnesota" was aground. So matters stood, when, at nine in the evening, a little vessel of insignificant appearance, looking, as one eye-witness has said, "like a capsized whale-ship," and, as another said, "like a cheese-box on a raft," steamed into

Hampton Roads. It was the "Monitor," commanded by Capt. John L. Worden, and invented by Captain Ericsson, an engineer of Swedish birth. In the morning the "Merrimack" got under way again, and bore down upon the frigate that lay aground. The "Monitor," steaming alongside the "Merrimack," opened fire. The "ram" fired in return. For two hours the contest

The conflict.

"MONITOR" AND "MERRIMACK."

lasted, both ships using more powerful ordnance than had ever before been used in a naval encounter, and this at a distance of one hundred and fifty yards; yet the cannonade was useless. Neither produced the slightest effect on the other, until at last the "Monitor" sent a shell through a porthole of her antagonist, doing severe execution among the crew. After that the

"Merrimack" retreated, leaving the victory with the little "Monitor." The whole nation was relieved when the news of this victory came; for, if the "Merrimack" had been left free to enter New York harbor, it might have destroyed every wooden vessel in port. The general substitution of iron vessels for wooden, in the navies of the world, may be said to have followed from this contest.

<small>Important Federal successes.</small> While these things were going on, by land and water, in Virginia, there were very important events happening elsewhere in the war. An expedition under General Burnside captured Roanoke Island, and several important points in North Carolina. The Union troops took Fort Pulaski and the seaports of Eastern Florida. On the Western rivers two strongholds were taken, — Fort Henry on the Tennessee, and Fort Donelson on the Cumberland. The latter was besieged by General Grant; and, on the Confederate commander's asking what terms the Union forces would accept, the message was returned, "Unconditional Surrender;" which afterwards became the nickname of Gen. U. S. Grant.

After the capture of Fort Donelson, the Confederate troops abandoned Nashville, the capital of Tennessee, and were driven from a strongly fortified island in the Mississippi River, called "Island No. 10." A severe <small>Battle of Pittsburg Landing.</small> battle took place at Pittsburg Landing (April 6, 1862), between the Union forces under Grant, and the Confederate forces under Johnston and Beauregard. On the first day General Grant was driven from his position with severe loss; but on the second day, with the aid of re-enforcements under General Buell, the Union troops recaptured the camps from which they had been

CAPTURE OF NEW ORLEANS.

dislodged. More than a hundred thousand men were engaged in the battle of Pittsburg Landing; and there were about ten thousand killed and wounded on each side.

One of the most important warlike exploits of this year was the taking of New Orleans by a naval force under Commodore Farragut, aided by a land force under General Butler. The city was very strongly defended. Seventy-five miles below it there were two strong forts; and below these a chain was stretched across the river, with earthworks at each end. Between the forts and the chain there were five rafts filled with inflammable materials, — besides thirteen gunboats, an iron-clad floating battery, and an iron "ram." Commodore Farragut cannonaded the forts in vain, but saved his vessels from the burning rafts by seizing and extinguishing each as it floated down. At last he decided to attempt to run by the forts with his fleet. He accordingly got under way on April 24, 1862; and while the forts, the steamers, and the battery, all poured their fire upon the fleet, it steamed steadily up the river till the danger was passed. A single Union vessel, the "Varuna," sunk or disabled six steamers; and Farragut anchored off the quarantine station that evening. The next morning he reached the city, and took possession; and the forts and fleet in the river

Capture of New Orleans.

COMMODORE FARRAGUT.

were surrendered a few days after. On May 1 General Butler, with a land force, entered New Orleans, and proclaimed martial law. Farragut afterwards penetrated farther up the river; and, though Vicksburg held out some time longer, the control of the lower Mississippi was thenceforth secured to the government.

Emancipation.

But the most important occurrence of this year was

COMMODORE FARRAGUT PASSING THE FORTS BELOW NEW ORLEANS.

a political event, — the President's proclamation for the emancipation of the slaves. The war had not been originally waged for the abolition of slavery, but to preserve the Union; and when Union generals — Fremont, Phelps, and Hunter — had, at different times and places, undertaken to set slaves free, the President had revoked their action, or limited it to the

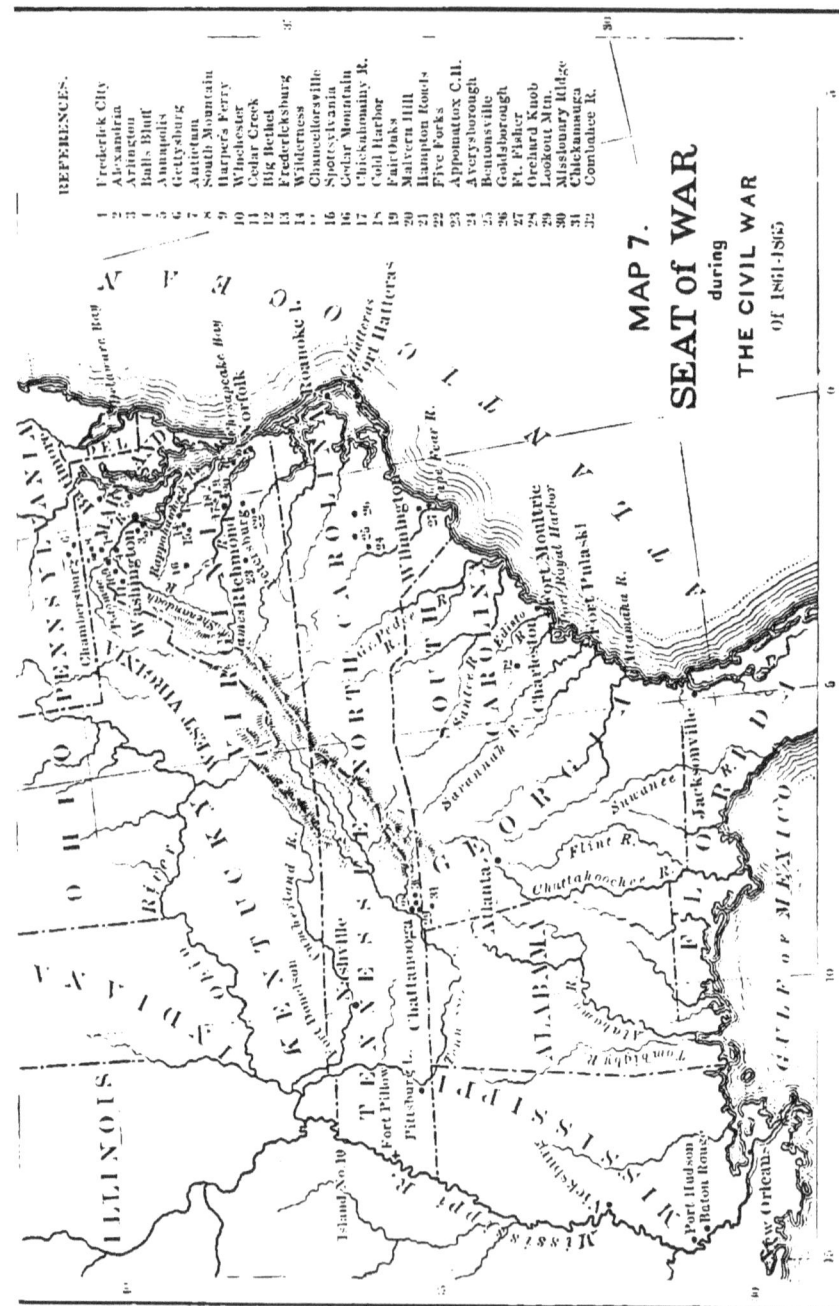

EMANCIPATION PROCLAMATION.   305

slaves actually employed against the government. It proved, at last, necessary to declare freedom to the slaves; and on Sept. 22, 1862, President Lincoln issued this proclamation: —

"That on the first day of January, in the year of our Lord one thousand eight hundred and sixty-three, all persons held as slaves within any State, or designated part of a State, the people whereof shall then be in rebellion against the United States, shall be then, thenceforth, and forever free; and the Executive Government of the United States, including the military and naval authority thereof, will recognize and maintain the freedom of such persons, and will do no act or acts to repress such persons, or any of them, in any effort they may make for their actual freedom."

In his message to Congress the President thus explained this act: —

"In giving freedom to the slave, we assure freedom to the free, honorable alike in what we give and what we preserve. We shall nobly save, or meanly lose, the last best hope of earth. . . . The way is plain, peaceful, glorious, just, — a way, which, if followed, the world will forever applaud, and God must forever bless."

Almost at the same time with this proclamation, the policy of raising colored troops began to be systematically adopted by the government. Already in May, 1862, Gen. David Hunter had organized in South Carolina, on his own responsibility, a regiment of blacks; and, though the government had disbanded the regiment, one company had been allowed to remain in service, and became the nucleus of the First South Carolina Volunteers, raised, with official authority, by Gen.

The raising of colored troops.

Rufus Saxton, in October. During the same summer the First Kansas Colored began to be enlisted by General Lane in Kansas. These were the first regiments composed of freed slaves. General Butler had, however, found some regiments of free colored troops partly organized for the Confederate service in New Orleans, and had taken them into the Union service.

The slaves set free.

On New Year's Day, 1863, President Lincoln issued a second proclamation, confirming his earlier one, and declaring the freedom of the slaves. Early in the year General Hooker succeeded General Burnside in command of the Army of the Potomac, but was defeated by General Lee at Chancellorsville, Va. In this battle fell General Jackson, called "Stonewall" Jackson, the most popular of the Confederate generals. A period of great reaction and discouragement followed. The cost of the war for the Union had become enormous; and large bounties had to be paid for soldiers, bringing into the service many "bounty-jumpers," as they were called, who enlisted merely for money, and soon deserted to enlist again. At one time more than two hundred a day were deserting from the Army of the Potomac. Soldiers were being drafted; but the draft was very unpopular. Under these circumstances General Lee resolved to invade the Northern States. He marched down the Shenandoah Valley, across the Potomac, and towards Chambersburg. Near Gettysburg his advance encountered the Union cavalry; and a general battle was brought on, without having been previously intended on either side. The Union forces were commanded by Gen. George G. Meade. The battle began July 1, and lasted three days; eighty thousand

The fourth advance on Richmond.

Lee's second invasion.

Gettysburg.

being engaged on each side, and the loss of each being more than twenty thousand. It ended in the defeat and retreat of Lee, and put an end forever to the thought of an invasion of the north.

The battle of Gettysburg may be regarded as the turning-point of the war. At the moment when the last charge of that battle was being repulsed, General

Surrender of Vicksburg.

SURRENDER OF VICKSBURG.

Grant was negotiating for the surrender of the stronghold of Vicksburg, which had, up to that time, rendered the Mississippi impassable for vessels. It was the most important fortified place in the south-west, being on a high bluff, thoroughly defended by batteries in all directions. It fell after a siege of forty-seven days, being surrendered on the Fourth of July. A cavalry raid by Col. B. R. Grierson occurred in connection with this siege. This officer, with about a thousand cavalry, swept through Mississippi, traversing in about a fortnight four hundred miles of territory, destroying bridges and military supplies. The Confederate General Morgan also made a daring raid through Kentucky into Indiana, with three thousand cavalry, but was defeated and captured at last.

Fall of Port Hudson.

Port Hudson, which had been besieged by General Banks for many weeks, was obliged to surrender soon after Vicksburg; and the Mississippi River was now open to the Union vessels once more. This was a great step forward. But, as time went on, it grew more and more difficult to raise soldiers for the war; and the draft was in many quarters bitterly opposed. In New York especially, a great riot took place, nominally occasioned by the draft, but aimed at the colored people and all who defended them. It began July 13, and lasted three days; the militia regiments of the city being absent for the defence of Pennsylvania, and the police force of the city being wholly unable to preserve order. Houses were burned, including an orphan asylum; and negroes were pursued and killed in the streets.

New York riot.

The campaign in East Tennessee.

Later in the year General Rosecrans, with a large Union force, met with a severe defeat near Chickamauga, Tennessee; and his army was besieged at Chattanooga, and was in danger of starvation. It was, however, relieved by General Grant in a masterly series of movements, including a three-days' battle, in which the Confederate army was dislodged from a series of strong positions upon the mountains which surrounded the town. "The opening movement of the battle was made with such regularity and precision, that the Confederate troops on the heights above took it for a mere review or drill." General Thomas captured Orchard Knob; General Hooker scaled the heights of Lookout Mountain, and fought a battle "above the clouds;" General Sherman attacked Missionary Ridge; and,

_{Lookout Mountain.}

BATTLE OF LOOKOUT MOUNTAIN.

finally, the whole army ascended the mountain side, under severe fire, and drove the opposing force from the intrenchments five hundred feet above. This was Nov. 25, 1863. The loss in these two battles was more than twenty thousand on each side. Their effect was to banish the Confederate forces from Tennessee.

During this time but little advance had been made

Operations against Charleston. in the "Department of the South;" though a successful attack on Charleston, S. C., had been made by Admiral Dupont with his "monitors," aided by General Hunter on land. There had been several expeditions up the Southern rivers, within the Confederate lines, but nothing on a large scale, until the arrival of General Gillmore, who planned a regular siege of Charleston, carried on chiefly from Folly and Morris Islands, with the aid of cannon of very long range. A severe attack and repulse took place at Fort Wagner (July 18, 1863), in which a regiment of colored troops was placed in front, and their brave young commander, Colonel Shaw, was killed. This important fort was taken in September; and the siege of Charleston became more close. On the whole, the prospects of the war for the Union were more favorable at the end of 1863. "Peace," said President Lincoln at that time, "does not appear so distant as it did. I hope it will come soon, and come to stay, and so come as to be worth keeping in all future time."

Some daring but fruitless movements. Early in the year 1864 some daring advances within the hostile lines took place on both sides, but without results. General Kilpatrick led his cavalry within three miles of Richmond, Va. General Seymour occupied Jacksonville, Fla., which had been twice before occupied and abandoned; and he was proceeding farther into the State, when he was checked at the severe battle of Olustee, Feb. 20. General Banks, in the South-west, conducted an expedition up the Red River, but was defeated and driven back; his gunboats being greatly endangered by the falling of the river, and being saved only by the skill of a volunteer officer,

Colonel Bailey, who built dams across the stream, and floated the vessels down. At the very time of the Red River Expedition, the Confederate general, Forrest, made a raid into Tennessee and Kentucky, captured Fort Pillow (April 12), and massacred three hundred colored soldiers who formed a part of its garrison.

But the event of greatest importance during this year was the appointment of General Grant to the command of all the armies (March 17), with the title of lieutenant-general. He soon planned two great movements, which were to proceed at the same time. One of these was to be directed against Richmond, Va., by the Army of the Potomac, which was commanded by General Meade, but under General Grant's immediate supervision. The other was under the exclusive charge of Gen. W. T. Sherman, who undertook to march an army across the interior of the States in rebellion, from the mountains to the sea.

Grand plan for 1864.

GENERAL GRANT.

When General Grant's movements in Virginia began, he wrote to President Lincoln, "I propose to fight it out on this line, if it takes all summer;" and though he was obliged to change his position more than once, he still persevered. In May and June he sustained terrible losses in the battles of the Wilderness, of Spottsylvania, and of Cold Harbor, losing seventy

Grant's advance on Richmond.

thousand men in all. He laid siege unsuccessfully to Richmond, and, in spite of the aid given in a brilliant raid by General Sheridan, the whole campaign of Grant in 1864 was discouraging. Meanwhile the Confederate general, Early, with twenty thousand men, made a raid into Pennsylvania in July, and burned the town of Chambersburg; and an incursion was also made into the town of St. Albans, Vt., by some Confederates from Canada, who took the inhabitants by surprise, robbed the banks, and retreated. General Early was pursued by General Sheridan, and defeated at Cedar Creek on Oct. 19. The forces of Sheridan had been attacked by Early during the temporary absence of their commander, and had been driven four miles with heavy loss. Sheridan had news of the fight when at Winchester, twenty miles away, and rode that distance at a furious speed. Meeting his retreating troops, he rallied them, and turned the defeat into victory, capturing fifty pieces of artillery, and many prisoners. This event has been made the subject of a ballad, called "Sheridan's Ride," by Buchanan Read.

Early's raid.

Raid on St. Albans, Vt.

Sheridan's ride.

Kearsarge and Alabama. At sea, the Confederate privateers had for some time been very destructive to American merchant-vessels. The "Shenandoah" had destroyed thirty-four whale-ships in the arctic seas; and the "Alabama" had taken sixty-five vessels. American ships had almost been driven from the ocean, or had been transferred to British ownership for protection. The Confederate privateers had escaped meeting United States men-of-war, until the "Alabama" was attacked by the "Kearsarge," Captain Winslow, off the coast of Cherbourg, France, June 19, 1864. During the action, the two vessels were steaming at the rate of seven miles an hour, and swinging round one another in circles, so as to bring their broadsides to bear. After they had described seven of these circles, and had come within a quarter of a mile of one another, the "Alabama"

SHERIDAN'S RIDE.

was sunk; Captain Semmes and his men being picked up by an English yacht.

Another brilliant naval action during this year was that won in Mobile Bay by Admiral Farragut, Aug. 5. The bay was a great resort for blockade-runners: it was defended by two forts, by torpedoes set in the narrow channel, and by an iron-plated ram of great power,

Capture of Mobile.

— the "Tennessee." Farragut had to meet these obstacles with wooden ships, aided by a few "monitors," one of which was soon struck by a torpedo, and went down with her crew. Farragut had provided false bows of iron with which his wooden ships might charge the ram; and this dangerous vessel was at length disabled, and surrendered with the forts.

DESTRUCTION OF THE "ALBEMARLE."

Destruction of the Albemarle. Still another encounter, and probably the most daring naval action of the war, was that in which a powerful ram, the "Albemarle," was destroyed at night (Oct. 27, 1864) by a torpedo from a steam-launch commanded by Lieutenant Cushing, who had volunteered for this dangerous duty. His boat was itself sunk by the shock of the torpedo; and only the com-

SHERMAN'S MARCH TO THE SEA.

mander and one of his crew were saved,—by swimming,—under close fire from the ram.

But the main event of this year was the campaign of General Sherman in Tennessee, and his march across the State of Georgia to Savannah. The object was to cut off the supplies of the Confederates, and break up their railroad communications. The campaign began early in May, 1864. Sherman had to conduct his army through a series of mountain regions and passes bristling with fortifications, which had to be carried with great loss. He took the important town of Atlanta, Ga., and then began his famous "March to the Sea." His course lay through a fertile region, where the army of sixty thousand men advanced in two columns, under Generals Howard and Slocum, subsisting largely on what could be found in the country passed through. After a march of three hundred miles, they reached the sea, and established communication with the forces at Hilton Head under General Foster, and with the fleet under Admiral Dahlgren. The Confederate forces retreated from Savannah, and the Union Army entered it; and General Sherman wrote to President Lincoln, "I beg to present to you as a Christmas gift the city of Savannah, with one hundred and fifty heavy guns, and plenty of ammunition, and also twenty-five thousand bales of cotton." He had lost in the march only sixty-three killed, and two hundred and forty-five wounded.

Sherman's march to the sea.

In January, 1865, General Sherman resumed his "Great March," from Savannah northward. He himself wrote, "Christmas found us at Savannah. Waiting there only long enough to fill our wagons, we began another march, which for peril, labor, and results, will

Sherman's great march northward

compare with any ever made by an organized army. The floods of the Savannah, the swamps of the Combahee and the Edisto, the high hills and rocks of the Santee, the flat quagmires of the Pedee and Cape Fear Rivers, were all passed in midwinter, with its floods and rain, in the face of an accumulating enemy; and, after the battles of Averysborough and Bentonsville, we once more came out of the wilderness to meet our friends at Goldsborough."

He met these " friends " — the troops under General Schofield — on the 23d of March. Sherman had proved by this exploit that the Confederacy had now become, as he said, "an empty shell;" the men having been necessarily withdrawn from the interior of the country to defend its borders. His triumphant success helped to give the finishing stroke to the war.

Fall of Charleston

This march aided, also, in the capture of Charleston, which had now been besieged for more than five hundred days. It was finally abandoned (Feb. 17) by the Confederate forces; fires being first set in different parts of the city. Some other successes took place this year, especially the capture by General Terry of Fort Fisher, which protected Wilmington, N.C. But these were only preliminary to the final movement of General Grant against Richmond.

Final movement of Grant's army.

On March 29, 1865, the movement of Grant's army began. He had become satisfied, both by his own observation and by the success of Sherman's attempt, that the Confederate armies were nearly exhausted, and that a resolute effort would bring the war to a close. Placing Sheridan in command of all the cavalry of the army, he sent out this daring officer with this order:

"In the morning push round the enemy, and get to his rear." Accordingly, on April 1, 1865, Sheridan, aided by Warren and Humphreys, fought the decisive battle of Five Forks, turning the flank of Lee's army and taking five thousand prisoners. Two days after, Petersburg and Richmond were occupied by the Union forces.

When General Lee found that he could no longer hold his position at Petersburg, he telegraphed to Jefferson Davis at Richmond, "My lines are broken in three places. Richmond must be evacuated this evening." The despatch reached Mr. Davis on Sunday, in church, and was handed to him amid the silence of the congregation. He hastily left the church, and the rumor was instantly spread that the city was to be abandoned. In a few hours wagons were seen at the department offices, carrying boxes away; and soon the streets were full of men, hurrying from the city, and carrying with them their valuables in all manner of conveyances. The sum of a hundred dollars in gold was offered for a wagon. Vast stores of provisions were sent away to the retreating army; and all that was left was freely distributed among the people, black and white. The city council gave orders to destroy all the liquor in the city to prevent intoxication; but much of it was seized by the soldiers, and made the confusion worse. Four large tobacco-houses were set on fire by the military authorities; the shipping was fired or blown up; and the bridges were also in flames. A scene of the wildest excitement raged that night in the city. On the next day (April 3) Richmond was occupied by colored troops of the Union army, under General Weitzel; and the Confederacy had no longer a capital.

Evacuation of Richmond.

Surrender of Lee.

Lee made courageous efforts to retreat with his army; but he was closely followed up by Sheridan, and the pressure of hunger and exhaustion upon his troops was so severe that, as an eye-witness said, "Hundreds dropped from exhaustion, and thousands let fall their muskets from inability to carry them farther." On the 9th of April, 1865, at Appomattox Court-House, Lee surrendered his army to Grant, on terms honorable to both parties. His surrender was soon followed by that of the other Confederate generals.

Capture of Jefferson Davis.

Jefferson Davis was captured in Georgia, disguised in woman's clothing; and the Great Rebellion, or civil war, was at an end.

Summary of the results of the war.

It had lasted four years; had cost during the last year more than three million dollars a day; and left the United States with a debt of more than two billion seven hundred million dollars ($2,749,491,745). It had also cost more than half a million lives, including both sides. But it had abolished slavery, a most important result, and one that few men could have anticipated. And it had established the principle that the United States must be regarded as a nation one and indivisible, and not as a mere alliance of independent States.

It had also proved, what some had doubted, that the strength, courage, and patriotism of the American people were still as great as in the period of the Revolution. There were few families, North or South, which did not suffer some bereavement during the long contest. On both sides the self-devotion of the women at home equalled that of the soldiers in the field; and in the Northern States, especially, the multitudes of women who worked for the "Sanitary Commission" rendered very valuable services to their country.

SINCERITY OF THE SOUTH.

The sacrifices made during the civil war were as great as those made in the Revolutionary War; while the armies and the battles were on a far larger scale. The Confederate army was, from the beginning, outnumbered by its opponents; but it had greatly the advantage of position, since it is far easier to defend any region than to conquer it. Each side learned to respect the courage and resources of the other, and to feel that, if Americans were once reunited, no foreign power could ever endanger their liberties. It was not, indeed, possible that those who had fought for the flag of their country could pay equal honor to those who tried to strike it down. But they could remember that most of these mistaken men had been taught from childhood that their first allegiance was due to their own State, not to the United States; so that they felt themselves loyal, in their own way, even when fighting against their nation. This delusion ended, let us hope, with the war; but it is necessary to remember it in order to do justice to those who fought for the Confederate side. So far as the object of the secessionists was to retain possession of their slaves, no excuse is to be made for them, except that the Union Government did not itself order the emancipation of the slaves until compelled to it by military necessity. For the cruelties inflicted by the Confederates on Union prisoners during the war no excuse at all is to be made, nor for deeds like the massacre of colored troops at Fort Pillow. But these were, after all, the acts of a few; and the general feeling in both armies was, no doubt, that of sincere and manly opponents.

Summary of the results of the war.

No one has ever expressed the feelings of thoughtful

and conscientious men at the close of the war, so simply and impressively as did President Lincoln in his second Inaugural Address, just before the fall of Richmond. The following is a portion of this address:—

Lincoln's second inaugural address.

"Neither party expected for the war the magnitude or the duration which it has already attained. Neither anticipated that the cause of the conflict might cease with, or even before, the conflict itself should cease. Each looked for an easier triumph, and a result less fundamental and astounding.

"Both read the same Bible, and pray to the same God; and each invokes his aid against the other. It may seem strange that any men should dare to ask a just God's assistance in wringing their bread from the sweat of other men's faces; but let us judge not, that we be not judged. The prayers of both could not be answered. That of neither has been answered fully. The Almighty has his own purposes. 'Woe unto the world because of offences, for it must needs be that offences come; but woe to that man by whom the offence cometh.' If we shall suppose that American slavery is one of these offences, which, in the providence of God, must needs come, but which, having continued through his appointed time, he now wills to remove, and that he gives to both North and South this terrible war as the woe due to those by whom the offence came, shall we discern therein any departure from those divine attributes which the believers in a living God always ascribe to him? Fondly do we hope, fervently do we pray, that this mighty scourge of war may soon pass away. Yet if God wills that it continue until all the wealth piled by the bondman's two

EXTRACT FROM MR. LINCOLN'S ADDRESS.

hundred and fifty years of unrequited toil shall be sunk, and until every drop of blood drawn with the lash shall be paid with another drawn with the sword; as was said three thousand years ago, so still it must be said, 'The judgments of the Lord are true and righteous altogether.'

"With malice towards none, with charity for all, with firmness in the right, as God gives us to see the right, let us strive on to finish the work we are in, to bind up the nation's wounds, to care for him who shall have borne the battle, and for his widow and his orphans, to do all which may achieve and cherish a just and a lasting peace among ourselves and with all nations."

CHAPTER XXXII.

AFTER THE CIVIL WAR. — GRANT.

<small>Assassination of President Lincoln.</small>

THERE was joy, with thanksgiving, over the greater part of the nation, when the news of Lee's surrender came over the telegraphic wires, and it was known that the weary war had ended. Five days after (April 14, 1865), the same wires sent far and wide another message, turning joy into mourning. It was the news that President Lincoln had been shot while sitting in the theatre at Washington, by an assassin, Wilkes Booth. A similar attempt was made upon the life of Mr. Seward, the secretary of state; and there was evidence of a plot to remove all the leading members of the government. It does not appear that the plot extended far, or that any of the Confederate leaders were responsible for it. But no one knew, at the time, how far it might reach; and so the excitement was very great, apart from the lamentation.

<small>Confidence in Lincoln.</small>

President Lincoln had greatly endeared himself to the nation during his difficult term of office. No president since Washington had been put to so severe a test; and no president, unless it were Washington, had so thoroughly won the confidence of the people. His simplicity, honesty, and fidelity, his fearless purpose, sympathetic heart, and quaint humor, had never failed in the darkest hours of the war; and he had been elected by an overwhelming vote to a second term of office. Every one felt that great and difficult problems were before the nation now that peace had come; and everybody looked to the future with more confidence, from having Abraham Lincoln as Chief Magistrate. When the news of his death came, the mourning extended through all parties, and to all regions of the country, even to the States lately in insurrection. The colored people, especially, felt that they had lost more than a father. And when the funeral procession of the president passed slowly by railway, with frequent pauses, from Washington to his former home in Springfield, Ill., it found every railway station filled with mourners and draped with signs of grief. *Mourning for Lincoln.*

But it showed the strength of republican government, that even this sudden death of the head of the nation produced no confusion, and no new rebellion. Vice-president Andrew Johnson of Tennessee at once took the place of Mr. Lincoln; and the wheels of government went on. The new president found difficult duties awaiting him. To be sure, some things that had seemed likely to be hard proved easy. It had been predicted that the volunteer army of a million men, drawn from the people, would not easily be merged into the people again, but would retain warlike habits, and be dangerous to the peace of the country. This fear proved groundless: soldiers and officers were alike glad to lay down their arms, and to return to the peaceful pursuits whence they came. But there was a vast debt to be provided for; and loans and taxes had to be planned for this purpose. Then all the region lately *Strength of our government. The disbanding of the army. The work now to be done* in rebellion had to be reorganized into a peaceful community; and opinions varied greatly as to the best way of doing this. Some thought that the seceding States had a right to come back whenever they would, with their former power, and without any new conditions. Others thought that, by seceding, they had forfeited all rights as States, and had again become Territories, with which the United States Government might do as it would. But neither of these views was fully adopted.

Opinions about the seceded States.

To begin with, the president issued a proclamation granting amnesty, or pardon, to most of those engaged in the Rebellion. Then Congress established the Freedmen's Bureau, an organization to provide for the loyal and suffering classes, black or white, of the Southern States. Slavery was then formally abolished by an amendment to the United States Constitution; and another amendment was passed looking toward the enfranchisement of the colored people. "Reconstruction acts" were passed, restoring the seceded States to their places in the Union, on condition that they should annul their acts of secession, declare void all debts incurred in fighting for the Rebellion, and adopt the constitutional amendment abolishing slavery. The new president was very much opposed to making any of these conditions, as he held that the seceded States had a right to come back at any time, unrestrained. He therefore vetoed several of these measures; and, though they were passed over his veto, it led to an increasing hostility between him and Congress. Finally, the House of Representatives accused or "impeached" him, demanding his removal from office. For the first

Acts of the president and of Congress.

Impeachment of Johnson.

JOHNSON'S ADMINISTRATION.

time in the history of the government, a president of the United States was put on trial before the Senate, sitting as a court of impeachment, with the chief justice of the Supreme Court presiding. In such a trial, a vote of two-thirds of the Senate is needed for conviction; and, as one vote was wanting to this number, Mr. Johnson was not removed. He was not, however, re-elected as president.

During his and his predecessor's terms there had happened events more important than any since the United States had existed. A great civil war had been fought and ended; and slavery had been abolished, first by presidential proclamation, and then by constitutional amendment, — an event which the most far-sighted philanthropist had scarcely expected to live to see. For other events, three States had been added to the Union. One of these, West Virginia, had been separated from the "Old Dominion," and admitted as a separate State, in 1863; this being done by request of the inhabitants, who were loyal throughout the war. The other two States were Nevada (1864), formed out of territory ceded by Mexico, and named from the Sierra Nevada, or Snowy Mountains; and Nebraska (1867), formed out of the Louisiana Purchase, and named from an Indian word meaning "Shallow River." The great region called Alaska had been also purchased from the Russian Government, in 1867, for more than seven million dollars ($7,200,000); and, though not likely to be largely inhabited by any but an Esquimau population, it was expected to be of great value for its furs. Its area was about half a million square miles (577,390), and brought the whole area of the

The great civil war and its result.

West Virginia, Nebraska, and Nevada admitted.

Purchase of Alaska.

nation to about three and a half million square miles (3,559,091), instead of the original eight hundred thousand (820,680). Instead of the original thirteen States, with three millions of people, there were now thirty-seven States and twelve Territories, with a population (in 1870) of more than thirty-eight millions (38,558,371).

Census of 1870.

The next president of the United States was Ulysses S. Grant of Illinois, whose great services during the civil war had won for him the gratitude of the nation. He was first inaugurated in 1869, and entered on a second term in 1873; but the events of his administration are yet too recent to be fully or fairly described. Many important things, however, took place during his term of office. All the seceded States became finally restored to the Union. The successive steps by which a great increase of territory was brought about will be found marked on the map which is prefixed to this volume. The enormous debt incurred during the war was very greatly diminished; more than one-fifth of it (six hundred million dollars) having been paid. An amendment to the Constitution (the Fifteenth), providing that the right of suffrage shall not be withheld from any citizen of the United States, "on account of race, color, or previous condition of servitude," was declared adopted March 30, 1870, having been proposed by Congress, and ratified by three-fourths of the States. A treaty was made with Great Britain (May 8, 1871), providing for an international tribunal to be held at Geneva, which should decide all claims of the United States for damages done by those Confederate privateers which had been built or refitted in English ports. This tribunal awarded fifteen and a

The eighteenth president.

The great debt reduced.

The fifteenth amendment

Geneva tribunal.

half million dollars, in gold, as the amount to be paid by Great Britain; and it was accordingly paid in 1873. This was a result very encouraging to those who hope that wars will gradually cease, and the disputes of nations, like those of individuals, be left to the courts to settle. Never before in the history of the world was there so important an example of peaceful arbitration.

Not long after the great civil war ended, the leading statesmen of the war passed away. President Lincoln himself; William H. Seward, his Secretary of State; Edwin M. Stanton, Secretary of War; Salmon P. Chase, Secretary of the Treasury, and afterwards Chief Justice of the Supreme Court; and Charles Sumner, the leader of the United States Senate, — all died. The questions upon which the war turned were found to have been settled; and new issues arose, upon some of which the political parties of the future will be based. There are various questions which are important, or are claimed as important, — currency reform, civil service reform, revenue reform, woman suffrage, the rights of labor, and matters pertaining to temperance, education, and religion. It is impossible to foresee what shape these questions may take in the future, which of them will prove most prominent, or which will lead to lasting reforms. *Death of eminent statesmen.* *New questions.*

CHARLES SUMNER.

Yet some things we may safely assume. We may take for granted that wealth will go on increasing; and that the immense activity and energy that have marked the American people will still continue. Much as has been accomplished in the way of material progress, more remains to be done. The Pacific Railway is now opened, and the Atlantic Cable successfully laid. These seemed, in their day, to be wonderful steps in communication among men, but it is probable that greater wonders are still in store for us. The greatest triumphs achieved in the United States have thus far been in the direction of mechanical ingenuity; and American literature, science, and art have not yet won the applause of the world quite so thoroughly as have American sewing-machines and agricultural implements. Yet the poetry of Bryant, Whittier, and Longfellow; the prose of Irving, Hawthorne, and Emerson; the scientific discoveries of Franklin, Morse, and Rumford; the paintings of Copley, Allston, and Page; the sculptures of Powers, Story, and Harriet Hosmer, — have obtained great and perhaps permanent reputation. The spread of popular instruction in America is very wide; higher education is constantly on the increase; and there is no reason why the United States should not become more and more the chosen home of literature, science, and art, as well as of mechanical ingenuity and business skill.

And we can safely assume something more than this. Habits and opinions alter with every generation; but the great principles of right and wrong do not change. Those who founded the American colonies left to their descendants many examples of noble lives and unselfish purposes; and we may be very sure that those who are

DUTY OF THE AMERICAN PEOPLE.

to carry on the institutions thus founded cannot prosper without something of the same high motive and religious self-devotion. The first great mission of the nation was that of proving to the world that republican government on a large scale was practicable. In this attempt success has been attained, in spite of the great difficulty resulting from the presence of slavery, and the annual arrival of many thousand immigrants, wholly untrained in republican institutions. The civil war has proved that the people of the United States, when at peace among themselves, are strong enough for self-protection against any foreign power. The thing now essential to Americans is to guard against internal as well as external dangers, to purify their own government, educate their own community, give to the world an example of pure lives and noble purposes; and so conduct the affairs of the Republic, that, as President Lincoln said in his Gettysburg Address, "Government of the people, by the people, and for the people, shall not perish from the earth."

Proof that our form of government is a success.

CHAPTER XXXIII.

HAYES. — GARFIELD. — ARTHUR.

Our Centennial celebration

GENERAL GRANT served two terms as President. In the last year of his second term (1876) there took place the centennial celebration of the independence of the United States. All over the land there were meetings and festivals, and a great International Exhibition was

THE CENTENNIAL EXHIBITION.

held at Philadelphia in honor of the event. The leading nations of the world sent specimens of their works in science and art, to be publicly inspected and compared; and prizes were given in all departments by skilled commissioners from various lands. The exhibition remained open for many weeks, and was attended by vast numbers of people. The whole effect was to give a great impulse to American industry. The exhibition showed that, while the United States surpassed all nations in inventive skill, the older nations still took the lead in art education, and could teach us a great deal in that way.

During this year (1876) Colorado was admitted as a State, making thirty-eight States with eleven Territories. *Colorado admitted.*

The next presidential election took place that same year, and led to much excitement, from the peculiar circumstances of the case. The Republicans nominated Rutherford B. Hayes of Ohio for president, and William A. Wheeler of New York for vice-president; while the Democrats nominated Samuel J. Tilden of New York and Thomas A. Hendricks of Indiana. *The presidential candidates.*

. RUTHERFORD B. HAYES.

There was also a third party, called the "Greenback" party, composed of those who desired to abolish bank-notes, and to have for currency only the paper money issued by the General Government and popularly called "greenbacks." This party nominated for president Peter Cooper of New York, but no electoral votes were thrown for him. The peculiar excitement about the election came from the fact that the votes of the States were very closely divided between the two leading candidates, and the decision had to turn upon the votes of two *The excitement about the election.*

doubtful States. It was generally admitted that the Democrats had legally chosen one hundred and eighty-four electors, and the Republicans one hundred and seventy-three; but the four votes of Florida and the eight of Louisiana were in doubt. If all of these were to be counted for Mr. Hayes he would have a majority of one. There could hardly be a closer vote. Now, the "returning boards" of these two States declared that both States had chosen Republican electors. These boards were bodies of men appointed after the war by the laws of these States; and they were authorized not merely to count the votes actually cast, but to throw out the votes of these neighborhoods where there had been violence or intimidation. This put a great deal of power, and a rather dangerous power, into the hands of these boards. The Republicans believed that this power had been justly exercised, but the Democrats took a very different view. The Democrats said that the majority of votes actually cast was on their side in each of these States, and that the returning boards had unjustly thrown out a great many Democratic votes which should rightfully have been counted. So they argued that Congress should refuse to treat the Republican electors as having been legally chosen by Louisiana or by Florida. But the Republicans claimed, on the other hand, that the fraud and violence of the Democrats in some parts of these States had been so great as to justify the action of the returning boards; and that at any rate these boards were the only legal bodies through which the voice of these States could come, and that Congress had no right to revise or reject their reports.

Who should decide a question so difficult? Unluckily,

The returning boards.

Different views about the action of these boards.

it turned out that the makers of the Constitution had not provided for any such state of things. The Constitution of the United States only provides that "the president of the senate shall, in the presence of the senate and house of representatives, open all the certificates, and the votes shall then be counted." But, supposing that there is doubt about the legality of the vote from any State, the Constitution does not say who shall settle that doubt. In the session of 1876-7 the senate was Republican, and its president was Republican, while the house of representatives was Democratic. It was very clear that the two bodies were not likely to agree about the votes of Florida and Louisiana; and who was to decide the matter? There was great excitement on the subject; and many angry things were said, and many people feared that the nation was on the verge of another civil war. But wiser counsels prevailed, and the moderate men of both parties in Congress hit upon a plan by which the decision was finally made. Both houses of Congress passed an act establishing an "Electoral Commission," to which all doubtful votes should be referred. *The difficult question before Congress.*

The Electoral Commission.

This body consisted of five senators, five representatives, and five justices of the Supreme Court; and it met and decided, by a vote of eight to seven, that the votes of Florida and Louisiana must be counted just as the returning boards had reported them, because these boards had been legally appointed by those States, and the other States could not revise or reject their returns. This added twelve electoral votes to the Republican side, so that Hayes and Wheeler had one hundred and eighty-five, and Tilden and Hendricks had but one hundred and eighty-four. Hayes and Wheeler were therefore declared *Their decision.*

to be elected, and were inaugurated March 5, 1877; but the circumstances of their election left a sore feeling which wore away very slowly, and indeed lasted during the whole of President Hayes's administration. If the "Electoral Commission" had been unanimous in its decision, there would have been much less of this feeling; but this close vote of eight to seven did not satisfy everybody, especially as all the eight were Republicans and all the seven were Democrats. It was, however, generally admitted that the matter was settled, and that Mr. Hayes was legally the President; but there was left a bitterness, very unlike the feeling of good nature which usually exists in the United States after an election. This state of things also showed the importance of some clearer and more definite law as to counting electoral votes in Presidential elections. Usually, in a republican government, a minority is very willing to submit to a majority; but there is always dissatisfaction unless it is known that the majority of votes has been fairly obtained. When a vote is very evenly divided, and the defeated party can point to anything that even looks like unfairness, men usually find it quite hard to keep their tempers.

Their decision not unanimous.

Importance of a new law.

The policy of the new president.

Under these circumstances the administration of Mr. Hayes began with an unusual amount of distrust and ill-feeling. It was fortunate, therefore, that the new president was a man of unusually mild and conciliatory disposition, and seemed very desirous to do justice to all. He had announced, when first nominated, that he should not be a candidate for re-election; and he began by making up his cabinet partly from both parties, a very uncommon thing. He showed a similar spirit in his early appointments to office. This gave great offence to some of his warmest supporters, but was approved by the nation as a whole. His next step was to withdraw all United States troops from the State-houses of any States formerly in rebellion, and to prohibit the interference of United States troops with the elections in those States. General Grant had begun this policy in Mississippi; but President Hayes completed it, even in South Carolina, where there had been the greatest complaints, and where many people still believed that the nation ought to interfere. This course was very much criticised at the time, but the President was firm in it; for, as he reasoned, these States were not now subject to the laws of war; they had been readmitted as States, and could not be treated as conquered territory. They must be controlled by the State governments and courts, except on matters expressly reserved to the national government; and, if any part of the people was wronged, time and the courts must set the matter right.

The result has proved that this course was wise, on the whole. Those States have steadily grown more peaceful since that time; and, where injustice has been shown toward the colored people, many of them have taken the remedy into their own hands, and have removed into some other State in hopes of better treatment. Many of them went to Kansas especially, where they were welcomed as settlers. But time has gradually diminished the sore feeling between the two races in the Southern States; and these States were never before, on the whole, prosperous and orderly as now. In the largest of them, — Virginia, — there has lately been a change of the old parties; and the white citizens have shown themselves quite willing that their former slaves should vote. *Better times at the south*

At a late election in Virginia the successful party, called the "Readjuster" party, was elected largely by the votes of the colored people.

<small>Census of 1880.</small> This prosperity has been shared by the whole nation. The census of 1880 showed an enormous increase of population in the United States, and there was no State or Territory which did not share this increase in a greater or less degree. Between 1870 and 1880 the

GOING WEST.

whole population increased from about thirty-eight and a a half millions (38,558,371) to more than fifty millions (50,155,783), this being a gain of more than a million a year. This estimate includes all persons residing within the limits of the United States, except the Indians within the Indian Territory, or supported elsewhere by the general government, and the inhabitants of Alaska. These are omitted because they are not regarded as being legally "citizens" of the United States.

Great as this increase has been, it is probable that the results of the next census in 1890 will be yet more surprising. The facts as to immigration alone are enough to show that the population of the United States is now increasing faster than ever before. During the five years preceding 1880, the number of foreign immigrants into this country never reached half a million a year. In

Our rapid increase in population

EMIGRANTS LANDING AT CASTLE GARDEN.

1880 it rose to 593,703; and in 1881, to 720,045. These immigrants now come more largely from Germany than from anywhere else. In 1881 there were 249,572 from Germany, 95,188 from Canada, 91,810 from Scandinavia (Norway, Sweden, and Denmark), 76,547 from England, and 70,909 from Ireland. These immigrants now go most largely to the States west of the Mississippi; some to Kansas and Colorado, there to engage in mining or

The immigrants now go west of the Mississippi

cattle-raising; some to Texas, where there is an immense extent of fertile country, under a mild climate ; and some to the new States of the North-west, where the wheat crop is found to be very abundant in spite of cold weather. Railways are being rapidly extended in all these directions, and there are already several of these great lines across the continent, instead of one, as at first.

The public debt.
This great increase of population has been only one evidence of the general prosperity of the nation. Another evidence of this has been the rapid payment of the public debt, which has gone on pretty steadily since the civil war closed. On July 1, 1865, this debt (after deducting cash in the treasury) was nearly three billion dollars ($2,756,431,571); whereas, on March 1, 1882, it was about one billion and three-quarters ($1,742,729,-369.10), more than a billion dollars having been paid. On Aug. 1, 1884, the total debt remaining (after deducting cash in the treasury) was $1,446,056,946.97, or less than a billion and a half, more than half of this great debt having been paid. Not only is the total amount of debt much diminished, but the rate of interest now paid on the remainder is very much lower than it was. The nation is now receiving, in taxes and duties, much more than is needed for the annual expenses of the government; and before long, at the present rate of progress, it will have paid all its debt, and be able to reduce its taxes.

Resumption of specie payments.
Another great advantage is that "specie-payments" have been restored. During the war the value of our national paper currency depreciated so much that a dollar in gold was worth in July, 1864, two dollars and eighty-

five cents in bank-notes. For nearly eighteen years neither the banks, nor the government, nor any private person would give a dollar in gold for a paper dollar; and the "promise to pay," upon the paper dollar seemed to mean very little. But the difference grew gradually less and less: and finally, on the 1st of January, 1879, specie payments were resumed; and ever since that time any one who has a dollar in paper can obtain for it a gold or silver dollar at any time without any difficulty.

Another evidence of prosperity is to be found in the increased industry of the nation. In 1878 this country imported one-third less goods from abroad than in 1873, — and this was partly because the people had learned to produce the same things themselves. Formerly almost every watch used in America was made in Europe; now the American watches rival European watches in the markets on the other side of the ocean. Formerly we imported a great deal of certain products of industry, such as medicines, perfumery, combs, soap, writing-paper, glassware, musical instruments, carriages, and furniture; now we supply ourselves almost wholly with these things, and send many of them abroad. Formerly the greater part of our cutlery and tools came from Sheffield in England; now American knives and tools are sold in Sheffield at a price lower than those made there. Between 1873 and 1878 our importation of foreign cottons and woollens fell off one-half; that of manufactured steel fell to one-third of what it had been; that of railroad iron to one-fifth of what it had been; that of carpets to one-tenth of what it had been; and all this time the exportation of provisions, especially of beef and grain, went on growing greater and greater. Before the aboli-

Increased prosperity of the nation.

Decline in our shipping interests.

tion of slavery it was supposed that without slave labor there could be no cotton crop; but more cotton is now raised and exported by the aid of free labor than was ever the case under slavery.

All branches of industry have gradually flourished more and more, except that of ship-building and ship-owning: the American nation has never to this day regained the prosperity that it once had in these ways. This came partly from the war, when foreign commerce under American flags almost stopped; and partly from the change from wooden to iron vessels. America has great advantages for building wooden vessels, but European nations, especially England, have great advantages for building iron vessels; so that all the great steamers which now cross the Atlantic are built and owned in Europe. It is hoped that at some time and in some way our old commercial prosperity will be restored. Until this is done it cannot be claimed that the welfare of the nation in business matters is in all respects complete.

The presidential candidates

JAMES A. GARFIELD.

In the national election of 1880 the Republicans nominated James A. Garfield of Ohio for president, and Chester A. Arthur of New York for vice-president. The Democrats nominated Winfield S. Hancock of New York for president, and William H. English of Indiana for vice-president; and the "Greenback" party and several smaller parties also made nominations. The Republican candidate was elected by a decided majority of electoral votes, so that there was none of the bitter feeling which had been left by the previous election. President Garfield was inaug- *The twentieth* urated March 4, 1881, and there was a general feeling of *president.* hopefulness and prosperity, when the nation was startled by a great shock. On July 2, 1881, while waiting for a train in the railway-station at Washington, President Garfield was shot and mortally wounded by an unknown stranger named Charles J. Guiteau. The President was at once taken to the White House, where he lingered between life and death for many weeks, amid the anxiety of the whole people.

During all this period the courage and patience *The anxi-* shown by the sufferer, and also by his heroic wife, *ety of the people.* were so great as to command peculiar respect and admiration. Day by day the telegraphic reports sent out by the physicians were read with the deepest interest, not only throughout the United States, but all over Europe. The state of the President's pulse, of his digestion, the temperature of his body, the condition of his mind, — all these things were reported by telegraph to anxious multitudes day by day. After eleven weeks of suffering the President died (Sept. 19, 1881) at Elberon, New Jersey, whither he had been removed; and then the mourning was universal. The story of his life was *Respect* told again and again, — how he had risen from the posi- *paid to his memory.* tion of a poor boy, through long and faithful service in the camp and in Congress, to the presidency of the nation. He seemed at the time of his death to be as well known and as much honored in Europe as in America; and in England especially his death created a feeling that showed itself through all classes of society. Five hundred different British societies and corporations passed resolutions in his honor; the English court went into mourning; and Queen Victoria, after repeated messages of sympathy to Mrs. Garfield, sent a wreath of honor to be placed upon his coffin.

The assassin of the president. His death was not the result of any conspiracy, nor did it proceed, like Lincoln's, from any political hostility; it was the act of one misguided man, who was angry at being refused an office. This fact created a new desire to have some better system of appointments to office, so that the president need not, as now, be responsible for them all. The murderer was tried and suffered death, although his counsel tried to prove that he was insane at the time of the assault.

CHESTER A. ARTHUR.

The twenty-first president. Vice-President Arthur succeeded to the presidency, taking the oath of office at New York (Sept. 20, 1881), and again, more formally, two days after, at Washington. For the first time in twenty years the inaugural address contained no reference to the Southern States as a distinct part of the nation. This signified that the long sectional contest, growing out of slavery, was at an end. Whatever evils might be left for the American people to deal with, the greatest evil was overcome. The nation was reunited, and was at peace with all the world.

ELECTION OF MR. CLEVELAND.

President Arthur served out his term of office, during which time the nation was at peace and no new States were added to the Union. For the presidential election of 1884, the Republican National Convention nominated James G. Blaine of Maine as President, and John A. Logan of Illinois as Vice-President; while the Democratic convention nominated Grover Cleveland of New York and Thomas A. Hendricks of Indiana. The Democratic candidates received 219 electoral votes, and their opponents but 182; so that the Republican party was defeated, after twenty-four years of power. Candidates were also nominated, at this election, by the prohibitory temperance party, and by the "citizens'" or "greenback" party, but these obtained no electoral votes. President Cleveland was inaugurated March 4, 1885, with Mr. Hendricks as Vice-President, who, however, died Nov. 25, 1885. After his death, a law was passed by Congress, providing that in case of the deaths of both President and Vice-President, the Secretary of State should be the successor to the Presidency. A law had been previously passed, known as the "Civil Service Act," under which the appointments to certain offices should thenceforth be made by competitive examination; the object of this law being to diminish arbitrary changes in office and secure greater permanence.

PRESIDENT CLEVELAND. Inauguration of President Cleveland

APPENDIX.

I.

BOOKS FOR CONSULTATION.

GENERAL WORKS.

Bancroft's, Hildreth's, and Bryant's "United States."
Ploetz's Manual of History (American portion).

EARLY INHABITANTS.

History. — Squier and Davis's "Ancient Monuments Smithsonian Contributions, vol. i.).
Baldwin's "Ancient America."
Foster's "Prehistoric Races of America."
Jones's "Mound-Builders of Tennessee."
Shaler's "Time of the Mammoths" ("American Naturalist," iv. 148).
Fiction. — Matthew's "Behemoth, a Legend of the Mound-Builders."

AMERICAN INDIANS.

History. — Schoolcraft's "History and Condition of the Indian Tribes."
Parkman's "Jesuits in America" (Introduction).
H. H. Bancroft's "Native Races of the Pacific Coast."
Ellis's "The Red Man and the White Man."
Fiction. — Cooper's "Leatherstocking Tales."
Poetry. — Longfellow's "Hiawatha."
Whittier's "Bridal of Pennacook."

DISCOVERERS AND EXPLORERS.

History. — Prescott's "Conquest of Mexico."
Parkman's "Pioneers of France in the New World" and "Discovery of the Great West."
T. Irving's "Conquest of Florida."
Anderson's "Discovery of America by the Northmen."

Voyages and Travels. — Hakluyt's "Voyages touching the Discovery of America."
    Kohl's "Discovery of the East Coast of America" (Maine Hist. Soc., 2d ser., vol. i.).
Biography. — W. Irving's "Columbus" and "Companions of Columbus."
Fiction. — Ballantyne's "Norsemen of the West" [Norsemen].
    Bird's "Calavar" and "Infidel" [Mexico].
    Wallace's "Fair God" [Mexico].
    Simms's "Damsel of Darien" [Balboa], "Vasconselos" [De Soto], and "The Lily and the Totem."
Poetry. — Whittier's "Norsemen."
    Longfellow's "Skeleton in Armor."
    Barlow's "Columbiad."
    Lowell's "Columbus."
    Rogers's "Columbus."

NEW ENGLAND COLONIAL HISTORY.

History. — Palfrey's and Elliott's "New England."
    State Histories: Williamson's "Maine."
        Belknap's "New Hampshire."
        Thompson's "Vermont."
        Barry's "Massachusetts."
        Arnold's "Rhode Island."
        Trumbull's "Connecticut."
    Young's "Chronicles of the Pilgrims" and "Chronicles of Mass'tts."
    Lodge's "English Colonies in America."
    Cheever's "Journal of the Pilgrims at Plymouth."
    Banvard's "Plymouth and the Pilgrims."
    Upham's "History of Witchcraft."
    Mather's "Magnalia."
Biography. — Winthrop's "Life and Letters."
    Sparks's "American Biographies:" Vane (vol. iv.), Mather (vi.), Phips (vii.), Williams (xiv), Gorton (xv.).
Fiction. — Miss Sedgwick's "Hope Leslie," "New England Tale," and "Redwood."
    Mrs. Child's "Hobomok."
    Hawthorne's "Scarlet Letter," and "Legends of the Old Province House" (in "Twice Told Tales").
    Thompson's "Green Mountain Boys."
    Motley's "Merry Mount."
    Mrs. Cheney's "Peep at the Pilgrims."
    Mrs. Lee's "Naomi."
    Holland's "Bay Path."
    Whittier's "Margaret Smith's Journal."
    Sears's "Pictures of the Olden Time."

Poetry. — Longfellow's "John Endicott," "Giles Corey," and "Courtship of Miles Standish."
Whittier's "Changeling," "Wreck of Rivermouth," "Exiles," and "Cassandra Southwick."
Pierpont's "Pilgrim Fathers."
Mrs. Hemans's "Landing of the Pilgrims."

COLONIAL HISTORY OF MIDDLE STATES.

History. — *State Histories:* Brodhead's and O'Callaghan's "New York."
Whitehead's "New Jersey."
Sypher's "Pennsylvania."
Irving's "Knickerbocker's New York."
Biography. — Clarkson's and Dixon's "Penn."
Sparks's "American Biographies:" Cleveland's "Hudson (vol. x.), Ellis's "Penn" (xxii.).
Fiction. — Irving's "Wolfert's Roost" and "Rip Van Winkle" (in "Sketch Book").
Paulding's "Dutchman's Fireside" and "Book of St. Nicholas."
Cooper's "Last of the Mohicans," "Water-Witch," and "Satanstoe."
Mrs. Grant's "Memoirs of an American Lady."
Myers's "First of the Knickerbockers" and "Young Patroon."
Bird's "Hawks of Hawk-Hollow."

COLONIAL HISTORY OF SOUTHERN STATES.

History. — Smith's "True Relation of Virginia" (reprinted, Boston, 1866).
State Histories: McSherry's "Maryland."
Campbell's "Virginia."
Williamson's "North Carolina."
Ramsay's "South Carolina."
Jones's "Georgia."
Jefferson's "Notes on Virginia."
Meade's "Old Churches of Virginia."
Biography. — "Sparks's "American Biographies:" Smith (ii.), Oglethorpe (xii.), Calvert (xix.).
Fiction. — Thackeray's "Virginians."
Cooke's "Virginia Comedians."
James's "Old Dominion."
Caruthers' "Cavaliers of Virginia" and "Knights of the Horseshoe."
Defoe's "Jaques" [Virginia].
Hopkins's "Youth of the Old Dominion."
Paulding's "Konigsmark" [Maryland].
Kennedy's "Rob of the Bowl" [Maryland].
Poetry. — Mrs. Sigourney's "Pocahontas."

INDIAN WARS.

History. — Drake's "Book of the Indians" and "Indian Wars."
  Parkman's "Conspiracy of Pontiac."
  Morgan's "League of the Iroquois."
  Warburton's "Conquest of Canada."
Biography. — Sparks's "American Biographies:" Lives of Eliot (v.), Brainerd (viii.), Mason (xiii.).
Fiction. — Cooper's "Last of the Mohicans" [Fort William Henry].
  Thackeray's "Virginians" [Braddock and Quebec].
  James's "Ticonderoga."
  Tiffany's "Brandon."
  Hall's "Twice Taken" [Louisburg].
Poetry. — Longfellow's "Evangeline."
  Whittier's "Pentucket," "St. John," "Mary Garvin," "Mogg Megone."

REVOLUTION.

History. — Winsor's "Reader's Handbook of the Revolution."
  Lossing's "Pictorial Field-Book of the Revolution."
  Frothingham's "Siege of Boston" and "Rise of the Republic."
Biography. — Sparks's "Washington" and "Franklin."
  Irving's "Washington."
  Franklin's "Autobiography."
  Parton's "Franklin," "Jefferson," and "Burr."
  Parker's "Historic Americans."
  C. F. Adams's "Life of John Adams," and "John Adams's Diary."
  Goodrich's "Lives of Signers of the Declaration."
  G. W. Greene's "Life of General Greene."
  Wirt's "Patrick Henry." Mackenzie's "Paul Jones."
  Sparks's "American Biographies:" Lives of Stark (i.), Allen (i.), Arnold (iii.), Pulaski (xii.).
Fiction. — Cooper's "Spy," "Pilot," "Lionel Lincoln," "Wyandotte," and "Chain-Bearer."
  Motley's "Morton's Hope."
  Mrs. Child's "Rebels."
  Thompson's "Rangers."
  Miss Sedgwick's "Linwoods."
  Kennedy's "Horse-Shoe Robinson."
  Simms's "Mellichampe" and "Partisan."
  Paulding's "Old Continental."
  Winthrop's "Edwin Brothertoft."
  Hawthorne's "Septimius Felton."
Poetry. — Longfellow's "Paul Revere's Ride."
  Bryant's "Song of Marion's Men."

Poetry. — Whittier's "Rangers."
Trumbull's "McFingal."
Calvert's "Arnold and André."
Moore's "Songs and Ballads of the Revolution."

FROM THE REVOLUTION TO THE CIVIL WAR.

History. — Cooper's "History of the Navy of the United States."
Griswold's "Court of Washington."
Lossing's "Pictorial Field-Book of the War of 1812."
Wilson's "Rise and Fall of the Slave Power."
Giddings's "Exiles of Florida."
Mayer's "History of the Mexican War."
Jay's "Review of the Mexican War."
Dunlop's "History of the Arts of Design in America."
Duyckinck's "American Literature."
Biography. — C. F. Adams's "Life of J. Q. Adams," "Diary" of J. Q. A.
Mrs. Adams's "Letters."
Parton's "Jackson."
E. Quincy's "Josiah Quincy."
Sparks's "American Biographies:" Fulton (x), Fitch (xvi.), Decatur (xxi.), Boone (xxiii.).
Benton's "Thirty Years' View."
"American Statesmen" (series).
Frothingham's "Theodore Parker."
Redpath's and Webb's "John Brown."
Travels. — "Lewis and Clarke's Expedition."
Fiction. — Wirt's "Letters of a British Spy."
Judd's "Margaret" [New England].
Paulding's "Westward Ho" [Virginians in Kentucky].
Bird's "Nick of the Woods" [Indians and Kentucky settlers].
Kennedy's "Swallow Barn" [Virginia].
Charles Brockden Brown's Novels.
Smith's "Jack Downing."
Hall's "Legends of the West."
Mrs. Stowe's "Minister's Wooing," "Uncle Tom's Cabin," "Dred."
Galt's "Lawrie Todd" [Western emigration].
Hildreth's "White Slave."
Poetry. — Colton's "Tecumseh."
Street's "Osceola."
Lowell's "Biglow Papers" (first series: Mexican War).
Whittier's "Angels of Buena Vista" and "Anti-slavery Poems."

CIVIL WAR.

History. — Moore's "Rebellion Record."
 Greeley's "American Conflict."
 Draper's "American Civil War."
 Pollard's "Lost Cause" (Confederate).
 "Campaigns of the Civil War" (series).
 Nichols's "Story of the Great March."
 Coffin's "Following the Flag" and "My Days and Nights on the Battlefield."
 Higginson's "Army Life in a Black Regiment."

Biography. — Badeau's "Military History of General Grant."
 Bowman's and Irwin's "Sherman and his Campaigns."
 Headley's "Farragut and our Naval Commanders."
 Pollard's "Jefferson Davis."
 Nason's "Sumner."
 Holland's and Raymond's "Lincoln."
 Chesney's "Military Biographies" (Grant, Lee, Farragut).
 Higginson's "Harvard Memorial Biographies" (Memoirs of Harvard Students and Graduates in the War).

Fiction. — Mrs. Child's "Romance of the Republic."
 Trowbridge's "Cudjo's Cave," "Three Scouts," and "Drummer Boy."
 De Forest's "Miss Ravenel's Conversion."
 Coffin's "Winning his Way."
 Mrs. Austin's "Dora Darling."

Poetry. — Moore's "Lyrics of Loyalty" and "Rebel Rhymes."
 Simms's "War Poetry of the South."
 Whittier's "In War Time."
 Lowell's "Biglow Papers" (second series) and "Harvard Commemoration Ode."
 Mrs. Howe's "Battle Hymn of the Republic."

LIST OF PRESIDENTS AND VICE-PRESIDENTS.

NO.	PRESIDENT.	STATE.	VICE-PRESIDENT.	TERM OF OFFICE.
1	George Washington	Virginia	John Adams	Two terms: 1789–1797.
2	John Adams	Massachusetts	Thomas Jefferson	One term: 1797–1801.
3	Thomas Jefferson	Virginia	Aaron Burr / George Clinton	Two terms: 1801–1809.
4	James Madison	Virginia	George Clinton / Elbridge Gerry	Two terms: 1809–1817.
5	James Monroe	Virginia	Daniel D. Tompkins	Two terms: 1817–1825.
6	John Quincy Adams	Massachusetts	John C. Calhoun	One term: 1825–1829.
7	Andrew Jackson	Tennessee	John C. Calhoun / Martin Van Buren	Two terms: 1829–1837.
8	Martin Van Buren	New York	Richard M. Johnson	One term: 1837–1841.
9	William H. Harrison	Ohio	John Tyler	One month: 1841.
10	John Tyler	Virginia		3 yrs., and 11 months: 1841–1845.
11	James K. Polk	Tennessee	George M. Dallas	One term: 1845–1849.
12	Zachary Taylor	Louisiana	Millard Fillmore	1 year and 4 months: 1849–1850.
13	Millard Fillmore	New York		2 yrs. and 8 months: 1850–1853.
14	Franklin Pierce	N. Hampshire	William R. King	One term: 1853–1857.
15	James Buchanan	Pennsylvania	J. C. Breckinridge	One term: 1857–1861.
16	Abraham Lincoln	Illinois	Hannibal Hamlin / Andrew Johnson	1 term and 1 month: 1861–1865.
17	Andrew Johnson	Tennessee		3 yrs., and 11 months: 1865–1869.
18	Ulysses S. Grant	Illinois	Schuyler Colfax / Henry Wilson	Two terms: 1869–1877.
19	Rutherford B. Hayes	Ohio	Wm. A. Wheeler	One term: 1877–1881.
20	James A. Garfield	Ohio	Chester A. Arthur	Six and a half months, 1881.
21	Chester A. Arthur	New York		3 years, 5½ months: 1881–1885.
22	Grover Cleveland	New York	Thos. A. Hendricks	

III.

LIST OF STATES AND TERRITORIES.

NO.	STATES.	DATE OF ADMISSION	NO.	STATES.	DATE OF ADMISSION
1	New Hampshire	*The thirteen original States.*	20	Mississippi	1817
2	Massachusetts		21	Illinois	1818
3	Rhode Island		22	Alabama	1819
4	Connecticut		23	Maine	1820
5	New York		24	Missouri	1821
6	New Jersey		25	Arkansas	1836
7	Pennsylvania		26	Michigan	1837
8	Delaware		27	Florida	1845
9	Maryland		28	Texas	1845
10	Virginia		29	Iowa	1846
11	North Carolina		30	Wisconsin	1848
12	South Carolina		31	California	1850
13	Georgia		32	Minnesota	1858
14	Vermont	1791	33	Oregon	1859
15	Kentucky	1792	34	Kansas	1861
16	Tennessee	1796	35	West Virginia	1863
17	Ohio	1802	36	Nevada	1864
18	Louisiana	1812	37	Nebraska	1867
19	Indiana	1816	38	Colorado	1876

NO.	TERRITORIES.	DATE OF ORGANIZ'N.	NO.	TERRITORIES.	DATE OF ORGANIZ'N.
1	New Mexico	1850	7	Montana	1864
2	Utah	1850	8	Wyoming	1868
3	Washington	1853	9	Dist. Columbia	No territo-
4	Dakota	1861	10	Indian Territory	rial organi-
5	Arizona	1863	11	Alaska	zation.
6	Idaho	1863			

IV.

AREA OF THE UNITED STATES.

	SQ. MILES.
Original limits of the Thirteen States	820,680
Louisiana, purchased of France in 1803, for $15,000,000 . .	899,577
Florida, purchased of Spain in 1819, for $5,000,000 . . .	66,900
Territory confirmed by the Oregon Treaty in 1842 and 1846 .	308,052
Texas annexed in 1846 (Texas debt, $7,500,000) . . .	318,000
New Mexico and California in 1847 (cost of the war $15,000,000),	522,955
"Gadsden Purchase" of Mexico in 1853, for $10,000,000 . .	45,535
Alaska, purchased of Russia in 1867, for $7,200,000 . . .	577,390
	3,559,099

[See Frontispiece.]

V.

THE DECLARATION OF INDEPENDENCE, ADOPTED BY CONGRESS JULY 4, 1776.

A DECLARATION BY THE REPRESENTATIVES OF THE UNITED STATES OF AMERICA, IN CONGRESS ASSEMBLED.

WHEN, in the course of human events, it becomes necessary for one people to dissolve the political bands which have connected them with another, and to assume among the powers of the earth the separate and equal station to which the laws of nature and of nature's God entitle them, a decent respect to the opinions of mankind requires that they should declare the causes which impel them to the separation.

We hold these truths to be self-evident, that all men are created equal; that they are endowed by their Creator with certain inalienable rights; that among these are life, liberty, and the pursuit of happiness; that, to secure these rights, governments are instituted among men, deriving their just powers from the consent of the governed; that, whenever any form of government becomes destructive of these ends, it is the right of the people to alter or abolish it. and to institute a new government, laying its foundation on such principles, and organizing its powers in such form, as to them shall seem most likely to effect their safety and happiness. Prudence, indeed, will dictate that governments long established should not be changed for light and transient causes; and, accordingly, all experience hath shown that mankind are more disposed to suffer, while evils are sufferable, than to right themselves by abolishing the forms to which they are accustomed. But when a long train of abuses and usurpations, pursuing invariably the same object, evinces a design to reduce them under absolute despotism, it is their right, it is their duty, to throw off such a government, and to provide new guards for their future security. Such has been the patient sufferance of these Colonies; and such is now the necessity which constrains them to alter their former systems of government. The history of the present king of Great Britain is a history of repeated injuries and usurpations, all having in direct object the establishment of an absolute tyranny over these States. To prove this, let facts be submitted to a candid world: —

He has refused his assent to laws the most wholesome, and necessary for the public good.

He has forbidden his governors to pass laws of immediate and pressing importance, unless suspended in their operations, till his assent should be obtained; and, when so suspended, he has utterly neglected to attend to them.

He has refused to pass other laws for the accommodation of large districts of people, unless those people would relinquish the right of representation in the legislature; a right inestimable to them, and formidable to tyrants only.

He has called together legislative bodies at places unusual, uncomfortable, and distant from the repository of their public records, for the sole purpose of fatiguing them into compliance with his measures.

He has dissolved representative houses repeatedly for opposing, with manly firmness, his invasions on the rights of the people.

He has refused, for a long time after such dissolutions, to cause others to be elected; whereby the legislative powers, incapable of annihilation, have returned to the people at large, for their exercise; the State remaining, in the mean time, exposed to all the dangers of invasions from without, and convulsions within.

He has endeavored to prevent the population of these States; for that purpose, obstructing the laws for the naturalization of foreigners; refusing to pass others to encourage their migration hither, and raising the conditions of new appropriations of lands.

He has obstructed the administration of justice by refusing his assent to laws for establishing judiciary powers.

He has made judges dependent on his will alone, for the tenure of their offices, and the amount and payment of their salaries.

He has erected a multitude of new offices, and sent hither swarms of officers, to harass our people, and eat out their substance.

He has kept among us, in times of peace, standing armies, without the consent of our legislature.

He has affected to render the military independent of, and superior to, the civil power.

He has combined with others to subject us to a jurisdiction foreign to our constitution, and unacknowledged by our laws; giving his assent to their acts of pretended legislation: —

For quartering large bodies of armed troops among us;

For protecting them, by mock trial, from punishment for any murders which they should commit on the inhabitants of these States;

For cutting off our trade with all parts of the world;

For imposing taxes on us without our consent;

For depriving us, in many cases, of the benefits of trial by jury;

For transporting us beyond seas to be tried for pretended offences;

For abolishing the free system of English laws in a neigboring province, establishing therein an arbitrary government, and enlarging its boundaries, so as to render it at once an example and fit instrument for introducing the same absolute rule into these Colonies;

For taking away our charters, abolishing our most valuable laws, and altering, fundamentally, the powers of our governments;

For suspending our own legislatures, and declaring themselves invested with power to legislate for us in all cases whatsoever.

He has abdicated government here, by declaring us out of his protection, and waging war against us.

He has plundered our seas, ravaged our coasts, burned our towns, and destroyed the lives of our people.

He is at this time transporting large armies of foreign mercenaries to complete the works of death, desolation, and tyranny, already begun with circumstances of cruelty and perfidy

DECLARATION OF INDEPENDENCE. 357

scarcely paralleled in the most barbarous ages, and totally unworthy the head of a civilized nation.

He has constrained our fellow-citizens, taken captive on the high seas, to bear arms against their country, to become the executioners of their friends and brethren, or to fall themselves by their hands.

He has excited domestic insurrections amongst us, and has endeavored to bring on the inhabitants of our frontiers, the merciless Indian savages, whose known rule of warfare is an undistinguished destruction of all ages, sexes, and conditions.

In every stage of these oppressions, we have petitioned for redress in the most humble terms; our repeated petitions have been answered only by repeated injury. A prince whose character is thus marked by every act which may define a tyrant is unfit to be the ruler of a free people.

Nor have we been wanting in attentions to our British brethren. We have warned them, from time to time, of attempts by their legislature to extend an unwarrantable jurisdiction over us. We have reminded them of the circumstances of our emigration and settlement here. We have appealed to their native justice and magnanimity, and we have conjured them, by the ties of our common kindred, to disavow these usurpations, which would inevitably interrupt our connections and correspondence. They, too, have been deaf to the voice of justice and of consanguinity. We must, therefore, acquiesce in the necessity, which denounces our separation, and hold them, as we hold the rest of mankind, enemies in war; in peace, friends.

We, therefore, the representatives of the UNITED STATES OF AMERICA, in general congress assembled, appealing to the Supreme Judge of the world for the rectitude of our intentions, do, in the name and by the authority of the good people of these Colonies, solemnly publish and declare, That these United Colonies are, and of right ought to be, *Free* and *Independent States;* that they are absolved from all allegiance to the British crown, and that all political connection between them and the State of Great Britain is, and ought to be, totally dissolved; and that, as *Free* and *Independent States*, they have full power to levy war, conclude peace, contract alliances, establish commerce, and do all other acts and things which *Independent States* may of right do. And for the support of this Declaration, with a firm reliance on the protection of DIVINE PROVIDENCE, we mutually pledge to each other our lives, our fortunes, and our sacred honor. JOHN HANCOCK.

NEW HAMPSHIRE. — Josiah Bartlett, William Whipple, Matthew Thornton.

MASSACHUSETTS BAY. — Samuel Adams, John Adams, Robert Treat Paine, Elbridge Gerry.

RHODE ISLAND, ETC. — Stephen Hopkins, William Ellery.

CONNECTICUT. — Roger Sherman, Samuel Huntington, William Williams, Oliver Wolcott.

NEW YORK. — William Floyd, Philip Livingston, Francis Lewis, Lewis Morris.

NEW JERSEY. — Richard Stockton, John Witherspoon, Francis Hopkinson, John Hart, Abraham Clark.

PENNSYLVANIA. — Robert Morris, Benjamin Rush, Benjamin Franklin, John Morton, George Clymer, James Smith, George Taylor, James Wilson, George Ross.

DELAWARE. — Cæsar Rodney, George Read, Thomas M'Kean.

MARYLAND. — Samuel Chase, William Paca, Thomas Stone, Charles Carroll of Carrollton.

VIRGINIA. — George Wythe, Richard Henry Lee, Thomas Jefferson, Benjamin Harrison, Thomas Nelson, Jr., Francis Lightfoot Lee, Carter Braxton.

NORTH CAROLINA. — William Hooper, Joseph Hewes, John Penn.

SOUTH CAROLINA. — Edward Rutledge, Thomas Hayward, Jr., Thomas Lynch, Jr., Arthur Middleton.

GEORGIA. — Button Gwinnett, Lyman Hall, George Walton.

VI.

CONSTITUTION OF THE UNITED STATES.

We, the People of the United States, in order to form a more perfect union, establish justice, insure domestic tranquillity, provide for the common defence, promote the general welfare, and secure the blessings of liberty to ourselves and our posterity, do ordain and establish this Constitution for the United States of America.

ARTICLE I.

SECTION 1. — All legislative powers herein granted shall be vested in a Congress of the United States, which shall consist of a Senate and House of Representatives.

SECT. 2. — The House of Representatives shall be composed of members chosen every second year by the people of the several States, and the electors in each State shall have the qualifications requisite for electors of the most numerous branch of the State legislature.

No person shall be a representative who shall not have attained to the age of twenty-five years, and been seven years a citizen of the United States, and who shall not, when elected, be an inhabitant of that State in which he shall be chosen.

Representatives and direct taxes shall be apportioned among the several States which may be included within this Union, according to their respective numbers, which shall be determined by adding to the whole number of free persons, including those bound to service for a term of years, and excluding Indians not taxed, three-fifths of all other persons. The actual enumeration shall be made within three years after the first meeting of the Congress of the United States, and within every subsequent term of ten years, in such manner as they shall by law direct. The number of representatives shall not exceed one for every thirty thousand; but each State shall have at least one representative; and, until such enumeration shall be made, the State of New Hampshire shall be entitled to choose three, Massachusetts, eight, Rhode Island and Providence Plantations, one, Connecticut, five, New York, six, New Jersey, four, Pennsylvania, eight, Delaware, one, Maryland, six, Virginia, ten, North Carolina, five, South Carolina, five, and Georgia, three.

When vacancies happen in the representation from any State, the executive authority thereof shall issue writs of election to fill such vacancies.

The House of Representatives shall choose their speaker and other officers; and shall have the sole power of impeachment.

SECT. 3. — The Senate of the United States shall be composed of two senators from each State, chosen by the legislature thereof, for six years; and each senator shall have one vote.

Immediately after they shall be assembled in consequence of the first election, they shall be divided, as equally as may be, into three classes. The seats of the senators of the first class shall be vacated at the expiration of the second year, of the second class, at the expiration of the fourth year, and of the third class, at the expiration of the sixth year, so that one-third may be chosen every second year; and if vacancies happen, by resignation or otherwise, during the recess of the legislature of any State, the executive thereof may make temporary appointments until the next meeting of the legislature, which shall then fill such vacancies.

No person shall be a senator who shall not have attained to the age of thirty years, and been nine years a citizen of the United States, and who shall not, when elected, be an inhabitant of that State for which he shall be chosen.

The Vice-President of the United States shall be president of the Senate, but shall have no vote, unless they be equally divided.

The Senate shall choose their other officers, and also a president *pro tempore*, in the absence of the Vice-President, or when he shall exercise the office as President of the United States.

The Senate shall have the sole power to try all impeachments. When sitting for that purpose, they shall be on oath or affirmation. When the President of the United States is tried, the chief justice shall preside; and no person shall be convicted without the concurrence of two-thirds of the members present.

Judgment, in cases of impeachment, shall not extend further than to removal from office, and disqualification to hold and enjoy any office of honor, trust, or profit under the United States; but the party convicted shall, nevertheless, be liable and subject to indictment, trial, judgment, and punishment, according to law.

SECT. 4. — The times, places, and manner of holding elections for senators and representatives shall be prescribed in each State by the legislature thereof; but the Congress may, at any time, by law, make or alter such regulations, except as to the places of choosing senators.

The Congress shall assemble at least once in every year; and such meeting shall be on the first Monday in December, unless they shall by law appoint a different day.

SECT. 5. — Each house shall be the judge of the elections, returns, and qualifications of its own members; and a majority of each shall constitute a quorum to do business; but a smaller number may adjourn from day to day, and may be authorized to compel the attendance of absent members, in such manner and under such penalties as each house may provide.

Each house may determine the rules of its proceedings, punish its members for disorderly behavior, and, with the concurrence of two-thirds, expel a member.

Each house shall keep a journal of its proceedings, and from time to time publish the same, excepting such parts as may in their judgment require secrecy; and the yeas and nays of the members of either house, on any question, shall, at the desire of one-fifth of those present, be entered on the journal.

Neither house, during the session of Congress, shall, without the consent of the other, adjourn for more than three days, nor to any other place than that in which the two houses shall be sitting.

SECT. 6. — The senators and representatives shall receive a

compensation for their services, to be ascertained by law, and paid out of the treasury of the United States. They shall, in all cases except treason, felony, and breach of the peace, be privileged from arrest during their attendance at the session of their respective houses, and in going to and returning from the same; and, for any speech or debate in either house, they shall not be questioned in any other place.

No senator or representative shall, during the time for which he was elected, be appointed to any civil office under the authority of the United States which shall have been created, or the emoluments whereof shall have been increased, during such time; and no person holding any office under the United States shall be a member of either house during his continuance in office.

SECT. 7.—All bills for raising revenue shall originate in the House of Representatives; but the Senate may propose or concur with amendments, as on other bills.

Every bill which shall have passed the House of Representatives and the Senate, shall, before it become a law, be presented to the President of the United States; if he approve he shall sign it, but if not he shall return it, with his objections, to that house in which it shall have originated, who shall enter the objections at large on their journal, and proceed to reconsider it. If, after such reconsideration, two-thirds of that house shall agree to pass the bill, it shall be sent, together with the objections, to the other house, by which it shall likewise be reconsidered, and, if approved by two-thirds of that house, it shall become a law. But, in all such cases, the votes of both houses shall be determined by yeas and nays, and the names of the persons voting for and against the bill shall be entered on the journal of each house respectively. If any bill shall not be returned by the President within ten days (Sundays excepted) after it shall have been presented to him, the same shall be a law in like manner as if he had signed it, unless the Congress by their adjournment prevent its return, in which case it shall not be a law.

Every order, resolution, or vote, to which the concurrence of the Senate and House of Representatives may be necessary (except on a question of adjournment) shall be presented to the President of the United States; and, before the same shall take effect, shall be approved by him, or, being disapproved by him, shall be repassed by two-thirds of the Senate and House of Representatives, according to the rules and limitations prescribed in the case of a bill.

SECT. 8. — The Congress shall have power: —

To lay and collect taxes, duties, imposts, and excises, to pay the debts, and provide for the common defence and general welfare, of the United States: but all duties, imposts, and excises shall be uniform throughout the United States:

To borrow money on the credit of the United States:

To regulate commerce with foreign nations, and among the several States, and with the Indian tribes:

To establish an uniform rule of naturalization, and uniform laws on the subject of bankruptcies throughout the United States:

To coin money, regulate the value thereof, and of foreign coin, and fix the standard of weights and measures:

To provide for the punishment of counterfeiting the securities and current coin of the United States:

To establish post-offices and post-roads:

To promote the progress of science and useful arts, by securing for limited times, to authors and inventors, the exclusive right to their respective writings and discoveries:

To constitute tribunals inferior to the Supreme Court:

To define and punish piracies and felonies committed on the high seas, and offences against the law of nations:

To declare war, grant letters of marque and reprisal, and make rules concerning captures on land and water:

To raise and support armies; but no appropriation of money to that use shall be for a longer term than two years:

To provide and maintain a navy:

To make rules for the government and regulation of the land and naval forces:

To provide for calling forth the militia to execute the laws of the Union, suppress insurrections, and repel invasions:

To provide for organizing, arming, and disciplining the militia, and for governing such part of them as may be employed in the service of the United States, reserving to the States respectively, the appointment of the officers, and the authority of training the militia according to the discipline prescribed by Congress:

To exercise exclusive legislation, in all cases whatsoever, over such district (not exceeding ten miles square) as may, by cession of particular States, and the acceptance of Congress, become the seat of government of the United States, and to exercise like authority over all places purchased by the consent of the legislature of the State in which the same shall be, for the erection of forts, magazines, arsenals, dockyards, and other needful buildings : — And,

To make all laws which shall be necessary and proper for carrying into execution the foregoing powers, and all other powers vested by this Constitution in the government of the United States, or in any department or officer thereof.

SECT. 9.— The migration or importation of such persons, as any of the States now existing shall think proper to admit, shall not be prohibited by the Congress prior to the year one thousand eight hundred and eight; but a tax, or duty, may be imposed on such importation, not exceeding ten dollars for each person.

The privilege of the writ of *habeas corpus* shall not be suspended, unless when in cases of rebellion or invasion the public safety may require it.

No bill of attainder or *ex post facto* law shall be passed.

No capitation or other direct tax shall be laid, unless in proportion to the census, or enumeration, hereinbefore directed to be taken.

No tax or duty shall be laid on articles exported from any State. No preference shall be given by any regulation of commerce or revenue to the ports of one State over those of another; nor shall vessels bound to or from one State be obliged to enter, clear, or pay duties, in another.

No money shall be drawn from the treasury but in consequence of appropriations made by law; and a regular statement and account of the receipts and expenditures of all public money shall be published from time to time.

No title of nobility shall be granted by the United States; and no person holding any office of profit or trust under them shall, without the consent of the Congress, accept of any present, emolument, office, or title of any kind whatever, from any king, prince, or foreign state.

SECT. 10. — No State shall enter into any treaty, alliance, or confederation; grant letters of marque and reprisal; coin money; emit bills of credit; make anything but gold and silver coin a tender in payment of debts; pass any bill of attainder, *ex post facto* law, or law impairing the obligation of contracts; or grant any title of nobility.

No State shall, without the consent of the Congress, lay any imposts or duties on imports or exports, except what may be absolutely necessary for executing its inspection laws; and the net produce of all duties and imposts laid by any State on imports or exports shall be for the use of the treasury of the United States: and all such laws shall be subject to the revision and control of the Congress. No State shall, without the consent of Congress, lay any duty of tonnage, keep troops or ships of war in time of peace, enter into any agreement or compact with another State or with a foreign power, or engage in war, unless actually invaded, or in such imminent danger as will not admit of delay.

ARTICLE II.

SECTION 1. — The executive power shall be vested in a President of the United States of America. He shall hold his office during the term of four years, and together with the Vice-President, chosen for the same term, be elected as follows: —

Each State shall appoint, in such manner as the legislature thereof may direct, a number of electors equal to the whole number of senators and representatives to which the State may be entitled in the Congress; but no senator or representative, or person holding an office of trust or profit under the United States, shall be appointed an elector.

The electors shall meet in their respective States, and vote by ballot for two persons, of whom one, at least, shall not be an inhabitant of the same State with themselves. And they shall make a list of all the persons voted for, and of the number of votes for each; which list they shall sign and certify, and transmit sealed to the seat of the government of the United States, directed to the president of the Senate. The president of the Senate shall, in the presence of the Senate and House of Representatives, open all the certificates; and the votes shall then be counted. The person having the greatest number of votes shall be the President, if such number be a majority of the whole number of electors appointed; and if there be more than one who have such majority, and have an equal number of votes, then the House of Representatives shall immediately choose, by ballot, one of them for President; and if no person have a majority, then, from the five highest on the list, the said house shall, in like manner. choose the President. But, in choosing the President, the votes shall be taken by States; the representation from each State having one vote; a quorum for this purpose shall consist of a member or members from two-thirds of the States; and a majority of all the States shall be necessary to a choice. In every case. after the choice of the President, the person having the greatest number of votes of the electors shall be the Vice-President. But, if there should remain two or more who have equal votes, the Senate shall choose from them, by ballot, the Vice-President.

The Congress may determine the time of choosing the electors, and the day on which they shall give their votes; which day shall be the same throughout the United States.

No person except a natural born citizen. or a citizen of the United States at the time of the adoption of this Constitution, shall be eligible to the office of President; neither shall any person be eligible to that office who shall not have attained to the age of thirty-five years, and been fourteen years a resident within the United States.

In case of the removal of the President from office, or of his death, resignation, or inability to discharge the powers and duties of the said office. the same shall devolve on the Vice-President; and the Congress may, by law. provide for the case of removal. death, resignation, or inability, both of the President and Vice-President, declaring what officer shall then act as President; and such officer shall act accordingly, until the disability be removed, or a President shall be elected.

The President shall, at stated times, receive for his services a compensation, which shall neither be increased nor diminished during the period for which he shall have been elected; and he shall not receive within that period any other emolument from the United States or any of them.

Before he enter on the execution of his office, he shall take the following oath or affirmation: —

"I do solemnly swear (or affirm) that I will faithfully execute the office of President of the United States, and will, to the best of my ability, preserve, protect, and defend the Constitution of the United States."

SECT. 2. — The President shall be commander-in-chief of the army and navy of the United States, and of the militia of the several States, when called into the actual service of the United States; he may require the opinion, in writing, of the principal officer in each of the executive departments, upon any subject relating to the duties of their respective offices, and he shall have power to grant reprieves and pardons for offences against the United States, except in cases of impeachment.

He shall have power, by and with the advice and consent of the Senate, to make treaties, provided two-thirds of the senators present concur; and he shall nominate and, by and with the advice and consent of the Senate, shall appoint, ambassadors, other public ministers, and consuls, judges of the Supreme Court, and all other officers of the United States, whose appointments are not herein otherwise provided for, and which shall be established by law: but the Congress may, by law, vest the appointment of such inferior officers as they think proper, in the President alone, in the courts of law, or in the heads of departments.

The President shall have power to fill up all vacancies that may happen during the recess of the Senate. by granting commissions, which shall expire at the end of their next session.

SECT. 3. — He shall, from time to time, give to the Congress information of the state of the Union, and recommend to their consideration such measures as he shall judge necessary and expedient; he may, on extraordinary occasions, convene both houses, or either of them, and in case of disagreement between them with respect to the time of adjournment, he may adjourn them to such time as he shall think proper; he shall receive ambassadors and other public ministers; he shall take care that the laws be faithfully executed; and shall commission all the officers of the United States.

SECT. 4. — The President, Vice-President, and all civil officers of the United States, shall be removed from office on impeachment for and conviction of treason, bribery, or other high crimes and misdemeanors.

ARTICLE III.

SECTION 1. — The judicial power of the United States shall be vested in one Supreme Court, and in such inferior courts as the Congress may from time to time ordain and establish. The judges, both of the supreme and inferior courts, shall hold their offices during good behavior; and shall, at stated times, receive for their services a compensation, which shall not be diminished during their continuance in office.

SECT. 2. — The judicial power shall extend to all cases, in law and equity, arising under this Constitution, the laws of the United States, and treaties made, or which shall be made under their authority; to all cases affecting ambassadors, other public ministers, and consuls; to all cases of admiralty and maritime jurisdiction; to controversies to which the United States shall be a party; to controversies between two or more States, between a State and citizens of another State, between citizens of different States, between citizens of the same State claiming lands under grants of different States, and between a State, or the citizens thereof, and foreign States, citizens, or subjects.

In all cases affecting ambassadors, other public ministers, and consuls, and those in which a State shall be a party, the Supreme Court shall have original jurisdiction. In all the other cases before mentioned, the Supreme Court shall have appellate jurisdiction both as to law and fact, with such exceptions, and under such regulations as the Congress shall make.

The trial of all crimes, except in cases of impeachment, shall be by jury; and such trial shall be held in the State where the said crimes shall have been committed; but, when not committed within any State, the trial shall be at such place or places as the Congress may by law have directed.

SECT. 3. — Treason against the United States shall consist only in levying war against them, or in adhering to their enemies, giving them aid and comfort. No person shall be convicted of treason unless on the testimony of two witnesses to the same overt act, or on confession in open court.

The Congress shall have power to declare the punishment of treason, but no attainder of treason shall work corruption of blood or forfeiture, except during the life of the person attainted.

ARTICLE IV.

SECTION 1. — Full faith and credit shall be given in each State to the public acts, records, and judicial proceedings of every other State. And the Congress may by general laws prescribe the manner in which such acts, records, and proceedings shall be proved, and the effect thereof.

SECT. 2. — The citizens of each State shall be entitled to all privileges and immunities of citizens in the several States.

A person charged in any State with treason, felony, or other crime, who shall flee from justice, and be found in another State, shall, on demand of the executive authority of the State from which he fled, be delivered up, to be removed to the State having jurisdiction of the crime.

No person held to service or labor in one State under the laws thereof, escaping into another, shall, in consequence of any law or regulation therein, be discharged from such service or labor, but shall be delivered up on claim of the party to whom such service or labor may be due.

SECT. 3. — New States may be admitted by the Congress into this Union; but no new State shall be formed or erected within the jurisdiction of any other State; nor any State be formed by the junction of two or more States, or parts of States, without the consent of the legislature of the States concerned, as well as of the Congress.

The Congress shall have power to dispose of and make all needful rules and regulations respecting the territory or other property belonging to the United States; and nothing in this

Constitution shall be so construed as to prejudice any claims of the United States, or of any particular State.

SECT. 4. — The United States shall guarantee to every State in this Union a republican form of government, and shall protect each of them against invasion; and on application of the legislature, or of the executive (when the legislature cannot be convened), against domestic violence.

ARTICLE V.

The Congress, whenever two-thirds of both houses shall deem it necessary, shall propose amendments to this Constitution, or, on the application of the legislatures of two-thirds of the several States, shall call a convention for proposing amendments, which, in either case, shall be valid, to all intents and purposes, as part of this Constitution, when ratified by the legislatures of three-fourths of the several States, or by conventions in three-fourths thereof, as the one or the other mode of ratification may be proposed by the Congress; Provided, that no amendment, which may be made prior to the year one thousand eight hundred and eight, shall in any manner affect the first and fourth clauses in the ninth section of the first article; and that no State, without its consent, shall be deprived of its equal suffrage in the Senate.

ARTICLE VI.

All debts contracted, and engagements entered into, before the adoption of this Constitution, shall be as valid against the United States under this Constitution, as under the Confederation.

This Constitution, and the laws of the United States which shall be made in pursuance thereof; and all treaties made, or which shall be made, under the authority of the United States, shall be the supreme law of the land; and the judges in every State shall be bound thereby, anything in the Constitution or laws of any State to the contrary notwithstanding.

The senators and representatives before mentioned, and the members of the several State legislatures, and all executive and judicial officers, both of the United States and of the several States, shall be bound by oath or affirmation to support this

CONSTITUTION OF THE UNITED STATES. 371

Constitution; but no religious test shall ever be required as a qualification to any office or public trust under the United States.

ARTICLE VII.

The ratification of the conventions of nine States shall be sufficient for the establishment of this Constitution between the States so ratifying the same.

Done in Convention by the unanimous consent of the States present, the seventeenth day of September, in the year of our Lord one thousand seven hundred and eighty-seven, and of the Independence of the United States of America the twelfth. In witness whereof, we have hereunto subscribed our names.

GEORGE WASHINGTON, *President,*
and *deputy from Virginia.*

NEW HAMPSHIRE. — John Langdon, Nicholas Gilman.
MASSACHUSETTS. — Nathaniel Gorham, Rufus King.
CONNECTICUT. — William Samuel Johnson, Roger Sherman.
NEW YORK. — Alexander Hamilton.
NEW JERSEY. — William Livingston, David Brearly, William Patterson, Jonathan Dayton.
PENNSYLVANIA. — Benjamin Franklin, Thomas Mifflin, Robert Morris, George Clymer, Thomas Fitzsimons, Jared Ingersoll, James Wilson, Gouverneur Morris.
DELAWARE. — George Read, Gunning Bedford, Jr., John Dickinson, Richard Bassett, Jacob Broom.
MARYLAND. — James McHenry, Daniel of St. Thomas Jenifer, Daniel Carroll.
VIRGINIA. — John Blair, James Madison, Jr.
NORTH CAROLINA. — William Blount, Richard Dobbs Spaight, Hugh Williamson.
SOUTH CAROLINA. — John Rutledge, Charles Cotesworth Pinckney, Charles Pinckney, Pierce Butler.
GEORGIA. — William Few, Abraham Baldwin.
Attest: WILLIAM JACKSON, *Secretary.*

AMENDMENTS TO THE CONSTITUTION.

ARTICLE I.

Congress shall make no law respecting an establishment of religion, or prohibiting the free exercise thereof; or abridging the freedom of speech or of the press; or the right of the people peaceably to assemble, and to petition the government for a redress of grievances.

ARTICLE II.

A well regulated militia being necessary to the security of a free state, the right of the people to keep and bear arms shall not be infringed.

ARTICLE III.

No soldier shall, in time of peace, be quartered in any house without the consent of the owner; nor in time of war, but in a manner to be prescribed by law.

ARTICLE IV.

The right of the people to be secure in their persons, houses, papers, and effects, against unreasonable searches and seizures, shall not be violated; and no warrants shall issue but upon probable cause, supported by oath or affirmation, and particularly describing the place to be searched, and the person or things to be seized.

ARTICLE V.

No person shall be held to answer for a capital or otherwise infamous crime, unless on a presentment or indictment of a grand jury, except in cases arising in the land or naval forces, or in the militia when in actual service in time of war or public danger; nor shall any person be subject, for the same offence, to be twice put in jeopardy of life or limb; nor shall be compelled, in any criminal case, to be a witness against himself; nor be deprived of life, liberty, or property, without due process of law; nor shall private property be taken for public use without just compensation.

AMENDMENTS TO THE CONSTITUTION. 373

ARTICLE VI.

In all criminal prosecutions, the accused shall enjoy the right to a speedy and public trial, by an impartial jury of the State and district wherein the crime shall have been committed, which district shall have been previously ascertained by law; and to be informed of the nature and cause of the accusation; to be confronted with the witnesses against him; to have compulsory process for obtaining witnesses in his favor; and to have the assistance of counsel for his defence.

ARTICLE VII.

In suits at common law, where the value in controversy shall exceed twenty dollars, the right of trial by jury shall be preserved; and no fact tried by a jury shall be otherwise reexamined in any court of the United States than according to the rules of the common law.

ARTICLE VIII.

Excessive bail shall not be required, nor excessive fines imposed, nor cruel and unusual punishments inflicted.

ARTICLE IX.

The enumeration in the Constitution of certain rights shall not be construed to deny or disparage others retained by the people.

ARTICLE X.

The powers not delegated to the United States by the Constitution, nor prohibited by it to the States, are reserved to the States respectively, or to the people.

ARTICLE XI.

The judicial power of the United States shall not be construed to extend to any suit in law or equity, commenced or prosecuted against one of the United States by citizens of another State, or by citizens or subjects of any foreign State.

ARTICLE XII.

The electors shall meet in their respective States, and vote by ballot for President and Vice-President, one of whom, at least, shall not be an inhabitant of the same State with themselves; they shall name in their ballots the person voted for as President, and in distinct ballots the person voted for as Vice-President; and they shall make distinct lists of all persons voted for as President, and of all persons voted for as Vice-President, and of the number of votes for each, which lists they shall sign and certify, and transmit sealed to the seat of the government of the United States, directed to the president of the Senate; the president of the Senate shall, in the presence of the Senate and House of Representatives, open all the certificates, and the votes shall then be counted: the person having the greatest number of votes for President shall be the President, if such number be a majority of the whole number of electors appointed; and if no person have such majority, then from the persons having the highest numbers, not exceeding three on the list of those voted for as President, the House of Representatives shall choose immediately, by ballot, the President. But, in choosing the president, the votes shall be taken by States, the representation from each State having one vote; a quorum for this purpose shall consist of a member or members from two-thirds of the States, and a majority of all the States shall be necessary to a choice. And if the House of Representatives shall not choose a President, whenever the right of choice shall devolve upon them, before the fourth day of March next following, then the Vice-President shall act as President, as in the case of the death or other constitutional disability of the President.

The person having the greatest number of votes as Vice-President shall be the Vice-President, if such number be a majority of the whole number of electors appointed; and if no person have a majority, then from the two highest numbers on the list the Senate shall choose the Vice-President: a quorum for the purpose shall consist of two-thirds of the whole number of senators, and a majority of the whole number shall be necessary to a choice.

But no person constitutionally ineligible to the office of President shall be eligible to that of Vice-President of the United States.

AMENDMENTS TO THE CONSTITUTION. 375

ARTICLE XIII.

SECTION 1. — Neither slavery nor involuntary servitude, except as a punishment for crime, whereof the party shall have been duly convicted, shall exist within the United States, or any place subject to their jurisdiction.

SECT. 2. — Congress shall have power to enforce this Article by appropriate legislation.

ARTICLE XIV.

SECTION 1. — All persons born or naturalized in the United States, and subject to the jurisdiction thereof, are citizens of the United States and of the State wherein they reside. No State shall make or enforce any law which shall abridge the privileges or immunities of citizens of the United States; nor shall any State deprive any person of life, liberty, or property, without due process of law, nor deny to any person within its jurisdiction the equal protection of the laws.

SECT. 2. — Representatives shall be apportioned among the several States, according to their respective numbers, counting the whole number of persons in each State, excluding Indians not taxed. But when the right to vote at any election for choice of electors for President and Vice-President of the United States, representatives in Congress, the executive and judicial officers of a State, or the members of the legislature thereof, is denied to any of the male inhabitants of such State, being twenty-one years of age and citizens of the United States, or in any way abridged, except for participation in rebellion or other crime, the basis of representation therein shall be reduced in the proportion which the number of such male citizens shall bear to the whole number of male citizens twenty-one years of age in such State.

SECT. 3. — No person shall be a senator, or representative in Congress, or elector of President and Vice-President, or hold any office, civil or military, under the United States, or under any State, who, having previously taken an oath as a member of Congress, or as an officer of the United States, or as a member of any State legislature, or as an executive or judicial officer of any State, to support the Constitution of the

United States, shall have engaged in insurrection or rebellion against the same, or given aid or comfort to the enemies thereof: but Congress may, by a vote of two-thirds of each house, remove such disability.

SECT. 4. — The validity of the public debt of the United States authorized by law, including debts incurred for payment of pensions, and bounties for services in suppressing insurrection or rebellion, shall not be questioned. But neither the United States, nor any State, shall assume or pay any debt or obligation incurred in aid of insurrection or rebellion against the United States, or any claim for the loss or emancipation of any slave; but all such debts, obligations, and claims shall be held illegal and void.

SECT. 5. — The Congress shall have power to enforce by appropriate legislation the provisions of this Article.

ARTICLE XV.

SECTION 1. — The right of citizens of the United States to vote shall not be denied or abridged by the United States, or by any State, on account of race, color, or previous condition of servitude.

SECT. 2. — The Congress shall have power to enforce this Article by appropriate legislation.

CHRONOLOGICAL TABLE.

[This table has been prepared solely for purposes of reference; and it is particularly advised that, if used in schools, it should not be committed to memory.]

A. D.		PAGE
1000.	Coming of the Northmen	25
1492.	Hispaniola discovered by Columbus	35
1497.	Continent of America discovered by the Cabots	40
1497-98.	South America visited by Americus Vespucius	37
1512.	Florida discovered by Ponce de Leon	43
1513.	Balboa sees the Pacific	43
1524.	The coast of North America explored by Verrazzano	44
1562.	Huguenot settlement at Port Royal	124
1565.	St. Augustine settled by Spaniards	50
1585.	Raleigh's first colony at Roanoke	51
1602.	Gosnold's explorations	51
1603.	New Hampshire visited by Martin Pring	66
1605.	French settlement of Nova Scotia	50
1606.	Formation of London and Plymouth Companies	52
1607.	Jamestown settled by London Company. Popham landed in Maine	53
1608.	Flight of Scrooby Independents to Holland	55
1609.	Hudson River discovered by Henry Hudson	88
	Champlain explored Vermont	67
1614.	Adrian Block explored the coast of Connecticut, and named Block Island	71
	New York settled by the Dutch	91
	Capt. John Smith explored the coast of New England as far as Maine	115

378 YOUNG FOLKS' UNITED STATES.

A. D.		PAGE
1619.	Negro slavery introduced in Virginia	117
1620.	Landing of Pilgrims at Plymouth	58
	Formation of second Plymouth company	117
1621.	Formation of Dutch West-India Company	92
1623.	Portsmouth and Dover settled. The Dutch began to colonize New York	66
1628.	Settlement by Endicott at Salem	61
1629.	Formation of Massachusetts Company. Francis Higginson's emigration. Winthrop's emigration	62
	Grant of Maryland to the first Lord Baltimore	121
1633.	Connecticut settled at Windsor	71
1634.	Maryland settled at St. Mary's	121
1635.	Colony at Saybrook, Ct., Hartford, and Wethersfield	71
1636.	Settlement of Rhode Island by Roger Williams	69
	Harvard College founded	86
1637.	Pequot War in Connecticut	134
1638.	New Haven settled	72
	Delaware settled by Swedes	107
1639.	Connecticut settlements united as the Connecticut Colony	72
	First printing-press in New England	86
1643.	First New England Confederation	83
1645.	Clayborne's Rebellion in Maryland	122
1663.	Carolina granted to Shaftesbury and others	124
1664.	New Netherlands taken by the English, and named New York	97
	Settlement of Elizabethtown in New Jersey	99
1665.	Connecticut and New Haven Colonies united	73
1675.	King Philip's War	137
1676.	Bacon's Rebellion in Virginia	139
1682.	Pennsylvania settled by William Penn	102
	La Salle explored the Mississippi	244
1687.	Connecticut charter hid in the Charter Oak	83
1689.	Andros seized and sent to England	83
	King William's War	143
1692.	Salem witchcraft delusion	81

CHRONOLOGICAL TABLE.

A. D.		PAGE
1692.	William and Mary College founded in Virginia	118
1700.	Yale College founded in Connecticut	86
1702.	Queen Anne's War	143
1703.	Delaware and Pennsylvania permanently separated	108
1729.	North and South Carolina permanently separated	127
1732.	Washington born in Virginia, Feb. 22	149
1733.	Georgia settled by Oglethorpe	128
1744.	King George's War	143
1745.	Louisburg taken from the French	148
1753.	Washington sent as a commissioner to the Ohio Valley	149
1754.	Washington defeated the French at Great Meadows	150
1755.	Expulsion of Acadians	151
	Braddock's defeat	153
1759.	Wolfe captured Quebec	155
1763.	Peace of Paris. Cession of Canada. Pontiac's War	156
1765.	Parliament passed the Stamp Act	161
	Patrick Henry's resolutions in the Virginia Assembly	163
	Congress of nine colonies met in New York. Declaration of Rights, and petition to the King. Stamp-officer hung in effigy	164
	Hutchinson House destroyed	165
1766.	Stamp Act repealed, May 1	165
1767.	Duty imposed on tea and other imports, June 29. British troops arrived in Boston, Sept. 27	166
1770.	Boston Massacre, March 5	168
1772.	Destruction of the "Gaspee." June 10	169
1773.	All duties repealed except on tea. Boston Tea Party, Dec. 16	171
1774.	Boston Port Bill put in force. June 1	173
	First Continental Congress met at Philadelphia, Sept. 5	176
1775.	Battle of Lexington, April 19	178-183
	Allen and Arnold captured Ticonderoga, May 10	183

A. D.		PAGE
1775.	Washington chosen commander-in-chief, June 15	189
	Battle of Bunker Hill, June 17	183-187
	Washington took command of the American army at Cambridge, Mass., July 3. Montreal surrendered to Montgomery. Nov. 13. Montgomery defeated and slain at Quebec, Dec. 31. . .	189
1776.	Boston evacuated by the British, March 17 . .	192
	Congress adopted the Declaration of Independence, July 4	198
	British repulsed at Fort Moultrie, S. C., June 28. Battle of Long Island, Aug. 27. [The American forces under Gen. Putnam were here hemmed in, and cut to pieces. Greenwood Cemetery is part of the battle-field.] Washington defeated at White Plains, Oct. 28. The British captured Fort Washington, Nov. 16. Washington victorious at Trenton, Dec. 26.	203
1777.	Washington victorious at Princeton, Jan. 3 Battle of Brandywine, Sept. 11. [An unavailable attempt of the American troops to save Philadelphia. The army was preserved from overwhelming defeat by Gen. Greene.] Howe occupied Philadelphia, Sept. 26. Army went into winter quarters at Valley Forge, Dec. 11 . . .	204
	Tryon's expedition against Connecticut, April 26. Ticonderoga captured by Burgoyne, July 5. Americans defeated at Hubbardton, July 7. Prescott captured by Barton, July 10. Battle of Bennington, Aug. 16	205
	Americans repulsed at Germantown, Oct. 4. Battle of Saratoga, Oct. 7. Burgoyne surrendered to Gates. Oct. 17	206
1778	France acknowledged the independence of the United States, Feb. 6	206
	British evacuated Philadelphia, June 18. Battle of Monmouth, June 28. [Washington, intercepting Clinton as he was withdrawing his army from	

CHRONOLOGICAL TABLE. 381

A. D.		PAGE
	Philadelphia, came up with him at Monmouth. Gen. Lee's forces, prematurely retreating, were met and rallied by Washington, who sharply rebuked their commander. The British, however, got away in the night, and escaped defeat.] Battle and massacre at Wyoming, July 3. American victory at Quaker Hill, R. I. Massacre at Cherry Valley, Nov. 11. Campbell captured Savannah, Dec. 29	207
1779.	"Mad Anthony" Wayne took Stony Point, July 15. Victory of Paul Jones, Sept. 23	207
1780.	Major André executed as a spy, Oct. 2	209
1781.	Articles of Confederation ratified by the States. Arnold's expedition against New London, Sept. 6. Battle of Eutaw Springs, Sept. 8. Yorktown besieged by Americans and French, Sept. 30	211
	Cornwallis surrendered at Yorktown, Oct. 19	212
1782.	A preliminary treaty of peace was signed at Paris between Great Britain and the United States, Nov. 30	212
1783.	Savannah evacuated by the British, July 11. New York evacuated by the British, Nov. 25. Charleston evacuated by the British, Dec. 14	212
	Washington resigned his commission to Congress, Dec. 23. A definite treaty of peace signed at Paris between Great Britain and the United States, Nov. 30	213
	The American army disbanded, Nov. 3	214
1786.	Shays' Rebellion in Massachusetts	214
1787.	Slavery excluded from Northwest Territory by act of Congress	231
	Philadelphia Convention adopted the Constitution of the United States	215
1788.	The Constitution of the United States went into effect	215
1789.	North Carolina accepted the Constitution	215

A. D.		PAGE
1789.	George Washington inaugurated President of the United States	217
1790.	Rhode Island accepted the Constitution	215
	Franklin died. Indian War	226
1791.	Vermont admitted to the Union	229
	United States Bank established at Philadelphia. John Adams elected President	231
1792.	Eli Whitney invented the cotton-gin	226
	Kentucky admitted to the Union	229
1795.	Jay's treaty with Great Britain ratified	220
1796.	Tennessee admitted to the Union	230
1797.	John Adams became President	231
1799.	Washington died at Mount Vernon	233
1800.	The city of Washington made the seat of government	232
	A treaty of peace made with France	233
1801.	Thomas Jefferson elected President	235
	Tripoli declared war against the United States	237
1802.	Ohio admitted to the Union	243
1803.	Louisiana bought of Napoleon	245
	Expedition of Lewis and Clark	246
1804.	Decatur destroyed the frigate "Philadelphia"	238
	Burr killed Hamilton in a duel	242
1807.	Robert Fulton launched his steamboat	241
	The "Leopard" attacked the American frigate "Chesapeake"	236
	Congress laid an embargo on American ships	236
1809.	Congress forbade commerce with England and France. Madison became President	248
1811.	Victory of Gen. Harrison at Tippecanoe	249
1812.	United States at war with Great Britain. Gen. Hull invaded Canada. Gen. Hull surrendered Detroit. American frigate "Constitution" captured the "Guerrière," Aug. 19. Americans defeated at Queenstown. The American sloop "Wasp" captured "The Frolic." American frigate "United States" captured "The Mace-	

CHRONOLOGICAL TABLE. 383

| A. D. | | PAGE |

donian." The American frigate "United States"
took "The Java." Convention at Hartford
called 248–9
Louisiana admitted to the Union 253
1813. The British frigate "Shannon" took "The Chesapeake," June 1 249
Perry gained his victory on Lake Erie, Sept. 10 . 250
Creek war 249
1814. The British entered Washington, and fired the public buildings. The treaty of peace signed at Ghent 251
1815. Jackson defeated the British at New Orleans, Jan. 8 251
1816. The Bank of the United States rechartered for twenty years. Indiana admitted to the Union . 253
1817. Monroe became President, March 4. First Seminole War 253
Mississippi admitted to the Union 257
1818. Jackson went against the Seminoles . . . 253
Illinois admitted to the Union 254
1819. Treaty made with Spain that gave Florida to the United States 254
Alabama admitted to the Union 255
1820. Maine admitted to the Union 255
Missouri compromise 256
1821. Missouri admitted to the Union 255
1824. Lafayette visited the United States . . . 256
1825. John Quincy Adams became President . . . 259
Erie Canal opened 260
1826. Deaths of Jefferson and Adams, July 4 . . . 261
1827. First railroad in the United States. Attempt to purchase Texas from Mexico 260
1829. Andrew Jackson became President . . . 262
1830. First appearance of Mormons 270
1831. Anti-slavery agitation. Benjamin Lundy. William Lloyd Garrison. Insurrection of Nat Turner . 266
1832. South Carolina declares the doctrine of Nullification 263

A.D.		PAGE
1832.	Black Hawk War	264
	Jackson vetoed the bill for the National Bank. Antislavery Society founded	265
1835.	Second Seminole War	264
1836.	Arkansas admitted to the Union	266
	Texas declares her independence of Mexico.	272
1837.	Michigan admitted to the Union	266
	Martin Van Buren became President	267
	Lovejoy killed. Mobs in Boston	268
1841.	William Henry Harrison became President, March 4. Death of President Harrison, April 4. John Tyler inaugurated President, April 6.	269
1842.	Seminole War ended	264
	Ashburton treaty completed. Dorrite War in Rhode Island. Anti-rent troubles. Mormons left Nauvoo	270
1845.	Florida admitted into the Union, March 3	271
	Tyler signed the bill for the annexation of Texas, March 1	272
	James K. Polk became President, March 4. First transmission of news by Morse's telegraph	273
	Texas admitted to the Union, Dec. 20	274
1846.	Treaty settling boundary of Oregon	273
	Outbreak of Mexican War	275
	Iowa admitted into the Union	278
1847.	Taylor defeated the Mexicans at Buena Vista	275
	Gen. Scott captured the city of Mexico	276
	Expeditions of Frémont and Kearney	277
1848.	Treaty of Guadalupe Hidalgo	277
	Gold fever	278
	Wisconsin admitted to the Union. Wilmot proviso defeated. Origin of Free-soil party	279
	Departure of Mormons to Utah	282
1849.	Zachary Taylor inaugurated President, March 5	280
1850.	President Taylor died, July 9. Millard Fillmore inaugurated, July 10. Henry Clay's Omnibus Bill passed. California admitted to the Union	280

CHRONOLOGICAL TABLE. 385

A. D.		PAGE
1850.	Fugitive Slave Bill passed	281
1853.	Franklin Pierce inaugurated	282
	Arizona and New Mexico purchased	284
1854.	Missouri Compromise repealed. Kansas-Nebraska Bill passed	282
	Treaty made with Japan	284
1855.	Struggle in Kansas	283
1857.	Buchanan became President	285
1858.	Dred Scott Decision	286
	Minnesota admitted to the Union	292
1859.	Oregon admitted to the Union	292
	John Brown's raid	286
1860.	Abraham Lincoln elected. South Carolina seceded, Dec. 20	289
	General Anderson occupied Fort Sumter, Dec. 26	290
1861.	Southern Confederacy formed	289
	Kansas admitted to the Union, Jan. 29	292
	Jefferson Davis President of the Confederacy, Feb. 18	290
	Fort Sumter attacked, April 12, 13	293
	Lincoln inaugurated, March 4. President Lincoln called for seventy-five thousand troops, April 15. Massachusetts troops mobbed in Baltimore, April 19	294
	Davis offered letters of marque and reprisal, April 17. Lincoln proclaimed a blockade of Southern ports, April 19. Union army routed at Bull Run, July 21	296
	England, France, Spain, and Portugal acknowledged the Confederate States as belligerents. Confederate victory at Ball's Bluff, Oct. 21. Union victory at Port Royal, Nov. 7. Gen. Scott succeeded by Gen. McClellan	297
	Seizure of Mason and Slidell, Nov. 8	298
1862.	Battle of Fair Oaks, May 31. June 1. Seven days' contest before Richmond, June 25, July 1	298
	Battle of Cedar Mountain, Aug. 9. Battles between	

A.D.		PAGE
	Manassas and Washington. Lee invaded Maryland. Sept. 5. Lee defeated at South Mountain, Sept. 14. Harper's Ferry surrendered to Confederates, Sept. 15. Lee defeated at Antietam, Sept. 17	299
1862.	Confederates repulsed at Corinth, Oct. 4. Confederate victory at Fredericksburg, Dec. 13	300
	Engagement between "Monitor" and "Merrimac," March 9	301
	Fort Henry captured by United States gunboats, Feb. 6. Union troops took Roanoke Island, Feb. 8. Island No. 10 captured by Unionists, April 7	302
	Union victory at Shiloh, April 7. New Orleans captured by Unionists, April 25. Fort Pulaski captured by Unionists, April 25. Memphis surrendered to Union troops, June 6	303
	Lincoln's first emancipation proclamation, Sept. 22	305
1863.	Lee's second invasion of Maryland, June 21	306
	Lincoln's second emancipation proclamation, Jan. 1	306
	Union defeat at Chancellorsville, May 3. Union victory at Gettysburg, July 3	306
	Capture of Vicksburg by Union troops, July 4	307
	Capture of Port Hudson by Union troops, July 8. Negro riot in New York, July 13–16. Morgan's raid in Indiana and Ohio, July. Confederate victory at Chickamauga, Sept. 20	308
	Union victory at Chattanooga, Nov. 25. Confederates repulsed before Knoxville, Nov. 29	309
	Fort Wagner taken by Confederates, July 18	310
	West Virginia admitted to the Union, June 20	325
1864.	Union defeat at Olustee, Feb. 20	310
	Grant appointed lieutenant-general, May 3. Grant made commander of Union army, March 12. Red River expedition, March and April. Confederates captured Fort Pillow, April 12. Army of Potomac began a forward movement, May 3. The battle of the Wilderness, May 5, 6. The	

CHRONOLOGICAL TABLE. 387

A. D.		PAGE
	battles near Spottsylvania, May 9. Unionists routed near New Market, May 15. Confederate defeat at Piedmont, June 5	311
1864.	The "Kearsarge" met and sank the "Alabama," June 19. Early invaded Maryland, July 4. Confederate victory on the Monocacy, July 9. Chambersburg sacked and partly burned, July 30. Confederate defeat at Winchester, Sept. 19. Confederate rout at Fisher's Hill, Sept. 22 .	312
	Union mine explosion before Petersburg, July 30. Union victory in Mobile Bay, Aug. 5 . . .	313
	Sherman began his march against Atlanta, May 7. Sherman's victories before Atlanta, July 20, 28. Sherman captured Atlanta, Sept. 2. Confederate repulse at Franklin, Nov. 30. Union victory at Nashville, Dec. 16. Savannah occupied by Sherman's army, Dec. 21.	315
	Union victory at Cedar Creek, Oct. 19. Nevada admitted into the Union, Oct. 31 . . .	325
1865.	Union victory at Averysborough, March 16. Confederate rout at Bentonville, March 20 . .	316
	Unionists captured Fort Fisher, Jan. 15. Sherman captured Columbia, Feb. 17. Charleston occupied by Union troops, Feb. 18. Wilmington taken by Union troops, Feb. 22	316
	Union troops occupied Petersburg and Richmond, April 3	317
	Lee surrendered to Grant, April 9. Gen. J. E. Johnston surrendered to Sherman, April 26. Jefferson Davis captured, May 10 . . .	318
	President Lincoln assassinated, April 14 . .	322
	Andrew Johnson became President, April 15 .	323
	Freedmen's Bureau Bill became a law, March 3. Slavery declared constitutionally abolished, Dec. 18. Conditional amnesty	324
1866.	Congress passed second Freedmen's Bureau Bill over veto, July 16	324

A. D.		PAGE
1867.	Congress passed reconstruction bill over veto, March 2. Congress passed Tenure of Office Bill over veto, March 2	324
	Nebraska admitted to the Union, March 1. Alaska purchased, June 20	325
1868.	House of Representatives impeached President Johnson, Feb. 24. Fourteenth constitutional amendment adopted, July 28	324
	President Johnson acquitted, May 26	325
1869.	Ulysses S. Grant became President, March 4	326
1870.	The fifteenth amendment declared adopted	326
1871.	The Alabama treaty concluded, May 6. The great fire of Chicago occurred Oct 7, 8, 9	326
1873.	Grant inaugurated for a second term	326
1876.	Centennial celebration. Colorado admitted.	330
	Disputed presidential election. Electoral commission	331
1877.	Rutherford B. Hayes became President, March 5	334
1879.	Resumption of specie payments, Jan. 1	338
1881.	James A. Garfield became President, March 4	341
	President Garfield shot and mortally wounded, July 2	341
	President Garfield died, Sept. 19	341
	Chester A. Arthur became President, Sept. 20	342
1885.	Grover Cleveland became President, March 4	343
1885.	The Civil Service Act becomes a law	343

INDEX.

A.

ACADIA, 152.
Acton, Mass., 180.
Adams, John, President, 176, 196, 197, 217, 221, 231, 239, 261.
Adams, J. Q., President, 259, 260, 261, 262, 268.
Adams, Samuel, 172, 179, 182, 221.
Alabama, 234, 255, 257, 289.
"Alabama," The, 312.
Alaska, 325.
Albany, N. Y., 90, 95, 151, 241.
"Albemarl," The, 314.
Alleghany River, The, 150, 152.
Alexandria, Va., 296.
Algonquins, The, 18.
Alien and Sedition Laws, 233.
Allen, Ethan, 68, 183, 229.
Allston, W., 328.
Alton, Ill., 268.
Americus Vespucius, 37.
Anderson, Major Robert, 290.
André, Major John, 210.
Andros, Sir Edmund, 83.
Animals, Extinct, 2.
Annapolis, Md., 173, 295.
Antietam, Md., Battle of, 299.
Antislavery Societies, 265, 268.
Appomattox, Va., Lee's Surrender at, 318.
Aquidneck, 70.
Arizona, 284.
Arlington Heights, Va., 296.
"Ark," The, 121.
Arkansas, 266, 291.
Arnold, Gen. Benedict, 209, 210, 211.
Arnold, Gov. Benedict, 25, 26.
Arthur, Chester A., 340-342.

Astor, J. J., 247, 253.
Astoria, 247.
Atlanta, Ga., Capture of, 315.
Atlantic Cable, The, 328.
Atlantic Ocean, 13, 31, 32, 33, 35, 52.
Attucks, Crispus, 169.

B.

BACON, NATHANIEL, 139.
Bainbridge, Captain, 237.
Bailey, Colonel, 311.
Balboa, 43.
Ball's Bluff, Va., 297.
Baltimore, Md., 273, 294, 295.
Baltimore, George, Lord, 121.
Baltimore, Cecil, Lord, 121, 122.
Banks, Gen. N. P., 298, 310.
Barré, Colonel, 162, 163.
Baton Rouge, La., 293.
Beauregard, General, 291, 302.
Bennington, Vt., 205.
Berkeley, Governor, 139.
Berkeley, Lord, 99.
Big Bethel, Va., 296.
Blaine, James G., 343.
"Blessing of the Bay," The, 84.
Block, Adrian, 71, 91.
Block Island, 79, 91.
"Bonhomme Richard," The, 207, 208.
Boone, Daniel, 230.
Booth, Wilkes, 322.
Border Ruffians, 283, 286.
Boston, Mass., 62, 83, 86, 87, 164, 166, 167, 169, 171, 172, 174, 175, 178, 179, 181, 182, 183, 184, 189, 191, 192, 200, 202, 227, 259.

Boston Massacre, The, 169.
"Boston Newsletter," The, 86.
Boston Port Bill, 173, 174, 175.
"Bounty-jumpers," 306.
Braddock, General, 153, 154, 157.
Bradford, Governor, 133.
Brainard, David, 136.
Brandywine, Battle of, 204.
Breed's Hill, 183, 184.
Brewster, Elder, 60.
Brown, Capt. John, 283, 286, 288.
Bryant, W. C., 328.
Buchanan, James, President, 285, 286.
Buell, Gen. D. C., 302.
Buena Vista, Battle of, 275, 276.
Bull Run, Battles of, 296, 299.
Bunker Hill, Battle of, 178, 183, 188, 189, 192, 194, 206.
Burgoyne, General, 205, 206.
Burke, Edmund, 174.
Burns, Anthony, 281.
Burnside, Gen. A. E., 300, 302.
Burr, Aaron, 242, 243.
Butler, Gen. B. F., 295, 303, 304.
Buttrick, Major, 180.

C.

CABOT, JOHN, 40, 41, 51.
Cabot, Sebastian, 38, 40, 41, 42, 51.
Calhoun, J. C., 263, 272.
California, 277, 278, 280, 281.
Calvert, Leonard, 121.
Cambridge, Mass., 86, 87, 136, 174, 184, 189, 191, 200.
Canada, 18, 45, 50, 51, 52, 66, 95, 136, 139, 146, 147, 148.
Canals, 260.
Canonicus, 69.
Cape Ann, 67, 115.
Cape Charles, 113.
Cape Cod, 49, 61, 71, 89, 92.
Cape Henry, 113.
Carolinas, The, 124, 127.
Carteret, Sir George, 99.
Carver, John, 59.
Casey, General, 298.
Castle, William, 169, 191.
Cedar Creek, Va., Battle of, 312.
Cedar Mountain, Va., Battle of, 299.
Census of United States, 231, 234,

252, 257, 266, 269, 282, 292, 326, 336.
Centennial Celebration, 330.
Central America, 7.
Cerro Gordo, 276.
Champlain, Lake, 205, 209.
Chapultepec, 276.
Charles River, 115, 179.
Charleston, S. C., 126, 173, 202, 205, 207, 208, 212, 290, 291, 310, 316.
Charlestown, Mass., 62, 178, 179, 184.
Charlestown, Va., 288.
Charters, 52, 82, 84, 101, 110, 130, 160.
Chase, S. P., 327.
Chattanooga, Tenn., Battle of, 309.
Chesapeake Bay, 112, 121.
"Chesapeake," The, 236, 249, 250.
Chickamauga, Tenn., 308.
Chickasaws, The, 263.
Chihuahua, 277.
Chilton, Mary, 58.
Choctaws, The, 263.
Christiana, Del., 107, 108.
Church, Captain, 138.
Churubusco, 276.
Civil Service Act, 343.
Civil War, The, 293.
Clark, Capt. William, 245, 246.
Clayborne, Capt. William, 121, 122.
Clay, Henry, 280.
"Clermont," The, 241, 242.
Cleveland, Grover, 343.
Clinton, De Witt, 260.
Clinton, General, 202.
Coddington, William, 70.
Coins, early, in New England, 85.
Colorado, 2, 337.
Colored Troops, 305, 311, 317, 319.
Columbus, Christopher, 31, 40.
Columbia River, 246, 247, 253, 273.
Columbia, District of, 280.
"Columbia," The, 246.
"Common Sense," 195.
Compromise Measures, 280.
Concord, Mass., 179, 180, 181, 198.
Confederacy, The, 297.
Confederation, The, 214, 215.
Congress, Continental, 164, 176, 189, 194, 200.
Connecticut, 66, 71, 72, 73, 83, 84, 87, 96, 137, 148, 159, 165, 183, 196, 268.
Connecticut River, 92.

Constitution, Federal, The, 215, 216, 254, 256, 333.
"Constitution," The, 249.
Continental Army, 199.
Cook, Captain, 155.
Cooper, Peter, 331.
Copley, J. S., 328.
Cotton Gin, The, 226.
Cotton, Rev. John, 136.
Crown Point, 154.
Cuba, 37, 47.
Cumberland, Md., 252.
Cushing, Lieutenant, 314.
Cushing, Mrs., 164.
Cuttyhunk, Mass., Settlement at, 51.

D.

DAHLGREN, ADMIRAL, 315.
Dare, Virginia, 52.
Dark and Bloody Ground, The, 230.
"Daughters of Liberty," 173.
Davis, Capt. Isaac, 180.
Davis, Jefferson, 290, 317, 318.
Debt, National, 318, 326.
Decatur, Lieutenant, 237, 238.
Declaration of Rights, 164.
Declaration of Independence, 194, 197, 199, 202, 213, 216, 228, 232, 235, 261.
Deerfield, Mass., 146, 147.
De Kalb, General, 204.
Delaware, 93, 105, 106, 108, 159.
De la Ware, Lord, 106, 117.
Delaware River, 108, 203, 241.
Democratic Party, 221, 235, 267, 273, 282, 285, 331.
De Soto, 230, 244.
Detroit, Mich., 157, 158, 249.
Dighton Rock, 26.
Doniphan, Colonel, 277.
Dorchester, Mass., 62.
Dorchester Heights, 183, 192.
Dorr War, The, 270.
"Dove," The, 121.
Dover, N. H., 66.
Dred Scott Decision, 285.
Druillettes, Father, 136.
Dudingston, Lieutenant, 169.
Dupont, Admiral, 310.
Duston, Thomas, 144.
Dutch Times in New York, 88.

E.

EARLY, GEN. JUBAL, 312.
East Cambridge, Mass., 179.
Elberon, N. J., 341.
Electoral Commission, 333.
Eliot, Rev. John, 136.
Elizabethtown, N. J., 99.
El Molino del Rey, 276.
Ellsworth, Colonel, 296.
Emancipation Proclamations, 305, 306.
Embargo, The, 236.
Emerson, R. W., 328.
Endicott, John, 61, 74.
English, William H., 340.
Ericsson, Captain, 301.
Erie Canal, The, 260.
"Essex," The, 250.
Everett, Edward, 265.
Everglades, The, 263, 264.

F.

FAIRBANKS, JONAS, 78.
Fair Oaks, Battle of, 298.
Fall River, Mass., 26, 137.
Faneuil Hall, 172.
Farragut, Admiral, 303, 313.
Fifteenth Amendment, The, 326.
Fillmore, Millard, President, 280.
Fitch, John, 241.
Five Nations, The, 127, 150.
Flag, United States, 199.
Florida, 42, 47, 52, 77, 126, 128, 129, 253, 254, 263, 264, 289, 331.
"Flying Machine," The, 106.
Flynt, Alice, 78.
Forrest, General, 311.
Fort Donelson, 302.
Fort Du Quesne, 152, 154, 177.
Fort Fisher, 316.
Fort Hatteras, 297.
Fort Moultrie, 290, 291.
Fort Pillow Massacre, 311, 319.
Fort Pulaski, 302.
Fort St. George, 53.
Fort Sumter, 290, 291, 293.
Fort Wagner, 310.
Fortress Monroe, 236.
Foster, General, 315.

Fox, C. J., 174.
Foxes, The, 263.
Franklin, Dr. Benjamin, 151, 194, 195, 206, 227, 328.
Frederic City, Md., 299.
Fredericksburg, Va., 300.
Freedmen's Bureau, 324.
Freesoil Party, 279, 280.
Frémont, Gen. J. C., 277, 305.
French and Indian Wars, 139, 141.
Frietchie, Barbara, 299.
Fugitive Slave Law, 281.
Fulton, Robert, 241.

G.

GADSDEN PURCHASE, THE, 284.
Gage, General, 178, 183, 184.
Garfield, James A., 340.
Garfield, Mrs., 342.
Garner, Margaret, 281.
Garrison, W. L., 264, 265, 268.
"Gaspee," The, 169.
Gates, General, 206.
Geneva Tribunal, The, 326.
"Genius of Universal Emancipation," The, 264.
Georgia, 127, 129, 130, 159, 226, 234, 253, 264, 289, 290.
Germantown, Pa., Battle of, 204.
Gettysburg, Penn., Battle of, 306.
Gillmore, General, 310.
Goffe, William, 138.
Gorton, Samuel, 78.
Gosnold, Bartholomew, 51.
Grant, U. S., President, 302, 311, 312, 316, 326, 335.
Gray, Capt. Robert, 246.
Great March, The, 315.
Greenback Party, 331.
Green Mountain Boys, 229.
Greene, Mrs., 226.
Greene, Gen. Nathanael, 183, 208, 209.
Greenland, 89.
Grierson, Colonel, 308.
Groton, Mass., 174.
Guadalupe Hidalgo, Treaty of, 277, 284.
Gudrid, 29.
"Guerrière," The, 249.
Guilford, Conn., Old House in, 77.
Guiteau, Charles J., 341.

H.

HADLEY, MASS., 137, 138.
Hale, Capt. Nathan, 210.
"Half-Moon," The, 88.
Halifax, N. S., 192.
Hamilton, Alexander, 215, 221, 242.
Hancock, John, 170, 197.
Hancock, Winfield S., 340.
Harper's Ferry, Va., 286, 287, 288.
Harrison, W. H., President, 239, 267, 269, 270.
Hartford, Conn., 71, 96, 173, 249.
Hartford Convention, The, 249.
Harvard University, 86, 118, 184.
Havana, 39.
Haverill, Mass., 144.
Hawley, Major, 176.
Hawthorne, N., 328.
Hayes, Rutherford B., 331-334.
Heights of Abraham, The, 155.
Hendricks, Thomas A., 331, 343.
Henry, Patrick, 163, 164, 176.
Hertel de Renville, 146.
Hessians, The, 193, 203.
Hiawatha, Legend of, 18.
Higginson, Rev. Francis, 62, 63.
Higginson, Rev. John, 87.
Hooker, Gen. J., 72, 306, 309.
Hopeton, O., Mounds at, 7.
Hosmer, Harriet, 328.
Howe, General, 185, 192.
Hudson, Henry, 88.
Hudson River, 90, 150, 181, 209, 241, 270.
Hudson's Bay, 42.
Huguenots, The, 125.
Hull, General, 249.
Humphreys, General, 317.
Hunter, Gen. David, 303, 304, 310.
Hurlgate, 70, 91.
Hurons, The, 13.
Hutchinson, Anne, 70.
Hutchinson, Chief Justice, 165, 172.

I.

ICELAND, 27, 31.
Illinois, 255, 270, 289.
Illinois River, 139, 244.
Immigration, 337.

INDEX. 393

Impeachment of President Johnson, 325.
Inauguration Ball, 224.
India, Voyages in search of, 33, 40, 4 , 49.
Indiana, 252, 256.
Indians, American, 14, 89, 91, 93, 96, 103, 106, 115, 131, 139, 142, 151, 154, 177.
Indians, American, Wars with, 131, 142.
Industry, 339.
International Exhibition, 330.
Iowa, 278, 283.
Iroquois, The, 13.
Irving, W., 328.
Island No. 10, 302.
Isles of Shoals, 115.

J.

JACKSON, ANDREW, PRESIDENT, 251, 253, 262, 263, 265, 306.
Jacksonville, Fla., 310.
Jamaica, 37.
James River, The, 113, 117.
Jamestown, Va., 50, 110, 113, 116, 117, 139.
Jay, John, 220.
Jefferson, Thomas, President, 183, 196, 221, 231, 235, 239, 241, 243, 255.
Jerry Rescue, 281.
Johnson, Andrew, President, 323, 324.
Johnston, Gen. A. S., 302.
Jones, Capt. John Paul, 200, 207.

K.

KANSAS, 282, 284, 286, 335, 337.
Kearny, Gen. Stephen, 277.
"Kearsarge," The, 312.
Kennebec River, 53, 57.
Kent Island, Md., 121.
Kentucky, 229, 230, 231, 252.
Kieft, William, 96.
Kilpatrick, General, 310.
King George's War, 143.
King Philip's War, 137, 138.
King William's War, 143.
King's College, 98.

Know-Nothing Party, 285.
Kosciusko, General, 205.

L.

LABRADOR, 41.
La Fayette, General, 205, 256.
Lake Champlain, 67.
Lake Erie, 250, 260, 285.
Lake Michigan, 243.
Lake Superior, 9.
Lane, Gen. J. H., 283, 306.
La Salle, 244, 271.
Lawrence, Captain, 249.
"Lawrence," The, 250.
Lawrence, Kan., 284.
Lee, Gen. R. E., 189, 299, 318.
Lee, Richard Henry, 195.
Leif the Lucky, 28.
Lewis and Clark's Expedition, 245, 273.
Lewistown, Del., First School for Girls, 105.
Lexington, Mass., 178, 181, 196.
Leyden, 133.
"Liberator," The, 264.
"Liberty and Prop rty," 165.
Liberty Party, 273, 279.
Liberty-Tree, 165, 166.
Lincoln, Abraham, President, 289, 294, 303, 320, 322.
Lincoln, Abraham, President, Extract from Inaugural Address, 320.
Lincoln, Abraham, President, Extract from Gettysburg Address, 329.
Livingston, R. R., 196.
Locke, John, 125.
Logan, John A., 343.
"Log-Cabin Candidate," 269.
London Company, The, 52.
Longfellow, H. W., 18, 26, 328.
Long Island, 71, 96.
Long River, 230.
Lookout Mt., Tenn., Battle of, 309.
Louisburg, 148, 176, 177.
Louisiana Purchase, 230, 244, 266, 278, 282, 292.
Louisiana, State of, 253, 280, 289, 293, 332.
Lovejoy, Rev. E. P., 268.
Lundy, Benjamin, 264.
Lyon, Gen. N., 297.

M.

McCLELLAN, GEN. G. B., 296, 297, 299, 300.
McDowell, General, 296.
Madison, James, President, 248, 253.
Maine, 52, 65, 83, 87, 115, 137, 209, 255, 257, 270.
Malvern Hills, Va., Battle of, 298.
Mammoth, The, 2.
Mandans, The, 246.
Manhattan Island, 91, 99.
Mann, Horace, 281.
Maps, Early, 34, 48, 49, 109.
Marblehead, Mass., 148, 174.
Marietta, O., Mounds at, 10.
Marion, Gen. Francis, 208.
Maroons, The, 264.
Maryland, 42, 70, 121, 122, 123, 159, 160, 165, 285, 295.
Massachusetts, The, 13.
Massachusetts Bay Colony, 60, 72, 74, 200.
Massachusetts, 81, 93, 96, 106, 136, 148, 159, 164, 173, 178, 183, 195, 214, 226, 231, 240, 257, 259, 295.
Mason, Capt. J., 134.
Mason, J. M., 298.
Mason and Dixon's Line, 123.
Mastodon, The, 2.
"Mayflower," The, 56, 57, 59, 61.
Mayhews, The, 136.
Meade, Gen. G. G., 306.
Med, a Slave-Child, 268.
Medford, Mass., 179.
"Merrimack" and "Monitor," Contest of, 300.
Merrimac River, 145.
Merry Mount, 74.
Mexican War, 273, 280, 281, 284.
Mexico, 44, 50, 271, 276, 284.
Mexico, Gulf of, 244.
Michigan, 266.
Minnesota, 292.
Mississippi, 6, 7, 12, 156, 234, 257, 335.
Mississippi River, 139, 230, 234, 243, 244, 252, 293.
Missouri, 255, 270, 283, 286, 297.
Missouri Compromise, The, 256, 282.
Missouri River, 283.
Mobile Bay, Naval Action in, 313.
Mohegans, The, 13.
"Monitor," The, 300.
Monitors, 310, 314.
Monongahela, The, 152.
Monroe, James, President, 2, 8, 253.
Montcalm, General, 155.
Monterey, Battle of, 275.
Monterey, Cal., 277.
Montgomery, General, 283.
Morgan, General, 308.
Mormans, The, 270, 282.
Morosa, a Name for Virginia, 52.
Morse, Prof. S. F. B., 273, 328.
Mound-Builders, The, 14.
Mount Hope, 137.

N.

"NARRAGANSETTS," THE, 13, 26, 69, 138.
Narragansett Bay, 169.
Nashville, Tenn., 302.
Natick, Mass., Indian Village at, 136.
National Road, The, 252.
Nauvoo, Ill., 270.
Nebraska, 282, 284, 325.
Nevada, 325.
New Amsterdam, 91, 93.
New Brunswick, 270.
New Hampshire, 66, 67, 83, 115, 148, 159, 183, 206, 229, 268.
New Haven, Conn., 72, 87.
New Jersey, 98, 99, 140, 159, 203.
New Mexico, 10, 277, 282, 284.
New Netherlands, 72, 91, 93, 95, 97, 107.
New Orleans, La., 150, 251, 252, 262, 303.
New Sweden, 107, 108.
New York, 67, 72, 98, 127, 140, 159, 165, 196, 198, 215, 229, 260, 267, 270, 272, 280, 295.
New York, City of, 44, 91, 103, 106, 166, 173, 109, 202, 203, 211, 212, 217, 218, 241, 260, 295.
Newfoundland, 156.
Newport, R. I., 25, 26, 44, 169, 211.
Newport, Captain, 110.
Niagara, 154.
North Carolina, 44, 159, 179, 215, 231, 291.

INDEX. 395

Northampton, Mass., 176.
Northmen, The, 25, 26, 28.
Northwest Territory, The, 231, 243, 266, 279.
Nova Scotia, 29, 44, 148, 177.
Nueces, River, 274.

O.

OGLETHORPE, GEN. JAMES, 127.
Ohio, 6, 149, 152, 248, 252.
Ohio River, 139, 231, 253.
Old French and Indian War, The, 151.
Old Stone Mill at Newport, R.I., 25.
Old Point Comfort, Va., 113.
Old South Church, Boston, 172.
Oliver, Andrew, 165.
"Onrust," or "Unrest," The, 91.
Ordinance of 1787, 231, 254, 266.
Oregon, 273, 292.
Orleans, Territory of, 253.
Osceola, 264.
Ossawattomie, Kan., 283.
Otis, James, 164.

P.

PACIFIC RAILWAY, THE, 327.
Pacific Ocean, The, 11, 43.
Page, William, 328.
Paine, Thomas, 195, 241.
Palo Alto, Battle of, 274.
Patroons, 92, 270.
Parker, Capt. John, 179.
Parker, Theodore, 281.
Penn, William, 101, 139, 140, 141.
Pennsylvania 101, 104, 107, 123, 139, 140, 159, 195, 203.
Pennsylvania Hall, Burning of, 268.
"Pennsylvania Journal," The, 199.
Pepperrell, Gen. William, 148.
Pequots, The, 13.
Percy, Lord, 182.
Perry, Com. M. C., 276, 284.
Perry, Com. O. H., 250.
Phelps, Gen. J. W., 303.
Philadelphia, Penn., 98, 103, 105, 151, 173, 176, 194, 200, 204, 212, 215, 224, 227, 232, 330.
"Philadelphia," The, 237.

Phillips, Wendell, 281.
Pierce, Franklin, President, 282.
Pilgrims, The, 56, 63, 67, 131.
Pinckney, C. C, 233.
Pine Tree Flag, The, 200.
Pitcairn, Major, 179.
Pitt, William, Earl of Chatham, 165.
Pittsburg, Penn., 152.
Pittsburg Landing, Tenn., Battle of, 302.
Plymouth, Mass., 115.
Plymouth, Mass., Colony, 55, 62, 64, 95, 131.
Plymouth Company, 52.
Pocahontas, 115.
Polk, James K., President, 273.
Pontiac, 249.
Poor Richard's Almanack, 227.
Popham, George, his Colony, 53.
Population, 336.
Port Hudson, Surrender of, 308.
Porter, Com. David, 250.
Port Royal, S. C., 124, 297.
Porto Rico, 37.
Portsmouth, N. H., 66, 67, 87.
Potatoes, Introduction of, 52.
Potomac, 241.
Powers, H., 328.
Powhatan, 115.
Prescott, General, 183, 184, 185.
Preston, Captain, 168.
Price, Dr., 195.
Princeton, N. J., 100, 204.
Pring, Martin, 66.
Privateers, Confederate, 312.
Provincial Congress, 178, 186.
Providence, R. I., 69, 169, 170.
Public Debt, 338.
Pueblo Indians, The, 10.
Pulaski, General, 205.
Puritans, The, 15, 62, 63, 81, 85, 104, 122, 136, 138.
Putnam, Gen. Israel, 177, 183, 184, 185, 186, 187, 191.

Q.

QUAKERS, THE, 80, 81, 99, 106, 119, 122, 140.
Quebec, 150, 155, 156, 177.
Queen Anne's War, 143.
Queen Victoria, 342.
Quincy, Josiah, 240.

R.

Rafn, Professor, 25.
Railroad, First American, 260.
Ramsey, James, 241.
Readjuster Party, 336.
Rebellion, War of the, 285, 291, 293.
Reconstruction Acts, 324.
Red River Expedition, The, 310.
" Redeemed Captive," The, 147.
Reed, Adjutant-General, 199, 207.
Republican Party, 279, 285, 289, 331.
Resaca de la Palma, 274.
Returning Boards, 331.
Revere, Paul, 179.
Revolutionary War, 159, 207, 221, 228, 232, 241, 253, 259.
Rhode Island, 29, 68, 70, 74, 83, 84, 87, 138, 159, 165, 173, 183, 191, 215, 270.
Ribault, Jean, 124.
Richmond, Va., 296, 317.
Rio Grande, The, 274, 277.
Roanoke Island, 51, 302.
Robinson, Rev. John, 56, 133.
Rocky Mountains, 244, 245.
Rosecrans, General, 308.
Roxbury, Mass., 62.
Rumford, Count, 328.

S.

Sacramento River, 277, 278.
Sacs, The, 263.
St. Augustine, Fla., 43, 50, 126, 129, 271.
St. Lawrence, The, 49.
St. Louis, Mo., 246.
" St. Mary's, Pilgrims of," 121.
St. Simons's Island, 129.
Salem, Mass., 61, 62, 63, 87, 95.
Salt Licks, Ky., 230.
Sandy Hook, 89.
San Francisco, Cal., 278.
Sanitary Commission, The, 318.
San Juan d'Ulloa, 276.
Santa Anna, General, 275.
Saratoga, N. Y., 206.
Savannah, Ga., 128, 129, 212, 226.
Saxton, Gen. Rufus, 306.
Schofield, Gen., 316.
Schoolcraft, H. R., 19.

Schuyler, Philip, 189.
Schuylkill River, The, 201.
Scott, Gen. Winfield, 206, 263, 275, 296, 297.
Seguin, 71.
Semmes, Captain, 313.
Seminoles, The, 253, 263.
" Serapis," The, 207, 208.
" Seven Days' Battles, The," 298.
Sewell, Chief Justice, 82, 87.
Seward, W. H., 322, 327.
Seymour, General, 310.
Shadrach Rescue, The, 281.
Shaw, Colonel, 312.
Shays' Rebellion, 214.
" Shenandoah," The, 312.
Sheridan, Gen. P. H., 312, 316, 317, 318.
Sherman, Gen. W. T., 309, 311, 315.
Shoshones, The, 246.
Six Nations, The, 13, 127, 150.
" Skeleton in Armor," The, 26.
Skraelings, The, 29.
Slavery, American, 87, 92, 104, 117, 123, 126, 268, 271, 279, 280.
Slidell, J., 298.
Smith, Capt. J., 58, 65, 110, 114, 116.
Smith, Joseph, 270.
South Carolina, 52, 129, 159, 173, 208, 238, 262, 263, 265, 289, 290, 297, 335.
South Mountain, Va., Battle of, 299.
Specie Payments, 338.
"Speedwell," The, 56, 57.
Spencer, General, 183.
Stamp Act, The, 161, 162, 163, 165, 166.
Standish, Lora, 59.
Standish, Capt. Miles, 58, 59, 78, 133.
Stanton, E. M., 327.
Stark, Gen. John, 183, 205, 206.
Stark, Molly, 206.
" Star of the West," The, 290.
State Rights, 289.
Staten Island, 91.
Steamboat, the first, 241.
Stephens, A. H., 290, 291.
Steuben, General, 205.
Stillwater, N. Y., Battle of, 206.
Stockton, Commodore, 277.
Stonington, Conn., 134.
Stony Mountains, The, 246.

INDEX. 397

Stony Point, N.Y., Storming of, 207.
Story, W. W., 328.
Stuyvesant, Peter, 97, 108.
Suffrage, Universal, 239, 327.
Sumner, Charles, 281, 327.
Sumter, Gen. Thomas, 208.
Sutter, Captain, 278.
Snorri, 29.
Sylvania, 102.

T.

TARIFF, THE, 261, 262.
Taylor, Zachary, President, 274, 275, 280.
Tea-party, Boston, 172.
Tecumseh, 249, 269.
Telegraph, the, 273.
Tennessee, 230, 231, 291.
" Tennessee," The, 314.
Terry, Gen. A. H., 316.
Texas, 267, 268, 271, 277, 289, 338.
" The Selling of Joseph," a tract, 87.
Thomas, General, 309.
Thompson, John, Hatter, 197.
Ticonderoga, 154, 183, 205.
" Tiger," The, 91.
Tilden, Samuel J., 331.
Tippecanoe, O., 249, 269.
Tobacco, Introduction of, 52.
Toleration, Religious, 68, 99, 103, 122, 216.
Tories, The, 176.
Townshend, Charles, 162.
Treaties, 19, 151, 156, 206, 213, 220, 233, 237, 251, 254, 277, 284, 326.
Trenton, N. J., 203, 217.
Tri-mountain, 62.
Turner, Nat., 265.
Tuscaroras, The, 126.
Tyler, John, 269, 270, 271.
Tyrker, 28.

U.

UNDERHILL, CAPTAIN, 134.
United Colonies, 177, 196.
United States, 199, 215.
United States Constitution, 215.
United States Troops, 335.
University of Pennsylvania, 105.
Upper California, 277.
Utah, 271, 282.

V.

VALLEY FORGE, PENN., 204, 206.
Van Buren, Martin, President, 267, 268, 269.
Van Rensselaer, General, 249.
Vera Cruz, Mexico, 275, 276.
Vermont, 67, 83, 206, 229.
Verrazzano, 44, 45.
Vespucius, Americus, 37.
Vicksburg, Miss., 304, 307.
Vinland, 29, 31, 33, 34.
Virginia, 51, 52, 53, 56, 86, 106, 109, 110, 139, 152, 154, 159, 163, 164, 175, 189, 190, 195, 196, 217, 229, 230, 233, 234, 236, 240, 248, 253, 254, 265, 270, 286, 288, 291, 296, 297, 335.

W.

WADSWORTH, WILLIAM, 83, 84.
Walking Purchase, The, 141.
Wampanoags, 13.
Warner, Seth, 229.
Ward, Gen. Artemas, 183, 189.
Warren, Gen. G. K., 317.
Warren, Gen. Joseph, 177, 184, 185.
Washington, George, President, 149, 150, 152, 153, 154, 177, 189, 190, 191, 192, 211, 212, 214, 215, 217, 218, 220, 221, 222, 224, 225, 226, 229, 231, 233, 239, 255, 283, 286, 288, 295, 296, 297.
Washington, Mrs. Martha, 223.
Washington, D. C., 232, 251.
Watertown, Mass., 69.
Wayne, Gen. Anthony, 207.
Webster, Daniel, 270, 281.
Weitzel, Gen. G., 317.
" Welcome," The, 102.
Wentworth, Benning, 67.
Wesley, Rev. Charles, 129.
Wesley, Rev. John, 129.
West Point, N. Y. 209, 210.
West Virginia, 325.
Whalley, Richard, 138.
Wheeler, William A., 331.
Wheeling, Va., 252.
White, Peregrine, 59.
Whitenfeld, Rev. George, 129.
Whitfield, Rev. Henry, 76.
White Plains, 203.

Whitney, Eli, 226.
Whittier, J. G., 299, 328.
William and Mary College, 118.
Williams, Rev. John, 146.
Williams, Rev. Roger, 68, 70, 134.
Wilmot Proviso, The, 279.
Windham, Conn., 174.
Windsor, Conn., 71.
Winslow, Captain, 138.
Winthrop, John, 62, 63, 64, 67, 69.
Wisconsin, 278, 279.
Wise, Governor, 288.

Wolfe, General, 155, 162.
Worcester, Mass., 178.
Worden, Commodore, 301.
Wyoming, Penn., 207.

Y.

Yale College, 86, 226.
York River, 211.
Yorktown, Va., 211, 212.
Young, Brigham, 282.

QUESTIONS.

CHAPTER I.

How much do we know about the first men and women who lived on the North American continent?

What changes have there been in the surface of the continent?

What animals, now extinct, have lived here in past times?

Describe the cloven-footed animals.

Describe the mammoth and the mastodon.

How is it supposed that these animals may have perished?

What reason have we to think that men may have lived at the same time with these animals?

CHAPTER II.

What race of men followed the period of the mammoths?

How do we know that they did not live at the same time with the mammoths?

What great works did they leave?

Describe the serpent-mound.

For what were the higher mounds probably built?

How did the mound-builders show engineering skill?

What arts did they understand?

How can we judge of their numbers?

Describe the mine left by them near Lake Superior.

How can we judge of the time when they lived?

How far did they resemble the American Indians?

Describe the Pueblo Indians.

How can we judge whence the mound-builders came?

How many Asiatic vessels have been driven across the Pacific by storms?
How do we know that the mound-builders had seen the ocean?

CHAPTER III.

Who occupied the coast of North America when the first European explorers came?
Give the names of some of the tribes.
To how many great families did they belong?
Describe the dwellings of the Indians.
Describe their pursuits and ways of living.
What were their habits of physical activity?
How did they dress?
What was their food?
What were their manufactures?
Describe their two most ingenious inventions.
How were their tribes distinguished?
What were their legends and beliefs?
What money did they use?
Show how they communicated with one another, by drawing on bark.
What were their virtues and vices?
Describe a war-feast.
Describe their modes of making war.
What has been their history, since the arrival of Europeans?

CHAPTER IV.

What is the "Old Stone Mill" at Newport, R.I.?
To what early explorers has it been attributed?
What is the "Dighton Rock"?
What was the "Skeleton in Armor"?
What is now supposed to have been the origin of these various objects?
Who were the Northmen?
What colonies did they found?
What are their traditions as to the discovery of Vinland?
What were the adventures of Leif the Lucky?

QUESTIONS. 7

Describe the interviews between the Northmen and the Skrael-ings.
What is supposed to have been the true position of Vinland?
Why is it hard to know this position with certainty?
Have we yet any positive knowledge as to the supposed visit of the Northmen?

CHAPTER V.

How long was it before any more Europeans crossed the Atlantic?
How was the tradition of the voyages of the Northmen preserved?
What sailors used to visit Iceland?
Who was Christopher Columbus?
What was his early life?
What plan of discovery had he formed?
How did ignorant people then suppose the earth to be shaped?
How did scientific men suppose it to be shaped?
Describe the map made by a friend of Columbus.
What names of places does it show on the American continent?
Where did Columbus expect to arrive, by crossing the Atlantic?
What evidence had convinced him that he could reach India?
What may he have heard in Iceland?
To whom did he go for aid?
Who aided him finally?
With what vessels did he sail?
When did he sail?
Describe the voyage.
How long was it?
Where did he land?
Describe his second voyage.
When was his third voyage?
What did Americus Vespucius discover?
When did he discover it?
How came the continent to bear his name?
Who reached the North American coast before Columbus?
What happened to Columbus on his third voyage?
What was the last voyage of Columbus?

What continent did he suppose himself to have visited?
When did he die?
Where was he buried?

CHAPTER VI.

Who was John Cabot?
What was his patent?
When did he sail?
Describe their voyage.
What honors were paid John Cabot?
Describe Sebastian Cabot's voyage.
Describe his old age.
Who was Ponce de Leon?
Why did he visit Florida?
When did he sail?
When did he see land?
From what did the name of Florida come?
Where did Ponce de Leon land?
When did he come again?
What did Balboa discover?
What did he do on reaching the Pacific Ocean?
What did Cortez conquer?
What did Pizarro conquer?
Who was Verrazzano?
When did he sail?
Describe his voyage.
How did he describe the Indians?
How did the coast look when he approached it?
What treasures did he think he had found?
What did the King of France say?

CHAPTER VII.

What voyages to America have been described in this book?
To whom may the first explorers be compared?
How did they describe the new country?
For what did the different nations seek?
Where did they suppose India to be?
How did their maps vary?

QUESTIONS.

How could they decide who should own the lands they visited?
What was the first permanent European settlement?
By whom was it made? and when?
By what names did they call what is now called North America?
How is it represented on the early globes?
What efforts did the English make to settle North America?
What did they call it? and why?
What unsuccessful colonies were founded?
What did Sir Walter Raleigh carry from America to England?
What companies did King James I. charter?
What territory did he give them?
How did the books of that day describe this territory?
How did King James divide it?
What were the two companies named?
What happened to the southern colony?
What happened to the northern colony?
What account did the colonists give?
Which was the first English colony?
What order will be followed in describing the colonies?

CHAPTER VIII.

What was the name of the earliest New England colony?
What troubles took place in England two centuries and a half ago?
Where did the persecuted Englishmen go?
How did they behave there?
Why did they leave that place?
Why were they called Pilgrims?
How many went first?
What vessels did they procure?
Describe their departure.
Did they have aid from government?
Did they have a royal charter?
How long was their passage?
Where did they intend to land?
Describe their arrival.
Describe their first landing.

When did the whole party land?
What was the harbor named?
Who is said to have landed first?
What government did they form?
Who were their first officers?
How were their soldiers armed?
What did they bring on shore?
What baby was born on "The Mayflower"?
What houses did they build?
Describe their way of living.
How many died the first winter?
How many went home in the spring?
What other colony was founded?
Where did the colonists land?
How long was their voyage?
Describe their approach to the shore.
Who had preceded them?
How many came with this colony?
Who was the leader?
When did they come?
Who followed them the next year?
How did this colony differ from that of Plymouth?
Did they have a charter from the king?
What towns did they found?
What was the difference between the Puritans and the Pilgrims?
What did their leader say on leaving England?
How did they live after landing?
What did they think of the climate?
What did Governor Winthrop say of the colony?
Which colony grew most rapidly?
When were they united?
What does the word Massachusetts mean?

CHAPTER IX.

Who first visited Maine? and when?
Why did the early colonies fail?
What did the name of Maine come from?
What was its connection with Massachusetts?

When were the first towns founded?
How did the Maine settlements differ from those elsewhere?
Was Maine counted as a separate colony?
Who first visited New Hampshire?
When were the first towns settled?
For what purpose were the first settlements?
Through what changes of government did New Hampshire pass?
What had it to do with Vermont?
Whence was the name of New Hampshire derived?
When was Vermont first explored? and by whom?
What was its early history?
What is the derivation of its name?
How, and by whom, was Rhode Island founded?
Who was the founder?
What were his opinions?
What led him to Rhode Island?
When did he arrive?
Whom did he invite to come?
Who were some of those who came?
What was the colony called?
What were their habits as to religious toleration?
What was the feeling of the other colonies towards Rhode Island?
Who first explored Connecticut?
Who were the rival nations who first settled it?
What were the first settlements?
What parties of emigrants came to Connecticut?
What two colonies were established?
How did the troubles between the English and Dutch end?

CHAPTER X.

In what respect were the New England colonies alike?
What was the character of their leaders?
Describe an early New England village on Sunday morning.
Describe the church services.
Describe the houses.
Describe the appearance of the people.

Describe the soldiers.
What were some of the laws of the Puritans?
What was the general aim of their laws?
What did they declare to be the object of their colony?
Why were they especially tempted to persecute those who differed from them?
Describe their treatment of the Quakers.
What foolish things did some of the more excited Quakers do?
Describe the witchcraft excitement.
Was it peculiar to Massachusetts?
What effect did it have?
What were the charters of the colonies?
What trouble did they have about these charters?
For what did Sir Edmund Andros come?
What did he accomplish?
What league existed among the New England colonies?
What colonies joined it?
How long did it last?
What effect did the contest about charters have?
What were the occupations of the people?
What did they use for money?
What were their habits as to food, and to amusements?
By what titles were people called?
When were the first colleges and presses established?
What newspapers and books were printed?
What was the history of slavery in New England?

CHAPTER XI.

Who was Henry Hudson?
What were his early voyages?
When did he sail for America?
Describe his voyage.
When did he arrive?
Describe his ascent of the Hudson River.
What became of Henry Hudson?
What is still said of him on the Hudson River?
How came Holland to claim his discoveries?
Who was Adrian Block? and what did he accomplish?

QUESTIONS.

What was New Amsterdam?
What did Manhattan Island cost?
For what was Staten Island named?
Who were the "Patroons"?
How came the Dutch and English settlers to quarrel?
What other troubles had the Dutch settlers?
Describe New Amsterdam and the Dutch way of living.
What festivals did the Dutch introduce?
What was their food?
Who were the "dominies"?
How did the people dress?
What were their pursuits?
Who was "William the Testy"?
Who was "Headstrong Peter"?
How came the colony to be transferred to the English?
What Dutch traits remained?
How many languages were spoken in New York when it was transferred?
What was the early history of New Jersey?
From what was the colony named?
Why was it commonly called "The Jerseys"?
What was the practice as to liberty of conscience?
When were the two provinces united?
What was said by a traveller as to the way of living in New Jersey?

CHAPTER XII.

Who founded the Pennsylvania colony?
Describe William Penn.
How did he obtain the territory?
Why was it named Pennsylvania?
When did William Penn come to America?
What did he promise to the colonists?
Describe his colony.
When did William Penn return to it?
How were the first settlers employed?
Describe Philadelphia in early times.
How many Germans came to the colony in a single year?
What was the rank of Pennsylvania among the colonies, at the time of the Revolution?

Who first explored Delaware? and when?
By what nation was it colonized?
Who was Gustavus Adolphus?
What sort of colony did the Swedes plan?
Who was Queen Christina?
When was the colony at last established?
How did the Dutch and the Swedes agree?
How long was Delaware an independent colony?
To what different nations did it belong?
Did it suffer much from the Indians?

CHAPTER XIII.

What was the first English colony?
Why is Virginia called "The Old Dominion"?
When was the first Virginia settlement made? Where?
Describe Capt. John Smith's early life.
What was the character of the first colony?
What did Captain Smith say about the colonists?
What were some of the punishments that he appointed for them?
How did he describe their way of living?
What voyages did he make along the coast?
What adventures had he with the Indians?
What became of Pocahontas?
What became of Capt. John Smith?
What became of the settlers?
What was the "starving time"?
How did the people of Virginia live?
How was slavery introduced?
How did the people obtain wives?
How did the early governors regard schools?
What were some of the early laws?
How large were the plantations?
How did an early governor go to church?
What old buildings remain in Virginia?
What position had Virginia among the colonies at the time of the Revolution?
How was Maryland settled?
Who obtained a charter for the colony?

When did the first expedition arrive?
Why was the colony called Maryland?
How was it to be governed?
What form of religion prevailed in it?
What religions were protected there?
What religious changes took place afterwards?
What were the habits of the people?
What was "Mason and Dixon's line"?
Why was it important?

CHAPTER XIV.

Who first applied the name of Carolina?
When did the French explorers arrive?
What grant did King Charles I. give?
What was John Locke's plan of government?
Who were the Huguenots?
How did the people live in the southern part of Carolina?
How in the northern part?
What enemies and wars did the colonies have?
How came North and South Carolina to be separated?
Who was the founder of Georgia?
Decribe his life.
When did he send a colony?
For what purpose was it established?
What intercourse did he have with the Indians?
Who were the Moravians?
Who visited him?
Describe the war between Georgia and Florida.
What were some of the laws of Georgia?
How did it become a royal province?
What was the Scotch settlement in Georgia?
What was the success of the silk manufacture there?
What position had Georgia among the colonies at the time of the Revolution?

CHAPTER XV.

Who were the first Indians seen by the Pilgrims at Plymouth?
Who was Samoset?
Who was Massasoit?

What was the first war between the Plymouth settlers and the Indians?
What was the mode of trading with the Indians?
Describe the Pequot War.
What clergymen taught the Indians?
Who was Dreuilletes?
Describe King Philip's war.
What is the tradition of the "Gray Champion" at Hadley, Mass.?
What expedition was sent against the Narragansetts?
What was the fate of King Philip?
What Indian wars took place in New York? In Virginia?
Who was Nathaniel Bacon?
What course did William Penn pursue towards the Indians?
Did he have to deal with the same tribes that inhabited New England and New York?
What was William Penn's elm-tree?
What was the "Walking Purchase"?

CHAPTER XVI.

How was the condition of the Indians altered after white settlers had come?
Why did they prefer the French to the English?
What were the names of the different wars with the French and Indians?
How were these wars carried on?
What was a block-house?
What were the adventures of the Duston family?
Describe the attack on Deerfield.
What had the French missionaries to do with the Indian wars?
What was the Louisburg expedition?
How much of North America did the French claim?
For what was George Washington sent into the wilderness?
What were his adventures?
Who were the "Five Nations"?
Who were the "Six Nations"?
What convention was held at Albany?
What advice did Dr. Franklin give?

What was the removal of the Acadians?
What led to the building of Fort Du Quesne?
Describe Braddock's expedition.
When did it take place?
What effect did it have?
Describe the capture of Quebec.
When was peace made?
Describe the conspiracy of Pontiac?
How did he capture Michilimackinac?
What was the fate of Pontiac?

CHAPTER XVII.

What were the "old thirteen" colonies?
What difference existed among them?
In what were they alike?
What led them to separate from England?
What reason was there for taxing the colonies?
Why did they object?
When was the Stamp Act passed?
What was the Stamp Act?
What did Colonel Barré say about it?
What did Patrick Henry propose?
What did James Otis propose?
What was the first American Congress?
What was it agreed to do in regard to British goods?
What popular excitement took place in Boston? In Maryland? In Rhode Island? In Connecticut? In New York?
What did the Earl of Chatham say?
What was the end of the Stamp Act?
What other act followed?
What complaint did the Boston boys make of the troops?
Describe the Boston Massacre.
When did it take place?
Describe the destruction of the "Gaspee."
What tax was finally insisted upon?
Describe the Boston tea-party.
What happened in New York? Philadelphia? Charleston? Annapolis?

What organizations were formed in New England?
What was the Boston Port Bill?
What effect did it have?
Describe Boston in 1774.
Who were the Tories?
What were their arguments?
What did the patriotic colonists reply?
Why did they feel self-confident?

CHAPTER XVIII.

What brought about the "Provincial Congress"?
What did it do?
What were the British doing?
What watch was kept over them from Charlestown?
What was Paul Revere's ride?
How many British soldiers went out from Boston?
On what day was the battle of Lexington?
Describe it.
What did the minute-men see from the bridge at Concord?
Describe the Concord fight.
Describe the retreat of the British soldiers.
How did it end?
What was said about it in England?
What did Samuel Adams and Thomas Jefferson say about it?
What troops were sent to Boston?
Who commanded them?
What was the state of affairs in Boston?
What was the occasion of the battle of Bunker Hill?
Describe the work done the night before.
Describe the approach of the British.
Describe the main battle.
How many times did the British soldiers advance?
How did the battle end?
What general fell?
What was said about him?

CHAPTER XIX.

What was the effect of the battle of Bunker Hill in America?
What was said about it in England?

What generals were appointed for the army?
Why was Washington appointed?
When did he take command of the army? and where?
What was his appearance?
How did the army appear?
What did it need most?
How was it supplied?
What was the condition of the British?
Describe the play called "The Blockade of Boston."
How did Washington finally drive out the British?
When did General Howe leave the city?
Who went with him to Halifax?
What did the British Government do?
What effect had this on the Americans?

CHAPTER XX.

What had the Continental Congress to do?
What did Dr. Franklin say about the situation?
What was the real state of the colonies?
What did Washington say?
What book had great influence?
Who proposed independence?
What were Lee's famous resolutions?
When were they offered?
What action did the separate colonies take?
Who wrote the Declaration of Independence?
Who criticised it?
What did Jefferson say about the debate?
When was the Declaration adopted?
What did Hancock and Jefferson say about it?
What change was made in it?
What colonies voted for it?
How was its adoption announced?
How did the Pennsylvania Journal describe it?
What was the real state of the army?
What did Adjutant-General Reed say?
What were the first American flags?
What flag was unfurled at Cambridge?

When was the present flag adopted?
Who first unfurled it?
What changes have been made in it?

CHAPTER XXI.

Where had all the fighting been before the Declaration of Independence?
Why did Washington send an army to New York?
What British troops went there?
What trouble did Lord Howe find in sending a letter to General Washington?
What ill success had the American troops?
How many men had Washington in Pennsylvania?
Who were the Hessians?
What plan of attack did Washington form?
How did it end?
What other victory did he gain?
Where did he spend the winter?
Describe the winter at Valley Forge.
What foreign officers had joined the Americans?
What criticisms were made upon Washington?
What did General Burgoyne do?
Describe the battle at Bennington.
What other battles followed?
How did General Burgoyne's expedition end?
What effect had the surrender?
What treaty was made?
What did parliament attempt?
How much aid did France give?
How much longer did the war last?
What was the battle of Stony Point?
What happened at Charleston?
What happened at Wyoming?
What victory did Paul Jones obtain?
What did Marion and Sumter do?
Who was Benedict Arnold?
What treason did he plan?
Describe the capture of André.

What was the fate of Arnold?
What French army had landed?
What led to the defeat of Cornwallis?
When did he surrender?
Describe his surrender.
How was it celebrated?
How long had the war lasted?
What had it cost England?
How long did the British still hold New York?
What was the treaty of Paris?

CHAPTER XXII.

When was the Revolutionary army disbanded?
What was the condition of the colonies?
What was the state of the army?
What was Shays' Rebellion?
What kind of government had the Americans during the war?
Why did they need a stronger one?
What convention was called?
When was the Constitution adopted?
Who urged its adoption?
Which States adopted it?
When did the colonies become a nation?
What celebration took place?
Who were the first President and Vice-President?
What celebration took place at Trenton?
How was Washington received in New York?
Describe the first inauguration.
When did his term of office begin?

CHAPTER XXIII.

In what condition did Washington find the affairs of the nation?
What was soon accomplished?
What was Jay's treaty?
How did Americans feel towards France?

Who were the "Federalists" and the "Democrats"?
How did they differ in regard to public forms and ceremonies?
What was President Washington's way of living?
How did ladies and gentlemen dress in those days?
What amusements prevailed?
What were the chief occupations of the people?
How did people live in the country?
What was the history of the cotton-gin?
What was the career of Benjamin Franklin?
When did he die?
What new States were admitted under Washington's administration, and when?
How did Vermont become an independent colony?
Who was Ethan Allen?
What was the early history of Kentucky?
Who was Daniel Boone?
Who first explored Tennessee?
Who was De Soto?
How was he buried?
What was the proposed State of Franklin?
How many States composed the Union at the end of Washington's administration?
What was the North-west Territory?
How had slavery been excluded from it?
What was the population of the United States in 1790?
How long was Washington president?
Who was his successor?
Where was the seat of government under President Adams?
What trouble was there between France and the United States?
What did the American ambassadors say about paying money to France?
How was war averted?
What made President Adams's administration unpopular?
What were the Alien and Sedition Laws?
How was Mr. Jefferson chosen president?
When did Washington die?
What was the feeling about him?
What was the population of the United States in 1800?

CHAPTER XXIV.

Who was President Jefferson?
How long was he president?
What influence had the war between France and England on American affairs?
What was the "right of search" claimed by the English?
What was the affair between the "Chesapeake" and the "Leopard"?
What was the embargo.
What had the United States to do with the Barbary States?
What gallant deed took place in the harbor of Tripoli?
What changes did President Jefferson introduce?
What law was passed about the African slave-trade?
What attempts were made to invent steamboats?
Who first successfully introduced them? and when?
Who was Aaron Burr?
Describe his career.
What State was admitted under Jefferson? and when?
What was the early history of Ohio?
What great purchase of territory took place in President Jefferson's time?
How was the Mississippi River first explored?
Who was La Salle?
Why was the region explored by him named Louisiana?
How came the United States Government to buy it?
What were its boundaries?
How large was its area?
What effect had its purchase on the size of the national territory?
What was Lewis and Clark's expedition?
Describe what they did and saw.
Who first visited the Columbia River?
Who settled the Pacific coast?

CHAPTER XXV.

Between what years was Madison president?
What caused the war of 1812?

What was the popular feeling about it?
What was the Hartford Convention?
How did the war open?
What had Tecumseh to do with it?
What naval battles took place?
Describe the battle of Lake Erie.
Describe the loss of the "Essex."
How long did the war last?
What took place in the last year?
Describe the battle of New Orleans.
What treaty closed the war?
Did it settle the disputed points?
How long before there was another war?
What was the population of the United States in 1810?
What was the "national road"?
Describe the western emigration.
How many immigrants came from Europe?
What new States were added under Madison?
From what was Louisiana formed?
What had it previously been called?
Whence came the name of Indiana?
Who succeeded Madison?
How long was his administration?
What was it called?
Describe the Seminole war.
How was Florida obtained?
What did it cost?
How did the antislavery question arise?
What four States were admitted under Monroe's administration?
How did it happen that free and slave States came in alternately?
What trouble finally came up about Missouri?
What was said in the discussion?
What was the Missouri Compromise?
What was it supposed to have settled?
What foreign visitor came to America?
How was the State of Illinois formed and named?
Mississippi?

Alabama?
Missouri?
Maine?
How many States were there now in the Union?
What was the population in 1820?
What was the "Monroe doctrine"?

CHAPTER XXVI.

What president followed Monroe?
How long was John Quincy Adams president?
What had he heard in his youth?
What internal improvements took place during his administration?
Describe the Erie Canal.
Describe the first American railroads.
What fears existed about them?
When did John Adams and Thomas Jefferson die?
Describe their deaths.
What was the tariff question?
What president followed John Quincy Adams?
How long did Jackson serve?
What had been his previous career?
What was his character?
What was nullification in South Carolina?
How did it end?
What was done with the Indian tribes at this time?
What was the Seminole war?
Who was Osceola?
What were his wrongs?
How did the war end?
What did it cost?
Who was Benjamin Lundy?
What did Mr. Garrison do?
Who was Nat Turner?
What law did the president propose?
How did people regard General Jackson?
What bad practice did he introduce?
What was the "surplus revenue"?

What was the population of the United States in 1830?
What two new States were added to the Union?
From what was Arkansas formed?
When was it admitted?
From what was Michigan formed?
When was it admitted?
Were they slave States, or free States?

CHAPTER XXVII.

What president followed Jackson?
How long did he serve?
How did the Whigs and Democrats differ?
What rebellion took place in Canada?
What events happened during the antislavery agitation?
What plan of annexation was brought forward in Congress?
What took place in Congress in regard to petitions?
Why was not Mr. Van Buren re-elected?
What was the population of the United States in 1840?
What president followed Van Buren?
Who was the "Log Cabin candidate"?
How long did General Harrison live?
Who followed him?
What was the "Ashburton treaty"?
What was the "Dorr war"?
What troubles took place along the Hudson?
Who were the Mormons?
What State was admitted under Tyler?
What was the history of Florida?
What foreign State was annexed?
What was the history of Texas?
What reason did Mr. Calhoun give for annexing it?
How large was it?
When was it annexed?
What did it cost?

CHAPTER XXVIII.

What president succeeded Mr. Tyler?
How long was his administration?

QUESTIONS. 27

What was the first news sent by telegraph in America?
What new party opposed Mr. Polk?
What was the claim of the United States to Oregon?
What was the Oregon treaty?
How did the Mexican war originate?
What did congress vote?
What victories did General Taylor win?
What city and fort did General Scott take?
What naval commander assisted?
What other battles took place?
When was the city of Mexico captured?
How large an army took it?
What other Mexican provinces were taken?
What did Captain Frémont accomplish?
What was the treaty of Guadalupe Hidalgo?
When was it made and ratified?
What was then known of California?
How rapidly did San Francisco grow?
What was the origin of the name California?
How many States were admitted under Polk's administration?
How many did they make in all?
When was Texas admitted?
When Iowa? and from what Territory was it made?
When Wisconsin? and from what Territory?
Why did the antislavery excitement increase?
What was the Wilmot Proviso?
What new party arose?

CHAPTER XXIX.

What president succeeded Mr. Polk?
When was Taylor inaugurated?
When did he die?
Who took his place?
What were the "Compromise Measures"?
What was the Fugitive Slave Law?
When did it pass?
What excitements grew out of it?
What new State came in during Fillmore's administration?

What Territories were organized out of territory gained from Mexico?
What was the population of the United States in 1850?
Who succeeded Mr. Fillmore?
What change of policy took place as to the Missouri Compromise?
What new Territories were proposed?
What took place in Kansas?
Who were the " Border Ruffians "?
Who were the Free State leaders?
Who was Capt. John Brown?
How did the Kansas struggle end?
What was the "Gadsden Purchase"?
How large was the area of the United States in 1854?
How did it compare with the area of the original thirteen States?
With that of the Roman empire?
What was the Japanese treaty?
What were the parties at the next presidential election?
Who was chosen president?
For what was his term chiefly remarkable?

CHAPTER XXX.

When was Mr. Buchanan inaugurated?
What was the "Dred Scott Decision"?
What were John Brown's plans?
Describe his raid.
What did Colonel Washington say of him?
What did Governor Wise say about him?
When was he executed?
What became of his companions?
Who was the next president?
What was thought of him?
What was the State-Rights doctrine?
What State seceded first?
What States afterwards?
Who were chosen as officers of the Southern Confederacy?
What was its main principle?

What did Major Anderson do?
Describe the attack on Fort Sumter.
What effect had this attack?
What did President Buchanan do?
What new States came into the Union while he was in office?
How did their names originate?
What was the population of the United States in 1860?

CHAPTER XXXI.

What was the feeling in the Northern States on hearing of the attack on Fort Sumter?
What had been the feeling before this?
What was President Lincoln's first step?
What happened in Baltimore?
How were troops sent to Washington?
What was the most essential thing at first?
How was the army collected?
What was the blockade?
When were troops sent into Virginia?
What happened to Colonel Ellsworth?
Where was the first fighting?
Describe the battle of Bull Run.
What other defeat took place?
What successes?
What change of commanders?
What was the condition of the navy?
What position did European governments take?
What took place in regard to Mason and Slidell?
How large was the Union army in 1862?
What was General McClellan's policy?
Describe the battle of Fair Oaks.
Describe the seven-days' battles.
Describe Lee's invasion of Maryland.
Describe the battle of Antietam.
What change of commanders took place?
Describe the contest between the "Monitor" and "Merrimack"?
What took place on the southern coast?

What at the west?
Describe the battle of Pittsburg Landing.
Describe the taking of New Orleans.
What was the original policy of the Union Government as to slavery?
What was the president's Emancipation Proclamation?
What were the first colored regiments?
What was the president's second proclamation?
What took place at the battle of Chancellorsville?
What discouragements occurred at this period of the war?
Describe Lee's invasion.
How many were engaged at Gettysburg?
What was the turning-point of the war?
Describe the surrender of Vicksburg.
Describe Grierson's and Morgan's raids.
How did the Mississippi become finally opened to Union vessels?
What were the draft riots in New York?
What defeat took place at Chickamauga?
Describe the battles at Chattanooga.
What was the siege of Charleston?
What took place at Fort Wagner?
What did President Lincoln say at the end of 1863?
What attacks were made early in 1864?
What two movements did General Grant plan?
What did he accomplish in Virginia?
What was Early's raid?
What was the St. Alban's raid?
What was "Sheridan's ride"?
What was the career of the Confederate privateers?
What was their final engagement?
Describe the naval action in Mobile Bay.
Describe the destruction of the "Albemarle."
What was Sherman's "march to the sea"?
What Christmas gift did he offer to President Lincoln?
What was Sherman's march from Savannah northward?
What did he prove the Confederacy to be?
When was Charleston captured?
What was Fort Fisher?

When did Grant's final movement begin?
What was the battle of Five Forks?
Describe the evacuation of Richmond.
Who finally occupied it, and when?
What was the condition of Lee's army?
When was it surrendered?
How was Jefferson Davis captured?
What had the civil war cost?
What good had it effected?
What did it prove?
What was the Sanitary Commission?
How did the war compare with the Revolutionary War?
What advantage had each side?
What justification could the Confederates offer for their position?
What acts of theirs were indefensible?
What was the general feeling of both armies?
What did Mr. Lincoln say about the war in his second Inaugural Address?

CHAPTER XXXII.

What tragedy took place just after the close of the war?
What was the character of President Lincoln?
What was his funeral?
Who took his place?
What became of the army?
What different views prevailed as to the reconstruction of th Southern States?
What successive steps were taken?
What conditions were made with the Southern States?
What were the president's vetoes?
Describe his impeachment trial.
What had happened during his term and President Lincoln's?
What three States had been added to the Union?
How and when were they formed?
Describe the purchase of Alaska.
What was its price and size?
How large had the nation become?
How many States and Territories?

What was the population of the United States in 1870?
Who was the next president?
How much of the national debt has been paid?
What is the "Fifteenth Amendment" to the Constitution?
What was the Geneva tribunal?
What statesmen of the war have since died?
What new political questions are under discussion?
What material progress has been made?
Name some of those who have gained intellectual distinction in the United States.
What example did the founders of the American colonies leave?
What had the nation first to prove?
What made the experiment difficult?
What is now the main duty of Americans?
What did President Lincoln say in his Gettysburg address?
How many terms did General Grant serve?
What important event took place in the last year of Grant's second term?
Give some account of the great international exhibition, and its effect on American industry.
Who succeeded General Grant as president?
What parties nominated candidates for the presidency?
Give some account of the excitement after the election had taken place.
What happened for which the Constitution had provided no remedy?
How was the decision of the election finally made?
What measure of conciliation did President Hayes adopt which was much criticised?
What has the result proved?
Give some account of the increase of population, as shown by the census of 1880.
Does it seem probable that the increase will be as great from 1880 to 1890 as in the preceding ten years?
From what European country are we now receiving the greatest number of emigrants?
What evidence of national prosperity exists with regard to the payment of the national debt, and the return to specie-payments?

Give some account of the evidence of prosperity, as shown by the increased industry of the nation.

Who were the Republican and the Democratic candidates in the national election of 1880?

Give some account of the assassination of President Garfield and the sympathy manifested throughout the civilized world.

What peculiarity of the inaugural address of President Arthur is mentioned? and what does it indicate?

Who were the candidates of the several parties in the election of 1884?

Who was elected twenty-second president of the United States?

Describe the Civil Service Act.

www.ingramcontent.com/pod-product-compliance
Lightning Source LLC
Chambersburg PA
CBHW022135300426
44115CB00006B/202